Nashua Public Library

Enjoy this book!
Please remember to return it on time
so that others may enjoy it too.

Manage your library account and
discover all we offer by visiting us
online at www.nashualibrary.org

Love your library? Tell a friend!

The Many Deaths
of Jew Süss

The Many Deaths of Jew Süss

The Notorious Trial and Execution of
an Eighteenth-Century Court Jew

Yair Mintzker

PRINCETON UNIVERSITY PRESS
PRINCETON AND OXFORD

Requests for permission to reproduce material from this work
should be sent to Permissions, Princeton University Press

Published by Princeton University Press, 41 William Street,
Princeton, New Jersey 08540

In the United Kingdom: Princeton University Press, 6 Oxford Street,
Woodstock, Oxfordshire OX20 1TR

press.princeton.edu

Jacket art: Adapted from Elias Beck's woodcut, *A True Depiction of the
Jew Süss and His Room in the Herrenhaus*, 1738. Courtesy of
Württembergische Landesbibliothek, Graphic Collection

All Rights Reserved

ISBN 978-0-691-17232-3

Library of Congress Control Number 2017934500

British Library Cataloging-in-Publication Data is available

This book has been composed in Minion Pro

Printed on acid-free paper. ∞

Printed in the United States of America

1 3 5 7 9 10 8 6 4 2

In memory of the Langberg and Satin families

אמר רבי יוחנן: האיקונים הזה אלף
בני אדם מביטים בה, כל אחד
ואחד אומר בי היא מבטת. (מדרש,
פסיקתא רבתי כא 6)

Contents

Acknowledgments   ix

Note to Readers   xi

Introduction   1

First Conversation   23

1. The Inquisitor   25

Part 1: *Vita Ante Acta*   25

Part 2: *Species Facti*   55

Second Conversation   100

2. A Convert's Tale   103

Third Conversation   171

3. Joseph and His Brothers   177

Fourth Conversation   224

4. In the Land of the Dead   231

Afterword   280

List of Illustrations   **287**

List of Abbreviations   **289**

Notes   **291**

Index   **323**

Acknowledgments

During the seven years it took me to research and write this book, I received generous financial support from the Institute for Advanced Study in Princeton and the Wissenschaftskolleg zu Berlin, as well as from Princeton's History Department, the Class of 1942 Preceptorship in History, and the University Committee on Research in the Humanities and Social Sciences. In Germany, my research was facilitated by conversations with a series of archivists, librarians, and fellow historians. I thank especially Gudrun Emberger, Sonja Grund, Alexandra Haas, Uwe Jens Wandel, Ronald Fischer, Reinhard Mayer-Kalkus, and the indefatigable Thomas Reimer. One of the greatest pleasures in working on this project was to meet and befriend Hellmut Haasis, whose courage and generosity I shall not soon forget. Hellmut: bleib xond. Keith Baker, David Bell, Elisheva Carlebach, Laura Kounine, Natasha Mhatre, H. C. Erik Midelfort, Hannah Mintzker, Lyndal Roper, James J. Sheehan, and Hari Sidhar read drafts of individual chapters or the manuscript as a whole. I am grateful for their comments and for saving me from many factual and interpretative errors. Any that remain are of course my very own. Carolina Alvarado, Brooke Fitzgerald, and especially Sara Marcus helped with crucial editorial advice during the final preparation of the manuscript; Tsering Wangyal Shawa prepared the maps; Daniela

Blei prepared the index; and Brigitta van Rheinberg and her team at Princeton University Press took extraordinarily good care of my manuscript. I am grateful to them all. My final thanks go to Katie, Naomi, and Lydia. I love you.

I dedicate this book to the loving memory of my grandparents, Dov and Sarah (Sala) Langberg, as well as to Dov, Elka, Manya, and Henya Satin. May their memory be a blessing and their souls forever bound in the bundle of life.

Note to Readers

I wrote this book for a broad audience. For that reason, I preferred using common English terms where such were available ("Rosh Hashana," "cheder"). Otherwise, I followed the romanization principles of the American Library Association–Library of Congress (ALA-LC), but refrained from using diacritical marks which might otherwise have confused and frustrated many a nonspecialist.

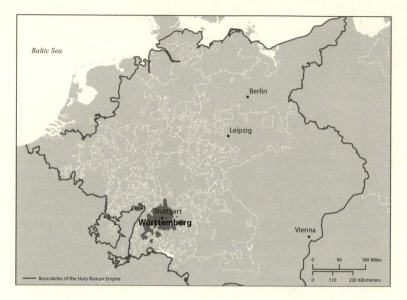

FIGURE 1. Central Europe in the early eighteenth century.

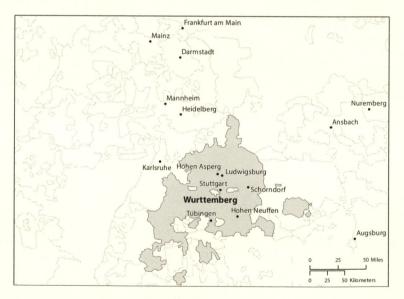

FIGURE 2. Württemberg and its environs, ca. 1730.

The Many Deaths
of Jew Süss

FIGURE 3. Bruno Rehab. Poster for the first screening of the film *Jud Süss*, 1940. *Source*: Deutsches Filminstitut / Postercollection.

Introduction

My business is to record what people say; but I
am by no means bound to believe it—and that
may be taken to apply to this book as a whole.
—Herodotus, *Histories*, 7.152.3

Joseph Süss Oppenheimer, better known as Jew Süss, is one of the
most iconic figures in the history of anti-Semitism. Originally
from the Jewish community in Heidelberg, in 1733 Oppenheimer
became the court Jew (personal banker and advisor) of the duke
of the small German state of Württemberg. When the duke died
unexpectedly in 1737, the Württemberg authorities arrested Oppenheimer, put him on trial, and finally executed him for what
they termed Oppenheimer's "damnable maltreatments of prince
and country."[1] Extremely well known in other parts of the world,
in the United States Oppenheimer is remembered today mainly
through a vicious Nazi propaganda movie made about him in
1940 (figure 3).

Though he was executed nearly three hundred years ago, Oppenheimer's trial never quite ended. Even as his trial was unfolding, it was already clear that what was being placed in the scales
of justice was not any of Oppenheimer's supposed crimes. Indeed,
the vague verdict pronounced in his case conspicuously failed to

provide any specific details about the reasons for the death sentence. The significance of his trial, and the reasons for Oppenheimer's public notoriety ever since the eighteenth century, is to be found not in the dry language of legal treatises but in the role his story has played as a parable about the rise and fall of prominent Jews in Christian Europe. Oppenheimer's meteoric ascendance during the years he spent in Württemberg and his no less spectacular fall have been viewed by many as an allegory for the history of German Jewry both in Oppenheimer's time as well as in the nineteenth and twentieth centuries. Here was a man who tried to fit in, and seemed to for a time, but was eventually rejected; a Jew who enjoyed much success but then fell from power and met a violent death. Thus, at every point in time when the status, culture, past, and future of Germany's Jews have hung in the balance, the story of this man has moved to center stage, where it was investigated, novelized, dramatized, and even set to music. It is no exaggeration to say that "Jew Süss" is to the German collective imagination what Shakespeare's Shylock is to the English-speaking world.

The historical figure of Joseph Süss Oppenheimer is incredibly elusive, and any understanding of him must begin with the political and legal regimes under which he lived and died. Oppenheimer spent almost his entire life in the southwest corner of the Holy Roman Empire of the German Nation (see figures 1 and 2). In the eighteenth century, the Holy Roman Empire was the general political organization that connected the hundreds of more or less sovereign polities in German-speaking central Europe, including large states like Bavaria and Saxony, Imperial and free cities like Frankfurt am Main and Nuremberg, and even some Imperial monasteries and knightly territories. The Empire was not a nation-state in the modern sense of the term—it possessed no central executive, no bureaucracy, and no standing army—but it did have some common features, such as a head (an emperor) and various representational bodies. Especially important for understanding Oppenheimer's case is the fact that the Empire's members shared a common legal system scholars term "inquisitorial."

An inquisitorial system is best contrasted with an adversarial one. In an adversarial criminal legal system, the court serves as a neutral referee between two principal adversaries: the prosecution and the defense. This is the system used today throughout the English-speaking world. In an inquisitorial system, on the other hand, judges are entrusted with actively investigating cases, rather than merely adjudicating between the two opposing sides. The inquisitorial system as such should not be conflated with the particular historical institutions of the Papal or Spanish Inquisitions, which are but two examples of a larger system. The judge-inquisitors in Oppenheimer's trial were not ecclesiastical officials entrusted with combatting heresy, but state servants who applied the inquisitorial procedures common in the Holy Roman Empire to Oppenheimer's particular case.

The specific corner of the Holy Roman Empire that Oppenheimer inhabited throughout his life was characterized by great political diversity. This part of central Europe contained important Imperial cities, many small territories belonging to Imperial knights and monasteries, and a series of small- and medium-size princely states that—as opposed to the Empire to which they all belonged—did have their own armies, executive organs, and state administrations. The political plurality in this part of the Empire was accompanied by considerable confessional diversity as well. German-speaking central Europe was the birthplace of the Protestant Reformation, the place where Martin Luther lived and where his message developed and prospered after 1517. But during Oppenheimer's time, over two centuries after Luther's break with the Catholic Church, the spread of Protestantism in the Empire had largely ground to a halt. While some polities in the Empire's southwest had turned Protestant (Lutheran or Calvinist) over the years, others remained devoutly Catholic, and yet a third group of states accommodated more than one confession within their borders. The duchy of Württemberg, the site of Oppenheimer's trial and execution, is a case in point. After 1733, this overwhelmingly Lutheran duchy was ruled by a Catholic duke.

Court Jews like Oppenheimer were a common feature of the Empire's diverse landscape. The number of Jews in the Holy Roman Empire wasn't large, partly because many territories and towns prohibited Jews from settling within their borders. In other places, though, Jews came to play a vital economic role as moneylenders, financiers, and traders. Jews lent money to princes who encountered difficulties in raising funds directly from their subjects; they supplied state armies with necessary provisions and military articles; they helped in the minting of coins; and they traded in many commodities, including precious stones and other luxury items. Such activities brought Jews like Oppenheimer to the courts of many princes in the Holy Roman Empire, where the most favored habitués were known as "court Jews."[2]

We do not know much about Oppenheimer's early life except that he was born in Heidelberg, probably in 1697 or 1698, to a Jewish tax collector by the name of Issachar Süsskind Oppenheimer and his wife, Michal. Starting in the mid-1720s, the young Oppenheimer served as a court Jew to several German princes in the Empire's southwest, first in the Palatinate, then in Hesse-Darmstadt, and finally in Württemberg, a duchy whose future ruler, Carl Alexander, Oppenheimer had met and befriended in

1732. In October 1733, the Catholic Carl Alexander ascended to the Württemberg throne, and Oppenheimer began to enjoy much success. He was first the duke's special representative in Frankfurt am Main, then his court Jew in Stuttgart. In this latter capacity, he ran the local mint and was involved in managing many aspects of the state's finances. These years of close collaboration with the Catholic duke did not last long, though. Less than four years after becoming duke of Württemberg, Carl Alexander suffered a sudden and fatal stroke. Oppenheimer was arrested that same night. During the next eleven months, he was kept under guard, first in his home in Stuttgart and then in two different jails. A special inquisition committee was appointed to investigate his case. Oppenheimer was interrogated daily for almost four months, met with many different people in jail, and was finally led back to Stuttgart, where he awaited his verdict in a room overlooking the marketplace.

On Friday, January 31, 1738, Oppenheimer's death sentence was read to him in a special session of the criminal court convened for his case. The court did not specify the exact basis for its verdict,[3] but the way it choreographed the subsequent execution clearly implied that Oppenheimer was guilty of corruption, the debasement of coins in the mint, and sexual transgressions.[4] Four days later, after a final public meeting of the court, the executioner's men escorted their prisoner to a site just north of Stuttgart and dragged him up a forty-foot-long ladder onto a bright red gallows. Anywhere between ten and twenty thousand people came to view the spectacle. On that Tuesday morning, February 4, 1738, they watched as Oppenheimer was strangled to death and his body then locked in a gibbet specifically constructed for the occasion. The caged corpse was supposed to serve, in the words of the public verdict, "as a hideous example for others."[5]

The Historiographic Predicament

Many scholars of the early modern period might look with envy at the profusion of documents left by Oppenheimer's trial. Today, in over one hundred cardboard boxes in the state archives in Stuttgart, one can read close to thirty thousand handwritten pages of documents from the time period of the trial. Among these pages are the materials collected by the inquisition committee assigned to the case; protocols of the interrogations of Oppenheimer himself, his alleged accomplices, and many witnesses; records of the committee's deliberations; documentation relating to Oppenheimer's confiscated property; descriptions of Oppenheimer's conversations with visitors; and a great number of poems, pamphlets, and essays about Oppenheimer's final months, days, hours, and even minutes. The state archives in Stuttgart contain a whole universe of sources about Oppenheimer's case, an unparalleled opportunity—or at least so it seems at first glance—to write an extraordinarily detailed history of the last years in the life of the notorious "Jew Süss."[6]

Yet while the abundance of sources about Oppenheimer's trial is remarkable, the sources themselves leave much to be desired. This is often the case with events that generate such an immense amount of discourse. As long as Oppenheimer was a nobody, there was little reason to falsify the basic facts about his life—hence both the scarcity and general reliability of sources about his early career.[7] Once Oppenheimer became famous and powerful, however, and especially after his arrest and downfall, few had reason to tell the truth, the whole truth, and nothing but the truth about his case. The inquisition committee assigned to the case lacked direct evidence against its Jewish prisoner, but wishing to make an example of him anyway, it left no stone unturned, no person unquestioned, and no fact in its right place in pursuit of its purpose. The testimonies of Oppenheimer's alleged accomplices, who were trying to save their own skins, are at least as problematic. The visitors who were allowed into Oppenheimer's cell often tried to convert him to Christianity, but having failed in their endeavors, they created what in all probability are highly polemical accounts of their encounters with him. Last but not least, Joseph Süss Oppenheimer himself was fighting for his life and can hardly be considered a reliable witness where his own deeds and misdeeds are concerned. Historians of Oppenheimer's case have to face a curious predicament: they possess few documents about Oppenheimer's early career, but what they have is fairly reliable; they have a huge amount of material about Oppenheimer's activities in Stuttgart and the last months of his life, but almost all of it is extremely tendentious. Therein lies the crux of the predicament of any historian of Oppenheimer's case: less proves to be more, and more proves to be less.

What is true for modern historians also applies to Oppenheimer's own contemporaries. Consider, for instance, the case of Johann Heinrich Zedler's *Universal-Lexicon*, a massive reference work published between 1731 and 1754 that was probably the easiest way for contemporaries to find information about Oppenheimer. The entry about Oppenheimer fits nicely within the long series of biographical sketches for which this lexicon has been famous since the eighteenth century. "Süß Oppenheimer, (Joseph)," the entry begins,

> was born in Frankfurt am Main, and saw the light of day in 1692. He was a descendant of one of the wealthiest and most honorable Jewish families in that place. Its origins can be traced back to the city of Oppenheim, hence its name, and

it enjoys great reputation among the Jews in Vienna and Prague. According to some sources, Oppenheimer was the bastard son of a Christian man. His Jewish mother, who had been known in times past for her great beauty, was still alive a few years ago, but his [Christian] father died when Oppenheimer was still a boy and replaced by a Jewish man, from whom he received his name and by whom he was raised. Most learned people, however, doubt the accuracy of this description.[8]

The first few sentences of this entry are worth quoting at length because they are representative of the inaccuracies one finds in many contemporary descriptions of Oppenheimer's life. Apart from the fact that Oppenheimer's birth date cannot be known with complete certainty (modern historians usually give dates in 1697 or 1698), it is clear that his birthplace was Heidelberg, not Frankfurt, and that his family was not a wealthy one. Indeed, over half the space in this entry's first paragraph is devoted to an anecdote whose accuracy, as the author himself is quick to admit, "[m]ost learned people . . . doubt."[9]

Doubt and uncertainty characterized contemporary stories about Oppenheimer not only for factual reasons. What, ultimately, was the meaning of the rise and fall of this man? How does it fit into the longer history of Jews and Christians in the Holy Roman Empire and beyond? Zedler's entry gives a fairly common description of Oppenheimer's life as a court Jew in Stuttgart and the duke's palace in nearby Ludwigsburg:

He shaved his beard, wore expensive clothes, maintained a well-stocked library, and had his own carriages and horses. He was present at all courtly events. He ate and drank whatever was laid before him except for pork, and he did not have

any objections to having affairs with Christian women—
indeed, he took many Christian concubines, of all social
classes, and led a libertine's life. As for the duke: Oppenheimer could enter his chambers at all times and hours, and
he bespoke his mind whenever he wished to do so. The entire fiscal business of the state went through him . . . and his
power at court grew day by day.[10]

Such a description does not simply paint a vivid (albeit questionable) picture of Oppenheimer's life at court. It also points to a
tension in Oppenheimer's life, often commented on by contemporaries, between following Jewish law (not eating pork) and discarding accepted norms (shaving his beard, having Christian concubines). Although it does so in a more nuanced way, the entry
might also point to a common biblical interpretation of Oppenheimer's story: "He ate and drank whatever was laid before him"
is probably an echo of Isaiah 22:13 and 1 Corinthians 15:32. "If
the dead are not raised," writes Paul in his epistle to the Corinthians, "let us eat and drink for tomorrow we die." Together with the
reference to Oppenheimer's libertinism, this biblical reference
signals that the end of Oppenheimer's story was foreshadowed
earlier in his life. Indeed, other contemporary texts would follow
biblical allusions more explicitly. Some compared Oppenheimer
to Ahitophel, King David's treacherous advisor; others viewed his
story as akin to that of Haman the Agagite, King Ahasuerus's evil
advisor from the Book of Esther; and yet others saw similarities
between Oppenheimer and Simon bar Kokhba, the leader of a
failed Jewish rebellion against Rome in the second century C.E.[11]
Contemporaries were not only interested in the facts of Oppenheimer's story, about which, more often than not, their knowledge
was sorely lacking. They were also very interested in what this

man's story could have meant, and here, as is often the case, there were as many interpretations as interpreters.

Finally, there is the question of Oppenheimer's own perspective. In many publications from the time period of the trial, contemporaries showed interest not only in the facts of the story and what it could mean but also in Oppenheimer's own reactions to what was happening around him and ultimately to him. These sources highlight the third reason for the inherent uncertainty in eighteenth-century depictions of Oppenheimer's case. Even if contemporaries had had access to all the facts about Oppenheimer's life (and they hadn't), and even if they had been able to agree on a single interpretation of his story (and they weren't), they still never would have been able to enter Oppenheimer's mind, access his innermost thoughts, feel his emotions and passions, view the world through his eyes. The legacy of the eighteenth-century uncertainty vis-à-vis Oppenheimer's story is consequently threefold: factual, interpretative, and psychological. Both contemporaries and later historians could never completely understand what Oppenheimer had actually done, what his story signified, and how Oppenheimer himself experienced his own rise, fall, and violent death.

Despite the suspect usefulness of the primary sources, Oppenheimer's story has fascinated many historians over the years, and for two main reasons. First, there is the sheer drama of the story: the fact that Oppenheimer was born a Jew, led a not altogether religious life, but decided to die as a Jew despite all attempts to convert him while in jail. His steep rise to power and his sudden downfall are the stuff from which great legends are made, complete with inquisitors, lengthy interrogations, torture sessions, a courtroom drama, and a horrific verdict. And then there is the execution itself: the red gallows and the iron gibbet; the bound Oppenheimer led up to the gallows; the moment of asphyxiation; and the decomposing cadaver left in the gibbet for years as a grave example for others. What historian, faced with these materials, would not be tempted to tell the story despite its many uncertainties?

The fascination with Oppenheimer's story, as we have already noted, has a second source as well. In the centuries after Oppenheimer's public hanging, his story came to represent the contested topic of Jewish integration into Christian society in Germany. Oppenheimer was neither the first nor the last prominent Jew to rise to fame and fall from power in a predominantly Christian country. But because his story took place right on the verge of the modern period, it became one of the most important allegories for the story of German Jews in modern times. Most important in that respect was the Nazi propaganda movie made about Oppenheimer in 1940 by the German director Veit Harlan, a movie so vicious, inflammatory, and patently false that in the wake of World War II, its director was put on trial for the mere fact of having created it. All of this explains why historians, writers, artists, and the German-speaking public at large never lost interest in Oppenheimer's story: why his trial, despite the many ambiguities, contradictions, and outright lies its records contain, has continued to fascinate people up through the present day.

What Is a Historian to Do?

What is a historian to do in such case, when none of the available sources can be trusted? When they often prevaricate, falsify, and distort, incessantly contradict one another and at times even contradict themselves? What is a historian to do when his or her sources are written by unreliable witnesses and for dubious purposes, paying little attention to well-documented events at the same time that they often describe at length dialogues that could never have taken place and events that probably never happened? When one of the historian's most basic tasks—to describe what happened—is impractical and probably impossible, what is a historian to do? Should he or she do anything at all?

Such is the predicament of any historian of Oppenheimer's case, and over the years, different scholars and writers have faced it in different ways. In the nineteenth and first two-thirds of the twentieth centuries, major treatments of the case included works by Manfred Zimmermann (1874), Curt Elwenspoek (1926), Selma Stern (1929), and Heinrich Schnee (1963).[12] To this list have been added more recently important books by Barbara Gerber (1990) and especially Hellmut Haasis (1998); edited volumes by Alexandra Przyrembel and Jörg Schönert (2006) and Gudrun Emberger and Robert Kretzschmar (2012); and a steady stream of essays in academic journals, encyclopedias, popular magazines, and newspapers.[13] Last but by no means least are the incredibly influential works of fiction about Jew Süss, including, among many others, an important novella by Wilhelm Hauff (1827), a seminal novel by Lion Feuchtwanger (1925), films by Lothar Mendes and Veit Harlan (1934 and 1940, respectively), and, more recently, Detlev Glanert's opera (1999) and a play by Yehoshua Sobol and Dieter Wedel (2013).[14] Leaving aside derivative works and the many books and essays that treat the historical Oppenheimer only in passing, one can detect in this large corpus four basic approaches to the historian's predicament vis-à-vis the sources. Each of them has its advantages, but each entails major disadvantages as well.

1. *When all of the sources lie, a historian should read them carefully and critically, compare them with each other and add new material, finally deducing from the analysis what really happened.* The best

example of a historian who professes to have followed this method is Hellmut Haasis, although one can, of course, also find similar attempts by earlier and later historians. The idea here is to use many testimonies in order to circumvent the limitations of any single document. Many sources are complete prevarications and others are only partly reliable. But a close and critical examination of a large number of documents could nonetheless lead to important conclusions about the events surrounding Oppenheimer's life, trial, and execution.

Certainly, part of the historian's job is to find out the truth about past events, and only the most skeptical of scholars would deny the historical existence of Joseph Süss Oppenheimer or the basic outlines of his life story. But although quite a few historians profess to have uncovered the one indivisible truth about this case, scholars regularly disagree about what that truth actually is. Thus, some historians see Oppenheimer as a conniving, greedy parvenu, unscrupulous in his relationships with women and in his treatment of the traditions of the duchy of Württemberg. Others disagree, viewing the famous court Jew as a victim of a conspiracy, a scapegoat sacrificed on the altar of intolerance. Disagreement also exists about the basic facts in the unfolding of the trial itself—what Oppenheimer said, how he looked, and what he did or did not do before and after his arrest—and of course about the meaning of the story within European, German, and Jewish history. Indeed, because of the extraordinary number of conflicting statements in the trial documents, there is hardly a narrative about Oppenheimer one could *not* support with some documentation. Finding out the truth in this case, though a noble endeavor, proves much harder in practice than in theory.

Empirical works on Oppenheimer have consequently left us with a mixed legacy. On the one hand, we have several remarkable studies about Oppenheimer's life that have without a doubt greatly advanced our knowledge of his case. One cannot help admiring especially Haasis's exemplary archival work, the full scope of which only a researcher who has spent many years reading the same sources can fully appreciate. The weaknesses of such empirical studies are not insubstantial, though. These accounts tend to reduce the incredible complexity of the case to the question of Oppenheimer's guilt—a kind of retrial, if you will, that once and for all would settle the truth of the matter definitively; they often do not explain why they choose to give credence to some testimonies while dismissing or ignoring others; and they pretend to have direct access to the past, although, like any work of history, they are to a large extent artificial constructions. Is there a way, then, to describe Oppenheimer's trial without pretending to always know the whole truth about it? Can one tell a story about what happened to Jew Süss without simultaneously dismissing anything that seems to contradict the author's particular interpretation? And can one treat empirical evidence both seriously and profitably while at the same time acknowledging that any story, and certainly any story about Jew Süss, is bound to contain fictional elements?

2. *When confronted by conflicting accounts of an event, historians should choose to keep silent about it.* Selma Stern and, more recently, Gudrun Emberger have confronted the predicament at least in part in this way, although keeping silent about certain topics is of course a characteristic of practically any work of history.

In her remarkable 1929 study *Jud Süss*, Stern depicted Oppenheimer as one of the earliest modern, secularized Jews. She viewed the tragedy of his life as the result both of his failed attempt to be accepted as a Jew in a Christian society and of the reformist economic measures he tried to introduce in Württemberg. Leaving the questions of Oppenheimer's modernity and his economic policies aside (they are both debatable), Stern's work was pathbreaking in many respects. She was the first historian to have full access to the documents in the state archives in Stuttgart and consequently also the first to discuss some of the case's central records. Being the serious historian that Stern was, however, she refused to tackle certain topics, even including the unfolding of Oppenheimer's very trial: the sources simply did not allow her to reach a definitive conclusion about many issues.

One can detect the same tendency in the work of Gudrun Emberger.[15] Few, if any, modern historians have studied the sources about Oppenheimer's trial as carefully as Emberger has, but few have also published so little. Despite the major differences between her patient and meticulous scholarship and the work by some of the other scholars of Oppenheimer's case, Emberger also seems to share the belief that historians should strive above all to recover the historical nucleus of Oppenheimer's story. Other historians believed that they had managed to do so and published their findings; Emberger, knowing the sources better than anyone, has been less sure about this possibility, and never published her long-awaited biography of the famous court Jew.

Stern's work and Emberger's depth of knowledge and caution are admirable. But isn't a story as important as Oppenheimer's worth more than silence? Have Stern and especially Emberger perhaps been a bit too cautious due to their pursuit of absolute and unquestionable truth? Is there a way to tell the story of Oppenheimer's trial without saying too much about it, but also without saying too little?

3. *When all of the sources are unreliable, one should leave history aside and turn to fiction instead.* This, over the years, has been the most popular approach to the story of Jew Süss. The most important examples in this respect are Hauff's novella, Feuchtwanger's novel, and particularly Harlan's notorious Nazi propaganda film.

There are of course many problems with fictional descriptions of Jew Süss. Although it is often very difficult to know what did take place in Oppenheimer's case, it is sometimes very clear what did *not* happen. The works by Hauff, Feuchtwanger, and Harlan are a case in point: they depict events that are pure fiction, characters that never existed, and dialogues that are nothing but figments of their authors' imaginations. Furthermore, Hauff's novella is tainted by early nineteenth-century anti-Semitism, and Harlan's 1940 film was supported and financed by none other than Joseph Goebbels. Under such circumstances, historians naturally tend to fight against the fictional accounts of the case. They rightly believe that setting the record straight is an important part of their job.

Dismissing out of hand any fictional account of Oppenheimer's case comes nonetheless at a price. One could leave aside here the old argument about art's ability to reach a higher truth despite, or perhaps because of, its "lies." (This was Aristotle's famous point in the *Poetics*, for instance.) The rabid anti-Semitism of some of the fictional accounts of Oppenheimer's life stretches this argument too thin. A similar objection can perhaps be made about the oft-repeated observation that works of history are always the result of the historian's creative interpretation and emplotment and consequently always contain a grain of the fictional. This observation is valuable, if by now also somewhat banal. Far more important to a scholarly treatment of Oppenheimer's story is the exact chronological ordering of truth and fiction within it. Some of the foremost historians of Oppenheimer's case—Stern, Haasis, and Emberger come immediately to mind—have argued for a clear distinction between the historical nucleus of the story (which came first) and the fictional depictions of "Jew Süss" (which came later).[16] As we shall see, there is reason to believe that this chronology is topsy-turvy. Oppenheimer's trial was the product of fictional stories as much as it was their cause; it was a case in which life imitated art before art began to imitate life.

4. *Finally, when a historian can't trust any of the available sources, he or she should concentrate on the history of the lies themselves. Such lies might tell us little about Oppenheimer himself, but when analyzed with the historian's tool kit, they do tell us a great deal about the society that produced them and how it did or did not change over time.* The fourth and most recent approach to Oppenheimer's story concentrates on the history of the stories about Oppenheimer, an approach that is known in German as *Rezeptionsgeschichte* ("history of reception") and associated with reader-response theory in the field of English literary studies.[17] Some works in this vein (Barbara Gerber's excellent book, for instance) concentrate on the flood of literature that appeared in the wake of Oppenheimer's execution, while others (Przyrembel and Schönert's edited volume, for example, and a recent book by Susan Tegel) concentrate on later time periods.[18] The brilliance of this approach derives from its recognition that while we do not have direct access to Oppenheimer's actions, we do have immediate access to sources *about* Oppenheimer's deeds. Practitioners of Rezeptionsgeschichte encourage us to use this distinction profitably and to read the many stories about Oppenheimer not as a way of learning something about the court Jew but as a means of

exploring common Christian attitudes toward German Jews much more generally.

Like any other approach to the historian's predicament vis-à-vis the sources about Oppenheimer's life, concentrating on the historical reception of the story has its drawbacks. Three are especially noteworthy. First, studies of historical reception have a tendency to be excessively technical and at times outright unreadable. (This is especially the case with Gerber's extraordinarily detailed study.) Second, they are based on the same problematic distinction we have noticed between historical truth (which supposedly came first) and legend (which allegedly came later). And last, they shift the attention away from Oppenheimer as a historical figure. Almost by definition, practitioners of Rezeptionsgeschichte focus on later echoes of Oppenheimer's story rather than on Oppenheimer himself.

Each of the four approaches outlined here has its flaws, but each also has its advantages. Empirical attempts to find out what really happened during the last several years of Oppenheimer's life are extremely important, but in their pretension to know the truth they often mislead the reader. Stern's and Emberger's decision to keep silent about important aspects of the case can be appreciated for exactly this reason, but the price they and their readers pay seems far too high. Fictional treatments of Oppenheimer's life solve the problem by dispensing with historical facts altogether: this is their strength from the reader's point of view, but also their fundamental weakness from the historian's perspective. And finally, Rezeptionsgeschichte brings the sources back in, albeit at the price of a very technical language and indeed a tendency to avoid questions of historical facts altogether.

New work on Oppenheimer's case needs to combine elements of previous approaches to the story as a way of overcoming their individual weaknesses. It should tell us something about the historical events of the trial (Haasis) without always pretending to know who Oppenheimer "really was." It should keep silent where appropriate (Stern, Emberger) without discarding the story altogether. It should take fiction seriously (Feuchtwander, history of reception) without turning itself into a novel. And it should redirect attention to the primary sources (Gerber, Tegel) without metamorphosing, like Echo in the ancient story, into nothing but sound. *Exeunt* Stern, Haasis, Emberger, Hauff, Feuchtwanger, Harlan, and Gerber. Enter polyphonic history.

Polyphonic History

When one can't trust any of the available sources, one should resist the urge to reduce all of them to a single narrative. One ought to follow the advice of the great Greek historian Herodotus and report what the sources say without necessarily believing them. One should quote the sources at length, giving the reader a taste of their complexity, their contradictions, and the personal writing styles of their authors. But the historian should never stop treating the sources critically. He or she should strive to differentiate between what is historically verifiable and what is probably or manifestly false. And he or she should always try to get beyond what the sources describe and reach toward the very act of their creation: who their authors were, when and how they were crafted, for whom they were composed, in what genre, and for what purpose. In a nutshell, when a historian can't trust any of the sources, he or she should write a polyvocal, critical work of scholarship: a polyphonic history.

Polyphonic history explores the lives of individuals in the past and the way they narrated events around them. Who were the people who wrote about the events of Oppenheimer's case? Why did they write, when, and for whom? What did these writers include in their stories, what did they exclude, and what cultural code guided them in making these decisions?

The pages of this book examine four such accounts, all fundamental to understanding Oppenheimer's trial and execution: three accounts that tell the same swath of the story from the perspective of people who met Oppenheimer in person, and a fourth that recounts the story from the point of view of a more distant observer. The book begins with the case of Philipp Friedrich Jäger, the judge-inquisitor who wrote the factual part of Oppenheimer's verdict and thus the basis for his death sentence. Although no other story in this book will take us closer to the issue of Oppenheimer's alleged crimes, the significance of Jäger's story goes well beyond factual issues alone. By reconstructing Jäger's life story and reading, as closely as we can, the document he submitted to the court, we shall be able to reveal important connections between anti-Semitism in general and Oppenheimer's particular case. Crucial in this respect will be Jäger's participation in another political trial in Württemberg less than two years before Oppenheimer's arrest.

Following closely on the footsteps of Jäger's story, the book will turn to the stories of two men who visited Oppenheimer during his last days. Christoph David Bernard was a university lecturer with a problematic past who met Oppenheimer on the eve of the execution and composed what is surely the most dramatic account of Oppenheimer in his last days. The question of its factual veracity aside, Bernard's story contains a profound theological truth and is furthermore key to deciphering many of the other testimonies during Oppenheimer's trial. The same could be said about the life and work of Mordechai Schloss, a Jewish notable who stood behind the publication of the only contemporary Jewish account of Joseph Süss's life and death. Schloss's own life story, and the important text he helped publish about Oppenheimer, together reveal much about the fraught relationships among Jews in 1730s Stuttgart. A careful reconstruction of this relationship will challenge many common assumptions about Oppenheimer's trial, its causes, and its implications.

The fourth and final chapter in this book concentrates on David Fassmann, one of the earliest known biographers of Joseph Süss Oppenheimer. Fassmann was a litterateur and fabulist from Leipzig who, though he lived far from Württemberg, somehow managed to anticipate some of the best modern literature on the historical figure of Jew Süss. Fassmann's life story and his several treatments of Oppenheimer's life story will help us understand at least some of the reasons why, even as it unfolded, the scandal surrounding Oppenheimer's trial reached well beyond the confines of the small duchy of Württemberg. It should also help us appreciate the tangled nature of Oppenheimer's case: how reality and repute, truth and fiction, were wound around each other in his story as if in a skein.

One can certainly read each of these four accounts separately or in a different order from that in which I present them in the following pages. This, indeed, is a fundamental aspect of this book. Taken together, however, the four accounts also create a whole that is larger than the sum of its individual parts. By exploring in quick succession the lives and works of Jäger, Bernard, Schloss, and Fassmann, we are about to see Oppenheimer portrayed from different angles: from up close and far away; in public, in the interrogation room, and in prison; in a legal, social, and theological light; and in Christian and Jewish terms. We will even see some of the storytellers portray each other in their separate accounts. We should not take a single word in these accounts for a faithful description of reality. But when we explore their authors' lives with care, and when we read them closely and patiently one after the other, we will learn, despite all the prevarications, fabrications, and contradictions they contain, a great deal that is meaningful and indeed true.

The polyphonic nature of this book is evident in its methodology, in its overall structure, and in the presence of long passages from the original sources among its pages. It is also manifest in my decision to include short dialogues between me and an imaginary reader after each chapter. It is highly unusual for this device to be used by a professional historian, and my employment of it is sure to cause some controversy. I use it, however, for a reason. Over the past several years, while presenting different parts of this book in the United States, Europe, and Israel, I was simultaneously fascinated and taken aback by my colleagues' reactions to my polyphonic methodology. The author-reader dialogues in the book are by no means an attempt to tell future readers of this book what to think. Rather, they are my way both of responding to some obvious objections to my methodology *and* of acknowledging their validity. Rather than seeing this as a contradiction in terms, I ask the reader to remember Plato's famous definition of thinking as a kind of discourse between the soul and itself, and, indeed, the multivoiced form of the Platonic dialogues themselves. Conflicting arguments are the stuff from which thinking is made. At least in that respect, all thoughtful historical writing, explicitly or implicitly, is always polyphonic history.

First Conversation

READER: This is all very fine and good. But this polyphonic history of yours, hasn't it been done already?

AUTHOR: To some extent, certainly. American historians such as Richard Price, Laura Otis, and above all James Goodman most definitely paved the way for the kind of multiperspectival, polyvocal history you will find in the pages of this book. I have learned a great deal from these historians' successes and not a little from what I consider their failures.[19]

READER: You're avoiding my question. If it has already been done, why do it again? After all, isn't the purpose of many of these works simply to show, by composing Rashomon-like accounts of historical events, that the truth is always in the eye of the beholder, that everything is socially constructed and therefore also relative?

AUTHOR: My friend, the realization that the world looks different from different perspectives cannot possibly be the bottom line of a good work of history. Indeed, as a conclusion for a historical study it seems to me to be utterly banal. What I am setting out to do in the following pages is different. I use the multiperspectival, polyphonic nature of lived experience as my starting point, not as my destination; it is a belief that informs what I'm about to do rather than a conclusion toward which I'm driving.

READER: I'm not sure I follow, but it certainly sounds very ambitious.

AUTHOR: Enough talk. Here comes our first protagonist. The year is 1745, the place is Stuttgart, the scene a funeral.

FIGURE 4. J. A. Fridrich, d. J. Portrait of Philipp Friedrich Jäger, 1745.
Source: UB Tübingen, L XVI 18.2.

CHAPTER 1

The Inquisitor

Part 1: *Vita Ante Acta*

> The hidden God has shown us this man
> for all too short a time. He was talented,
> industrious, honest, and a lover of truth and
> justice; it is as if he was born solely for the
> benefit of his community and country.
> —W.J.J. Cleß eulogizing Philipp Friedrich Jäger,
> August 1745[1]

Dr. Philipp Friedrich Jäger died in his Stuttgart home on Monday evening, August 2, 1745. He was only thirty-seven years old at the time, a man in the prime of life (see figure 4). Descended from a long line of provincial civil servants, Jäger had accumulated an impressive list of titles by the time of his death. He was doctor of both laws (civil and canon), governmental councilor to the duke of Württemberg, president of one of Württemberg's most prestigious administrative bodies, and a judge on the duchy's high court of appeals. The reported cause of death was typhus (*hitzige Krankheit*). In eighteenth-century Europe, it was not uncommon for a judge to contract this so-called jail-fever from those who stood trial before him. The damp and often over-crowded prison cells served as ideal breeding grounds for the lice that carried the typhus bacteria.[2]

The funeral took place three days after Jäger's passing at the cemetery of the Spitalkirche, a few streets north of Stuttgart's main marketplace. Many came to pay their respects: fellow judges and councilors, several church officials, a theologian and three law professors from Württemberg's renowned university in Tü-bingen, representatives of the city of Stuttgart, government secre-taries, the ducal archivist, and an unknown number of relatives, friends, and acquaintances. Presiding over the ceremony was the deacon of the Spitalkirche, Wilhelm Jeremias Jacob Cleß, who also happened to be a relative of the deceased.[3] According to Cleß, the scene was especially somber because it bore a close resem-blance to other recent events in the Jäger household. Dr. Jäger's wife, Charlotte Regina, had died two years earlier and of the nine children she had borne her husband over the years, only four girls were still alive.

In eighteenth-century Württemberg, it was part of the respon-sibility of clergymen like Cleß to deliver a particular type of eu-logy at funerals, especially at those of eminent men. Known in Lutheran Germany as a "body sermon" (*Leichenrede*), the eulogy was composed of two equally important parts. The first was a sermon that highlighted the deceased's piety by way of an inter-pretation of an appropriate biblical passage, while the second con-sisted of a more straightforward description of the life and death of the newly departed. Following the funeral, friends and family members would sometimes issue a printed (and edited) version of the eulogy, to which they would often add other materials such as individual elegies (*epicedia*).[4]

What we know of Jäger's funeral comes from just such a printed eulogy. It tells us that the topic Cleß chose for the funerary sermon was King David's pleas and complaints in Psalm 80:

Turn us again, O God, and cause thy face to shine; and we shall be saved.

O Lord God of hosts, how long wilt thou be angry against the prayer of thy people?

Thou feedest them with the bread of tears; and givest them tears to drink in great measure.

Turn us again, O God of hosts, and cause thy face to shine; and we shall be saved.

Cleß deemed this psalm particularly fitting for the occasion of Dr. Jäger's burial. By allowing this man to die, God had hidden his face from his flock and fed it with the bread of tears. What could possibly have driven God to deprive the deceased's elderly mother and four little girls, as well as "the princely house of Württemberg and indeed our entire fatherland [Württemberg] of such a devoted servant of the government, one of the duchy's most assiduous and talented councilors, protector of so many orphans, loyal member of our city and community through his many talents, erudition, experience, dexterity, industriousness, and fear of God?" "Why are you tearing this man away from us," Cleß began one of his many pathos-filled protestations during the sermon, "a man who is so indispensable for the public good and who furthermore had still so much to accomplish?"[5]

Cleß's funerary sermon repeatedly praised the deceased's piety, industriousness, and many accomplishments, but it also contained echoes of lives less worthy than Jäger's. Quoting from

Scripture again, Cleß invoked the words of the prophet Jeremiah. "O Lord . . . let me talk with thee of thy judgments: Wherefore doth the way of the wicked prosper? Wherefore are all they happy that deal very treacherously?" (Jeremiah 12:1). The deacon wanted to know why God would let such a beautiful flower as Jäger wither while tares prospered. "You let this man die, but so many others, who are nothing but a burden on this earth, you let live?" There was nothing left to do but to place one's trust in God's infinite wisdom. "Lord, thy ways are mysterious and thy path in the great waters. The Lord gave and the Lord hath taken away; Blessed be the name of the Lord."[6]

After the sermon came the second part of the eulogy, consisting of a description of Dr. Jäger's pious and extraordinarily industrious life. Cleß, who had first-hand knowledge of these matters, talked about the deceased's parents, birth, upbringing and education, marriage, children, final disease, and death. He did not forget to list Dr. Jäger's many important positions, including his membership in "several important princely committees" whose existence and significance were apparently so well known to his audience that Cleß felt no need to elaborate. "Dr. Jäger," Cleß finally said, "was amicable to all. . . . Deferential to his superiors, sincere and forthcoming toward his colleagues, obliging and unassuming to his inferiors, he was a personification of the good family member and friend."[7]

Later, when Jäger's colleagues, friends, and relatives prepared the eulogy for print, they added over fifty pages of elegies to Cleß's text. Councilor Günther Albrecht Renz, for instance, recalled in rhyme the common purpose that had driven him and Jäger in many an intense working hour together; the two law professors Georg Friedrich Harpprecht Sr. and Wolfgang Adam Schöpff bemoaned (in Latin) the death of a man they both had known and admired for many years; Christian Friedrich Sattler, Württemberg's ducal archivist, reminisced about the many years of friendship he had enjoyed with Jäger; and Johann Philipp Pregizer, a government secretary who at one point spent four years living in the Jäger household in Stuttgart, wrote an especially emotional elegy. Addressing the dead man directly, Pregizer wrote that "[a]ll I can and know I owe to the many hours / Which you have devoted to me," and "Go now with the faithful servants [of the Lord to heaven] / And inherit there the due rewards of the pious and righteous."[8]

Philipp Friedrich Jäger was the judge who composed the factual part of the verdict in Joseph Süss Oppenheimer's case. If one trusts what was said at his funeral, his was a truly exemplary life.

Early Life

Joseph Süss Oppenheimer's future judge was born in the town of Schorndorf, about fifteen miles east of Stuttgart as the crow flies. His father was Georg Friedrich Jäger, Schorndorf's town secretary (*Stadtschreiber*); his mother, Anna Maria, was daughter of a town secretary herself.[9] One nineteenth-century genealogist traced the Jägers' roots to the early seventeenth century, when the forester Georg Jäger, Philipp Friedrich's great-great-grandfather, migrated to Württemberg from the northern German territory of Anhalt. The next three generations of Jägers occupied important administrative positions in several Württemberg districts. The forester's son served as ducal commissioner (*Untervogt*) in the important district of Urach, and the latter's son held the same position in Herrenberg. Philipp Friedrich's father's position as town secretary in Schorndorf was only slightly less important than that of his father and his father's father before him. In Schorndorf, as in each of Württemberg's several dozen district towns, the town secretary was one of the ducal commissioner's closest aids.[10]

The Jägers belonged to a particular social group that had long dominated the ranks of Württemberg's administrators. Known as the *Ehrbarkeit* (the "worthies"), in the first half of the eighteenth century this group numbered a few thousand individuals out of a population of about 350,000 in the duchy as a whole.[11] The Ehrbarkeit's prominence in Württemberg owed to the fact that the local nobles had basically seceded from the duchy—the exact details of this story should not concern us here—and came under the direct protection of the Holy Roman emperor as so-called Imperial knights. The duke of Württemberg ruled his territory from Stuttgart (and later, Ludwigsburg), assisted by a group of close aides and a series of governmental bodies such as the administrative and privy councils (*Regierungsrat, Geheimrat*) as well as a few main general departments (war, church affairs, treasury, and so on). Issuing orders from the court was not enough, however. In order to implement ducal policies on the ground and deal with local administrative and legal matters, the duke placed his commissioners throughout the duchy, each in a town that served as the administrative center of a district (*Amt*). Such administrative centers were the historical power base of the Ehrbarkeit.

Over the years, the Ehrbarkeit managed to dominate each district's main political offices and through them the district's representation in Württemberg's general territorial assembly (*Landtag*). Influencing the latter institution was crucial, because according to Württemberg's constitution (*Tübinger Vertrag*, 1514), the territorial assembly was the only political body with the authority to raise new taxes from the general population. At a time when the dukes needed more and more money to finance their military expenditures and some grandiose Baroque building projects, a political conflict between the dukes and the Ehrbarkeit was a constant possibility, if never an unavoidable fact. The dukes needed a stronger army and more money, but also good administrators in the districts; the Ehrbarkeit was reluctant to vote for new taxes, but it also depended on the duke as the source of its social and political legitimacy.

The ongoing tensions between the dukes and the Ehrbarkeit did not affect the latter's political hegemony in towns like Schorndorf. The Ehrbarkeit was too entrenched in such towns for this to happen. The situation at the ducal court, on the other hand, was quite different. Because the pool of educated and experienced administrators in the duchy was quite small, the Ehrbarkeit manned not only the administration in the districts, but many positions in the central government as well. (The absence of a native nobility whose members would normally fill many of these positions was crucial in that respect.) In the decades leading up to Philipp Friedrich Jäger's birth, this situation was rapidly changing. According to one estimate, as late as the 1650s, seventy percent of Württemberg's administrative councilors still belonged to the Ehrbarkeit; by the first decade of the eighteenth century, not a single one did. A recent study called into question some aspects of this estimate, though not its overall conclusion.[12] In the late seventeenth and early eighteenth centuries, the dukes of Württemberg were increasingly turning to foreign advisors to replace native ones they deemed politically unreliable.

The general political circumstances in Württemberg aside, we also know a substantial amount about the particulars of Jäger's youth in Schorndorf. Information comes from three groups of sources. In addition to the individual elegies and Cleß's eulogy of 1745, we have quite a few archival documents about the Jäger family and a lot of evidence about early eighteenth-century

Schorndorf itself. It goes without saying that all three sources must be treated with great caution. The eulogy and the materials from the local archive, though they contain valuable biographical information, may be especially tendentious. A funeral is not the time or place to enumerate the darker sides of the deceased's life, and many of the archival documents in Schorndorf were created and conserved by members of Jäger's own family, three generations of which—Philipp Friedrich's maternal grandfather, his father, and his brother-in-law—served as town secretaries.

Early eighteenth-century Schorndorf was a small but important town.[13] With a population of about 2,000, it was one of those typical early modern hometowns where everybody knew everybody else. A view of the town from the north, drawn two decades before Philipp Friedrich's birth, depicts Schorndorf in an almost idyllic fashion. Nestled within green vineyards, Schorndorf is a compact and well-fortified town, surrounded by drawbridges, a wide moat, bulwarks, and medieval fortifications. On the far left-hand side is the Burgschloss, a fortified castle that helped make Schorndorf one of Württemberg's military fortresses. Picturesque to the modern observer, the castle was not necessarily viewed in the same way by the town's burghers.

Part of the problem was that the Burgschloss garrison, though small, was manned by the duke's, rather than Schorndorf's, men, thus introducing a foreign element into the community. Worse still was the fact that the town's strong fortifications, which were supposed to protect Schorndorf, only served to attract invading French troops to its gates. This happened several times in the decades before Philipp Friedrich's birth, including once in 1687 (an event Philipp Friedrich's father later described in print[14]) and again during Anna Maria Jäger's pregnancy in 1707. In June of that year, Schorndorf surrendered to French troops who threat-

ened to burn down the entire town if it did not immediately ca-
pitulate. The occupation of Schorndorf over the next three years
cost its burghers an estimated 300,000 gulden, a financial shock a
later chronicler deemed a major factor in the town's decline. "One
can boldly claim," the chronicler argued not without some hyperbole, "that had Schorndorf never been a fortress, it would have
become the most important provincial town in Württemberg."[15]

In addition to the strong fortifications and the castle, the
cityscape of early eighteenth-century Schorndorf was also dominated by the local Lutheran church. This was a late Gothic construction with an imposing tower over 180 feet high, which cast
a long shadow over the town both physically and symbolically.
Jäger, Oppenheimer's future judge, was baptized here on October
14, 1707, during the French occupation, and here, in front of the
confessional, he took his first communion on the second Sunday
of Lent fourteen years later.[16] As was common among the Ehrbarkeit, many Jägers served as pastors. While young Philipp
Friedrich was growing up, his uncle served as deacon in Stuttgart;
by the time of Jäger's funeral in 1745, his brother occupied the
same position in the nearby town of Bad Canstatt.[17]

Across from Schorndorf's churchyard was a building that
housed the office and personal quarters of the town's ducal commissioner,[18] and next to it was the town's grammar school. During
Jäger's youth, the schoolmaster was Sigmund Wisshack, an ener-
getic educator who also held an honorary position as Schorndorf's subdeacon. The grammar school had been held in high
esteem even before Wisshack took over as schoolmaster in 1709,
but under Wisshack's leadership it acquired a high reputation and
became a veritable factory of future pastors and state officials. The
situation with girls' education in the town was slightly different.
Wisshack certainly believed girls should be educated, because, as

he once wrote, "most household conflicts stem from the arrogance, avarice, and obstinacy of women who had not been educated properly in their youths." Still, girls should not study too much. "They should not be too smart or curious." In Wisshack's social worldview, everyone had his or her appropriate, God-ordained place.[19]

During the funeral of 1745, Cleß quoted a long passage Jäger once wrote about his old Schorndorf schoolmaster. "He spent so much time and effort on my education: the study of the Latin and Greek languages, Latin and German poetics, also the fundamentals of history, moral philosophy, and physics. I could never even begin to thank him [for all he did for me]."[20] Wisshack, who attended his former student's funeral, replied with an ode. "It went fast with thee, from tender years of youth / Thou hastened to sound mind, with quick steps, further on // Thy mind was fixed by wisdom, virtue, and the truth / of God's Word, thy guiding star, thy true icon."[21] The parting was hard for the aging schoolmaster. He confessed that he had written the ode with "more tears than ink," then addressed the deceased directly: "Thy all too early death oppresses my breast so."[22]

At the center of Schorndorf, not far from the Lutheran church and the grammar school, was the town's elongated marketplace, running north to south. Jäger's father worked in the town chancellery in the southern part of the marketplace, and there is reason to believe that Georg Friedrich's family lived in the same house as well. Immediately opposite this house stood in the 1720s the temporary building of the town hall (the old one had burned down a few years before), a monument to Schorndorf's civic identity and self-administration but also, at least in retrospect, to the close ties between Wisshack and Philipp Friedrich. In November 1717, on the occasion of the two-hundredth anniversary of the

Lutheran Reformation, Wisshack hand-picked Jäger to represent the grammar school in the celebrations by giving a speech from the town hall's balcony.[23] What the young boy said on that occasion is not irrelevant to his eventual involvement in Oppenheimer's case.

Early that day, the two town pastors held commemorative sermons in the church, followed by a procession of the grammar school children to the town hall, where "many important officials, residents, and other burghers had already assembled." After speeches by Wisshack and other dignitaries, it was young Philipp Friedrich Jäger's turn. According to Wisshack's notes from that day, Jäger used his speech to make three related points. He spoke about Luther and his church, which had "freed us from Papal darkness" and replaced "the heavy, cloudy skies which blocked the sun of Jesus Christ's justice" with the "light of the gospels." He acknowledged man's original sin by reminding the crowd that "[w]e know that we are all conceived and born in sin, already full of lust and desire in our mothers' wombs, which would have drawn God's eternal wrath on us had we not been baptized." And he prayed for God to inscribe "these truths in all of our hearts so that we, our children, and our children's children remain fast in the Lutheran faith and honor for ever and ever."[24] When he uttered these words, Philipp Friedrich Jäger was barely ten years old. Even if Wisshack did not write the speech for him, its content was undoubtedly profoundly influenced by the charismatic schoolmaster.

From the balcony of the town hall on that November day in 1717, Jäger could survey much of his hometown: the fortifications and the Burgschloss, the church and its imposing tower, the public buildings and the many timber-framed burgher houses. For us, who are interested above all in the young boy's eventual involvement in Oppenheimer's trial, one last detail about this view is of relevance. In 1717, as in previous centuries, there was no synagogue in sight nor any other trace of Jewish life in the town, Jews having never lived before in Schorndorf, or in almost any other Württemberg town, for that matter. Whatever young Philipp Friedrich Jäger thought about Jews at the time was consequently not the result of interacting with them in person.

Education

In the fall of 1722, shortly before he turned fifteen, Philipp Friedrich Jäger left his hometown. He first moved to Stuttgart, where he spent a year attending the local gymnasium (a highly selective preparatory high school), then on to Tübingen, where he matriculated at the university. Three of Philipp Friedrich's brothers eventually followed him and left Schorndorf. Their father died in 1731, but their mother and the remaining siblings still resided in Schorndorf during Joseph Oppenheimer's ordeal, and they were still there seven years later when Philipp Friedrich passed away. In his 1745 elegy, the Schorndorf magistrate made a special mention of the elderly mother, who was apparently quite frail. "You [that is, Jäger] have left us a special pawn. The mother who laid you in our bosom, she still lives among us."[25]

The gymnasium Jäger attended in Stuttgart was very near the Spitalkirche, the site of his final resting place. Here young men prepared for university by deepening their knowledge in a range of subjects, including Latin, theology, law, history, physics, and mathematics. According to Cleß's funerary oration, Jäger counted among his Stuttgart teachers several representatives of distinguished Ehrbarkeit families, including a Hochstetter and a Bardili.[26] His metaphysics teacher was Georg Konrad Rieger, a Lutheran pastor who, fifteen years later, would play a small but important role in the drama of Joseph Oppenheimer's trial.

While in Stuttgart, Jäger stayed at the house of his uncle, David Friedrich Jäger, the deacon of the local Collegiate church. Just across the street from the church was the palace of the dukes of Württemberg, an impressive stone building complete with turrets, a grand staircase, an internal courtyard, and a three-story loggia. The palace was occupied at the time only by the duchess, Johanna Elisabetha. Fifteen years earlier, Duke Eberhard Ludwig had begun a decades-long affair with Christina Wilhelmina von Grävenitz (later, von Würben), the sister of one of his courtiers, and soon thereafter he, his mistress, and most of the court moved out of the city.[27] Their destination was a newly constructed palace named Ludwigsburg, after the duke. Only the duchess and her private retinue stayed behind in the old Stuttgart palace.

Later in life, Jäger had much to say about the relationship between the duke and his mistress—much that bore directly on the ultimate fate of Joseph Oppenheimer. What Jäger thought about the affair in the early 1720s, on the other hand, is harder to gauge. The only evidence comes from a 1723 celebratory poem Jäger composed as class valedictorian of the Stuttgart gymnasium. The poem never once mentions the scandalous side of Eberhard Ludwig's life. Quite the contrary: "Long live Eberhard, whom Mompelgard and all of Württemberg admire / His happiness and joy should last forever and entire."[28] Whether this adolescent rhyme reflected any authentic feelings on Jäger's part is anyone's guess.

Jäger's next stop after Stuttgart was Tübingen, the site of Württemberg's renowned university. With a population of 4,500, early eighteenth-century Tübingen could have given one the initial impression of a run-of-the-mill German hometown.[29] It had the archetypal medieval fortifications and castle, the simple but symbolically important city gates, a centrally located Lutheran church, a town hall, two marketplaces, and, of course, many streets, alleys, and burgher houses. Just like Schorndorf and several dozen other

Württemberg towns, Tübingen was also a district administrative center. The ducal commissioner and his aides worked from several buildings throughout the town.

Despite its archetypal façade, Tübingen was anything but an ordinary place. Serving as one of the historical residence towns of the dukes of Württemberg, Tübingen hosted a range of important institutions as well as a strong military garrison. The latter's story was not dissimilar to the one Jäger knew from Schorndorf. Adjacent to Tübingen's walls was a castle that had been originally built as the ducal residence but over the years turned more and more into a military fortress manned by the duke's hired soldiers. By the time Jäger moved to Tübingen, this process had long been completed.[30]

Tübingen's many students were perhaps less intimidating than the duke's soldiers, but they were certainly no less raucous. From near and far, they flocked to the town to attend one of its numerous high-quality educational institutions. These included a famous theological seminary, an important academy for the education of young nobles, and above all the local university, the destination of Jäger's own journey in October 1723. According to Cleß's account, Jäger arrived in Tübingen on October 8. Ten days later, the young student also entered his name in the university's records. A "Philipp Friedrich Jäger of Schorndorf" appears in the university's matriculation records for October 18.[31]

Just as in the case of his Schorndorf childhood and the one-year stay in Stuttgart, there is no shortage of sources about Jäger's years in Tübingen. The basic facts are mentioned in Cleß's eulogy and are easily complemented by city, university, and court records. That we can know so much about a single individual in the early eighteenth century is significant in and of itself. Unlike many of the other participants in Joseph Oppenheimer's trial, basic information about Jäger's life—his family, hometown, education, career, and general whereabouts—is known to us today just as it was to his contemporaries in the early eighteenth century. In this respect, one can say about Philipp Friedrich Jäger that he had been well known long before he became famous.

The future main inquisitor in the Oppenheimer case, Jäger spent his first four years in Tübingen as a law student. At least for a while, he lived in the old university dormitory (*Bursa*), a fifteenth-century construction located very near the university's main building in the southern part of town.[32] His daily schedule was busy and often started as early as six o'clock in the morning. Like all his peers, Jäger had to attend mandatory daily lectures by the senior law faculty, lectures that covered a wide range of topics, including canon, civil, feudal, criminal, and inheritance law; he took part and often participated in disputations, a form of academic debate about which a later chapter in this book will have much more to say; and he attended colloquia, a rather flexible form of academic instruction that included, beside dictation and repetition of lecture materials, open discussions between professor and students. If enrolling in a colloquium required extra tuition, it was known as a "private colloquium" (*collegium privatum*) and took place at the professor's house. Otherwise, colloquia were free and held at the university's main building.[33]

Jäger's professors, all of whom are known to us by name, were much more than pure academics.[34] For one, senior faculty members were sworn in as ducal councilors (*Räte*) and at times even called to act as such. (Thus, one of the codefendants in Oppenheimer's trial, Johann Theodor Scheffer, was at the time of his arrest both a top court official and an acting professor of law in Tübingen.)[35] A crucial role of the senior faculty was also to give its learned opinion about important legal cases and—a curiosity of the legal system in the Holy Roman Empire—to compose a proposed final verdict in a large number of trials after reading the evidentiary materials collected by court officials in the districts. Finally, it was the custom that one or two members of the Tübingen law faculty also serve as judges on the *Hofgericht*, Württemberg's high court of appeals for civil cases. The court met once a year for four intensive weeks on the fourth floor of Tübingen's town hall.[36]

The lectures, disputations, and colloquia Jäger attended as a law student are too numerous to be listed here, let alone treated in any length. But two particular colloquia should be mentioned nonetheless, because they allow us to establish a preliminary connection between Jäger's education in the 1720s and his involvement in Oppenheimer's trial in 1737–1738. The first of these two colloquia was taught by Georg Friedrich Harpprecht Sr., a forty-eight-year-old specialist in criminal law and a member of a renowned family of Württemberg jurists. The second was taught by Wolfgang Adam Schöpff, a forty-four-year-old scholar originally from the city of Schweinfurt, up the river Main from Frankfurt. Both Harpprecht and Schöpff served as judges on Württemberg's Hofgericht in the 1720s, and both would ultimately sit next to Jäger on the special criminal court that condemned Joseph Süss Oppenheimer to death. In fact, we have already met the two jurists: they both attended and composed elegies for Jäger's funeral in Stuttgart's Spitalkirche in August 1745.

We know from Cleß and from the printed program of a 1730 university degree ceremony that Jäger learned some of the basic practical aspects of the legal profession in a practical colloquium (*collegium practicum*) taught by Schöpff and in a private colloquium on practical matters (*in rebus practicis*) led by Harpprecht.[37] Both colloquia could very well have included visits to the

Hofgericht, where students could observe firsthand a court in session. (The lectures, disputations, and some of the other colloquia in Tübingen could be quite abstract.[38]) The heart of the practical colloquia, however, lay in supervised exercises in the composition of legal documents in both civil and criminal cases. Jäger not only met Harpprecht and Schöpff in 1720s Tübingen, then; he also learned from the two law professors how to create the basic written records of a trial. Since Jäger would be responsible for creating just such records in Oppenheimer's case, it is worth exploring their nature at this point, if only briefly.

Among the records of a typical trial in the Holy Roman Empire, the *Relation* held a special place. It was a composite document created at the final stage of a trial, once the court completed its inquiries into a case and the consultations over the final verdict were about to begin. Composed by one or two of the court's members (known as the *Referent* and, where such existed, the *Korreferent*), the Relation contained three interrelated parts: (1) a summary of the main facts and circumstances of the case (*species facti*); (2) excerpts from the trial documents that exemplified the main lines of argument pursued by the accusation and the defense (*extractus actorum*); and (3) a learned evaluation of the case by the author(s) of the Relation, complete with justification and a preliminary text for the final verdict (*rationes decidendi, Urthel*). In the early modern period, it was the common practice in many German territories that during the verdict consultations the Referent read the Relation to the other judges, who then voted in a predetermined order whether to accept it or not. In the case that a judge agreed with the proposed verdict, a single word of assent ("placet") was sufficient. If a judge objected to the proposed verdict, his reasons were entered into the protocol and, depending on the circumstances, sometimes taken into account.[39]

Cleß reports that Jäger's years as a law student went by quickly and were so successful that "everyone entertained great hopes for him."[40] In April 1727, with the end of his formal studies in sight, Jäger embarked on a four-month trip to the Rhine Valley and the Low Countries, where he attended lectures by famous law professors at the universities of Heidelberg, Leiden, and Utrecht. He did not travel very long, however. In August of the same year, Jäger was already back in Tübingen, and four months later he passed the exam necessary for attaining the degree of licentiate or doctor of law.[41] It was very early: university regulations prescribed a minimum time period of five years between entering the university and taking this exam, unless one received an exemption on account of a former degree (which Jäger did not have) or demonstrated sufficient knowledge of the material (which he apparently did). The preparatory year in Stuttgart must have played a role in this accelerated course of study, as had the connection with Schöpff and Harpprecht. Indeed, on September 5, 1727, three months before he passed his final exam, Jäger had already been sworn in as advocate of Württemberg's Hofgericht, the same court on which his two mentors had been serving for years.[42]

The rest of Jäger's university career was a mere formality. He submitted a short but learned dissertation on inheritance law in May 1728 and officially became a doctor of both laws after defending his thesis on June 25, 1730.[43] By then, Jäger had already left Tübingen to practice law in Stuttgart, where he soon married Charlotte Regina Cleß, the twenty-one-year-old daughter of the ducal commissioner of the district town of Kirchheim unter Teck.[44] Philipp Friedrich Jäger, the son of Schorndorf's town secretary, was now a well-connected and married doctor of jurisprudence, who practiced law in Stuttgart and served as advocate on Württemberg's high court of appeals. He was barely twenty-three years old.

The Hofgericht

Jäger spent his mid- and late twenties working as a Hofgericht advocate. As such, he gave year-round legal advice to contending parties, presented oral arguments during the court's annual meetings, and sometimes served as independent arbitrator in local civil disputes. Some advocates remained in their positions their entire lives, but more often than not advocacy served as a springboard to higher callings in state administration and academe. Oppenheimer's codefendant, Johann Theodor Scheffer, was a court advocate for five years before embarking on his long career in academia and then politics; Christian Friedrich Sattler, the future ducal archivist (and one of the attendees at Jäger's funeral), started out as an advocate as well; and Jäger's own teacher, Wolfgang Adam Schöpff, also served as an advocate before becoming first professor of law and then judge on the court's bench. Schöpff's unique experience made him a perfect candidate for explaining the court's role within Württemberg's legal system. In 1720, he published one of the most influential treatises on the subject.[45]

The Württemberg Hofgericht dealt mainly with civil disputes and had no jurisdiction over capital cases. The latter were handled in Württemberg principally by district courts as both first and last instances. Because the duke was the ultimate source of law in the land, he could always pardon convicted criminals and, in cases of special importance, could also circumvent usual practice by convening a special (or "princely") criminal court. It had been the controversial claim of Schöpff and other Württemberg jurists that no verdict of a Württemberg court could ever be appealed to a higher instance outside the duchy (*privilegium de non appelando illimitum*).[46] Whether found guilty by a district or a special criminal court, men and women convicted of capital crimes could not consequently appeal their sentence, only hope for ducal pardon.

Readers already familiar with Oppenheimer's trial may recognize two further names among the list of Hofgericht officers in the late 1720s and early 1730s apart from Jäger, Sattler, Scheffer, Schöpff, and Harpprecht. The first is Christoph Ludwig Gabler, the future secretary of the special criminal court against Oppenheimer. For many years, Gabler served as a Hofgericht advocate and in 1735 he became the assistant to the court's permanent secretary. By the mid-1740s at the latest, Gabler seems to have suffered from some serious mental health issues.[47] Even more important than Gabler is Ernst Conrad von Gaisberg,[48] the vice president of the Hofgericht after 1730, who in May 1737 also became the president of the special criminal court against Oppenheimer. Thus, one can say with certainty that already in the 1720s, Harpprecht, Schöpff, Sattler, Scheffer, Gabler, von Gaisberg, and Jäger all knew each other quite well.

And Jäger himself? What kind of person was he? How well did he do his job as an advocate? The destruction of much of the Hofgericht archive in the twentieth century makes it difficult to reconstruct Jäger's exact whereabouts and activities from 1728 to 1735, let alone the intricacies of his professional life.[49] Nevertheless, one anecdote and one general observation about these years might still be quite telling. In his very first year as an advocate, Jäger was entrusted with the arbitration of a small land dispute between two villages in his home district of Schorndorf. According to a surviving account of the case, the dispute was straightforward in both point of fact ("what happened") and point of law (the relevant laws to be applied).[50] After the case had dragged on for several years, representatives of the two sides appeared in front of the Hofgericht on June 9, 1728, and two weeks later Jäger (as arbitrator in the case) submitted his learned opinion to the court. Jäger's document ran for more than two hundred dense pages of learned quotations, references, and relevant, as well as not-so-relevant, legal hairsplitting. Whatever else one might say about Philipp Friedrich Jäger at this point in his life, laziness does not seem to have been one of his faults.

No less telling is a more general observation about Jäger's years as a Hofgericht advocate. We have already noted how by the early eighteenth century the Württemberg Ehrbarkeit had lost much of its influence at court. Jäger's story may be a case in point. Despite his social background, education, many personal connections, and industriousness, Jäger's career progress, very rapid at first, seems to have ground to a halt in the early 1730s. It has been calculated that in seventeenth-century Württemberg, a doctor of law was practically guaranteed a well-paid government position. Not so in Jäger's case in the 1720s and early 1730s. He was a Hofgericht advocate in 1728 and was still one seven years later. Indeed, as late as the spring of 1735, Philipp Friedrich Jäger still had not served as a judge or state councilor, and his expertise was limited to civil and administrative cases rather than criminal law. Why would he, of all people, end up serving as a leading judge-inquisitor in the criminal court against Oppenheimer?

The Grävenitz Affair

Unbeknownst to Jäger and Oppenheimer, in 1731 a series of unexpected events began drawing their lives together. It all began in the spring of that year, when Duke Eberhard Ludwig decided to reconcile with his long-estranged wife, Johanna Elisabetha. The reason for the duke's surprising move—he had been living with his mistress in Ludwigsburg for almost twenty years at that point—was the deteriorating health of his only son and heir, Friedrich Ludwig. If the successor to the throne passed away and the duke died childless, Württemberg's next ruler would be Carl Alexander, Eberhard Ludwig's Catholic cousin. A Catholic prince reigning over a proudly Lutheran population was a clear recipe for trouble. Consider the anti-Catholicism of Jäger's speech from the balcony of Schorndorf's town hall in 1717. If the pope was indeed "the heavy, cloudy skies that blocked the sun of Jesus Christ's justice,"[51] how could a Catholic prince be trusted to rule Württemberg?

Once Eberhard Ludwig finally ended his relationship with Christina Wilhelmina von Würben (née Grävenitz), he went all in. On the night of October 15, 1731, he had his former mistress and many of her close allies arrested, and soon thereafter he appointed a special inquisition committee to investigate the prisoners' yet-to-be-determined crimes. In the meantime, Grävenitz-Würben and her associates were incarcerated in different fortresses throughout the duchy, including Urach, Hohen Asperg, and Hohen Neuffen. Despite all this trouble, the reconciliation with the duchess proved fruitless. The ailing heir passed away on November 23, 1731, and Eberhard Ludwig himself died two years later. That his wife did not bear him another son in the meantime should not have taken anyone by surprise. By the time the duke finally reconciled with her, Johanna Elisabetha was already fifty-one years old.

The rise and fall of Christina Wilhelmina von Grävenitz on the one hand and Joseph Süss Oppenheimer on the other hand are usually told as two separate, if similar, stories.[52] Clearly, they share many leitmotifs. Both Grävenitz and Oppenheimer were foreigners who came to play important roles at the Württemberg court; both were perceived as enemies of the Ehrbarkeit and champions of political and financial reform; and both were eventually arrested, incarcerated in a fortress, and put on trial alongside their alleged accomplices. It is nonetheless a mistake to emphasize the similarities between the two stories without stressing that the connections between them run much deeper than that. Grävenitz-Würben's and Oppenheimer's stories are marked not so much by parallelism as by intermingling. The biographies of Philipp Friedrich Jäger and some of his associates prove this point beyond any doubt.

The first stage of the legal proceedings against Grävenitz-Würben took place during the reign of her former lover, Eberhard Ludwig. It started with the arrests of October 1731 and ended with Grävenitz-Würben's release from prison in the spring of 1733 before the main part of her trial could even begin. Württemberg criminal procedure followed here the general practice in the Holy Roman Empire: once an arrest had been made, a state-appointed judge-inquisitor or group of judges ("inquisition committee") interrogated the suspect and began gathering evidence against him or her through interrogations, depositions, and the collection of other relevant material. If the evidence in this pre-trial inquisition was deemed damning enough, the main part of the trial could commence.[53]

In the spring of 1733, Grävenitz-Würben agreed to pay Eberhard Ludwig a sum of 150,000 gulden in exchange for her liberty. Shortly thereafter, she left the duchy and settled first in Frankfurt and then in Berlin. She would never visit Württemberg again. After Carl Alexander's ascension to the throne, however, the duke reopened the criminal case against his predecessor's mistress and allowed the court to proceed to the main part of the trial, complete with a *Fiskal* (prosecutor) and judges. Among the latter, we see familiar names—Schöpff, Harpprecht, and von Gaisberg—but also Johann Christoph von Pflug, Eberhard Ludwig Bardili, and Abel Weinmann, all of whom we shall encounter again soon. The court secretary was Christoph Ludwig Gabler, Jäger's associate from the Hofgericht.

It was then that a new series of unexpected events catapulted Jäger onto center stage. First came the death of one of the appointed judges, then of another. By early June 1735, the Fiskal, Moritz David Harpprecht, was also suffering from deteriorating health and unable to proceed. A relative of the Tübingen professor and himself a former colleague of Jäger's on the advocates' bench of the Hofgericht, Moritz David Harpprecht recommended Jäger as his replacement. The latter was "to appear in my [M. D. Harpprecht's] name before the court, with the complete and free power to negotiate and observe, just as I would have done myself."[54] Two days later, Harpprecht succumbed to his illness, and three days after that Carl Alexander appointed Jäger to Harpprecht's vacated position of Fiskal in the criminal case against Grävenitz-Würben and her accomplices.[55]

In his role as Fiskal, Moritz David Harpprecht had already drawn the outlines of the accusations against Grävenitz-Würben and her "system" (retinue). According to his list of accusation charges (*Anklageschrift*), Grävenitz-Würben was guilty of a long series of what Harpprecht termed "great crimes" and "abominable excesses," including assisting abortion, bigamy, aggravated adultery, fraud, embezzlement, perjury, lèse-majesté, and even attempted murder.[56] Had Grävenitz been convicted of even a fraction of these allegations, she would have ended up on the gallows.

Once he replaced Harpprecht as Fiskal, Jäger pursued further his predecessor's line of attack against Grävenitz-Würben's supposedly "atrocious crimes."[57] We see this most clearly in the catalogue of questions (*articulos probatoriales*) Jäger prepared in the early summer of 1735, shortly after assuming the role of Fiskal. The catalogue was supposed to serve in the interrogations of close to two hundred witnesses Jäger intended to summon, and though at first glance its 310 questions seem to include everything but the kitchen sink, a closer look reveals five more or less clear lines of questioning.

Some of Jäger's questions were related to Grävenitz-Würben's alleged ability to control who would have direct contact with the duke. "Is it true that [Grävenitz-Würben] did all she could to prevent others from having access to the duke? . . . Is it true that no issue [at court] could ever be resolved without her knowledge and permission?" (questions 3, 6). A second set of questions had to do with Grävenitz-Würben's alleged crimes against the state and the estates, including misuse of the criminal justice system, the selling of government offices, and the creation of state monopolies. "Is it true," Jäger asked, "that state offices were sold to the highest bidder rather than to those who were best qualified to perform them?" and, "Is it true that all state councilors who were not members of [Grävenitz-Würben's] close circle were chased away, and sometimes even prosecuted?" (questions 14, 91). These and similar questions were asked in a very general way. At stake were not specific incidents so much as an alleged policy against Jäger's own social milieu, the Ehrbarkeit. In one of his questions, Jäger put it quite bluntly. "Is it true that [Grävenitz-Würben] made the duke hate the estates [that is, essentially the Ehrbarkeit]?" (question 214). Another, very early on, even asked, "Is it true that the country's great misfortune [*Verderben*] has happened because of her?" (question 9).

When it did come to specific questions, Jäger was interested in three main issues. One was Grävenitz's personal life. Some of the questions here related to the countess's sexual behavior. "Is it true that she was impregnated by a trumpeter? . . . Is it true that a small baby, about a finger long, was once found in her night stool?" (questions 224, 226). At other times, Jäger concentrated on the countess's alleged use of black magic. "Is it true that everyone suspected she was employing secret arts [*verbotene Künste*]?" or, "Is it true that she took from the duke samples of his blood and hair to use [in her magic]?" (questions 248, 258). Most important of all, however, were questions about the exchange of money during her many years in Eberhard Ludwig's court: who paid what to whom, when, for what purpose, and by what means. Of the 310 questions listed in Jäger's catalogue, about seventy percent belong to this category.

Considering what Jäger was about to do during Oppenheimer's trial, this last group of questions might take one by surprise. Both Grävenitz-Würben and Duke Eberhard Ludwig had maintained many contacts with court Jews.[58] In his interrogation of witnesses during the Grävenitz-Würben trial, Jäger questioned some of these Jews, and his questions to them make clear that he suspected they had been misused, robbed, and criminalized by the countess and her retinue. "Is it true that she targeted especially the court Jews, interrogated and even arrested them [for no reason]?" (question 49); "Is it true that [she] extorted 70,000 gulden from the Jew Levin?" (question 50); "Is it true that she had the Jew Model arrested and kept in prison for six years for no reason at all?" (question 52).[59]

Surprising though it may sound, Philipp Friedrich Jäger, one of the driving forces behind the interrogation and criminalization of Joseph Süss Oppenheimer, was only a few years earlier concerned about the unjustified treatment of Württemberg's court Jews. One faces two interpretative possibilities here: either Jäger was an especially opportunistic and hypocritical Fiskal, for whom achieving a conviction always justified the means; or else his attitude toward Jews, his involvement in Oppenheimer's case notwithstanding, was more complicated than previously assumed.

* * *

Exactly one year after Jäger became the Fiskal in the Grävenitz-Würben case, Duke Carl Alexander reached a financial settlement with his predecessor's mistress. On top of the 150,000 gulden she had already paid Eberhard Ludwig, Grävenitz-Würben was to pay another 350,000 gulden to Carl Alexander in exchange for a final settlement of her case.[60] Joseph Süss Oppenheimer played a significant role in striking this deal. He seems to have built a good relationship with Grävenitz-Würben when they were both living in Frankfurt, so Carl Alexander appointed him as ducal representative in the negotiations.[61] Two years later, during Oppenheimer's own trial, one of the judges asked him directly about his involvement in Grävenitz-Würben's defense. According to Gabler's protocol of the interrogation of August 28, 1737, Oppenheimer replied that he had in fact done very little for Grävenitz-Würben. He did not mention a plea he had sent to Carl Alexander on the countess's behalf and indeed claimed that he had been sick during much of the Grävenitz-Würben affair.[62]

As for Jäger, he was clearly disappointed by the way the Grävenitz-Würben trial ended. He had suspected that something was afoot as early as October 1735, when he politely complained in a letter to Duke Carl Alexander about the frequent and unexplained delays in the trial.[63] A few weeks later, he wrote again to the duke that he had "already devoted 20 weeks to the trial, to the great detriment of my law practice . . . and despite a series of illnesses and other household calamities."[64] (What these calamities were he did not specify.) Half a year later, with the conclusion of the financial settlement between Carl Alexander and Grävenitz-Würben, Jäger could not hide his frustration anymore. He called the whole affair "as tedious and odious a thing as one can imagine."[65] All his hard work over the previous year, attested to by the mountains of paperwork one can still see in the Stuttgart state archives today, seemed to have been in vain.

As it turned out, it was not all for naught. A little over a year after the sudden conclusion of the Grävenitz-Würben trial, one last series of unexpected incidents caused Jäger and Oppenheimer to finally confront each other face-to-face. On March 12, 1737, Carl Alexander died in his Ludwigsburg palace, and over the next few days, a regent was appointed to stand in for the dead duke's nine-year-old son. On the very night of the duke's sudden death, Oppenheimer, his servants, and many other court officials were arrested, and soon a special inquisition committee was convened in order to investigate the court Jew's "atrocious crimes"—exactly the same expression used against Grävenitz-Würben only a short time earlier.

The similarities between Grävenitz's and Oppenheimer's trials did not end with this one expression. Schöpff, Harpprecht, and von Gaisberg, whom Jäger had met in Tübingen and then worked with in the Hofgericht and the Grävenitz-Würben trial, were involved in the legal proceedings against Oppenheimer as well. Even more important were von Pflug, Bardili, Weinmann, Gabler, and Pregizer, who, like Jäger himself, were appointed to different positions in Oppenheimer's inquisition committee itself (to be distinguished from the criminal court as a whole). The similarities between the Grävenitz and Oppenheimer trials were consequently neither coincidental nor merely structural. The two trials took place in quick succession, in the same duchy, against a similar type of accused (a foreign courtier), with an almost identical cast of characters, and with a very similar list of accusations.

The connection between Grävenitz-Würben's and Oppenheimer's trials was especially decisive with respect to Jäger. Without his experience as Fiskal in the Grävenitz-Würben case—indeed, without the long series of unexpected events that made his involvement in the trial against Grävenitz-Würben a possibility and then a reality—there would have been no reason to appoint him to the criminal inquisition committee against Oppenheimer. No wonder that Cleß, in his eulogy of 1745, referred to Jäger's membership in several "princely [inquisition] committees" as decisive stepping-stones in the deceased's illustrious career; so, indeed, they were. The exact nature of these committees and the connections between them were so well known to the crowd assembled in the Spitalkirche on August 5, 1745, that Cleß felt no need to say much about them. Only the modern reader, three centuries later, needs to be reminded how Philipp Friedrich Jäger came to play such an important role in the criminal case against Joseph Süss Oppenheimer, the notorious "Jew Süss."

FIGURE 5. Unknown artist. Three scenes from Oppenheimer's trial, 1738. From top to bottom: Interrogation by the inquisition committee; Jews bewailing Oppenheimer's fate; Oppenheimer transported to the execution site.
Source: WLB, Grafische Sammlung.

Part 2: *Species Facti*

He was without any religion at all,
without conscience, without honor, without
culture, without loyalty, without faith.
—Philipp Friedrich Jäger on Oppenheimer,
December 1737

At the time of Carl Alexander's death, Jäger's wife was in the last stages of pregnancy. Four days later, on March 16, 1737, she gave birth to a girl she and her husband named Maria Rosine.[66] This was the couple's third child, after Anna Friderika (born 1732) and Charlotte Regina (1735). Because, in the next few months, Philipp Friedrich Jäger's involvement in Oppenheimer's trial required his presence away from Stuttgart for long periods of time, it is safe to assume he saw little of his newborn daughter, her sisters, or his wife until at least early September, possibly even later.

In Stuttgart, the week of Maria Rosine's birth was characterized by extreme political uncertainty. The dead duke's son was a minor, the dowager was a Catholic like her late husband, and there were rumors—never to be confirmed—of a Catholic plot to invade Württemberg and topple the government. Later in the year, Jäger himself would have difficulties reconstructing the exact details of those days. On August 4, 1737, during one of his many interrogation sessions with Oppenheimer, he would ask the prisoner to enlighten him in this respect. According to Gabler's protocol of the interrogation, Oppenheimer too was unclear about what had happened in the days immediately following Carl Alexander's death. He replied to Jäger's question by describing a period of "great confusion."[67]

Eight days after the duke's death, things had stabilized at least a little. The dowager had been pushed aside, and Carl Rudolph, a sixty-nine-year-old scion of a sideline of the ducal family, had been appointed regent. It was around this time that Jäger's name began to appear in the official records concerning Oppenheimer.[68] On March 20, Carl Rudolph appointed three men to a special inquisition committee to investigate the case: Johann Jakob Dann, a thirty-seven-year-old government councilor and former member of the Hofgericht in Tübingen; Wilhelm Eberhard Faber, another government councilor and Hofgericht veteran; and Abel Weinmann, a former judge in the Grävenitz-Würben case who would soon be transferred off the committee.[69] Also on that day, Oppenheimer and two other arrestees, Johann Christoph Bühler and Jacob Friedrich Hallwachs, were transported from Stuttgart to the prison fortress of Hohen Neuffen, about half a day's march south of Stuttgart.[70]

In the days following the formation of the inquisition committee, the regent strengthened it with three additional members. On March 21, he appointed Jäger and Eberhard Ludwig Bardili to the committee, and by March 23 the sources mention von Pflug as another member.[71] That the three new commissars were all veterans of the Grävenitz-Würben case could hardly have been a coincidence; that all six commissars had known each other long before March 1737 is worth reiterating.

On the same day, Jäger was appointed commissar, but before he, Bardili, or von Pflug could physically join the inquisition committee, Faber, Dann, and Weinmann met for the first time. Gabler served as their secretary. The location of the meeting was the "small heated room of the [administrative council] library" in Stuttgart.[72] From that point on, our knowledge of the commissars' activities is extremely detailed. During their first meeting, the three original members of the committee promised to keep a *diarium* (logbook) of what they did every day. Over the next few months, the committee's scribes also created meticulous protocols of the various interrogations and depositions, while the commissars themselves engaged in extensive correspondence both with one another and with various people and agencies in Württemberg and abroad. The result is a remarkable collection of documents about who did what, where, and when in the course of the investigation.

From the very beginning, one can observe a division of labor among the commissars. During the trial's first (preliminary) phase, Faber, Dann, Gabler, and Weinmann (while he was still a commissar) remained in Stuttgart, performing their tasks in at least three different locations: the library of the administrative council, Oppenheimer's seized house in the city, and a room in the personal residence of the president of the administrative council, Christoph Peter von Forstner. This group of commissars had much on its plate: receiving orders from the regent and his administrative council (March 22: "the members of the committee should be careful to follow all the instructions studiously and carefully, and accelerate the trial as much as possible"); interrogating Oppenheimer's arrested domestic servants; supervising the creation of a general inventory of Oppenheimer's possessions; and exchanging letters with various people, both near and far.[73]

Jäger and von Pflug had a different task. Accompanied by a scribe, they left Stuttgart on Wednesday, March 27, for the fortress of Hohen Neuffen, where Oppenheimer, Bühler, and Hallwachs were being kept under guard. The small party arrived at the fortress at 6 o'clock in the evening and remained there until April 8.[74] The morning after their arrival in Hohen Neuffen, Jäger, von Pflug, and their secretary began working, "in the room adjacent to the Chamber of State."[75] The hierarchy in the inquisition committee must have been very clear: von Pflug was the senior member, Jäger second in command, and Johann Heinrich Hochstetter Sr. (the secretary) a distant third (figure 5). First on the agenda was the preliminary interrogation of Oppenheimer himself. The secretary described a scene in which "they had the Jew, Süß Oppenheimer, brought before them by the guard, informed him of the task assigned to them by His Highness [the regent], and then formulated the questions and began interrogating him."[76]

Throughout the following interrogation, the scribe wrote down Oppenheimer's answers using the third person. This common practice in the early modern period highlights the important role of the scribe in the inquisitorial procedure as a translator of live speech into writing.[77] Some historians of Oppenheimer's case have been cautious about not conflating the oral testimony with the written record.[78] Jäger's contemporaries would not have disagreed. Like many early modern jurists, they realized the power and responsibilities invested in the person of the scribe.[79]

According to Hochstetter's protocol, Oppenheimer's first interrogation began with the usual preliminary questions about the arrestee's name, age, profession, and religion. These questions were known as the *interrogatoria generalia* in contemporary jurists' Latin, the standard interrogatory questions with which any new interrogation was supposed to open:

1. What is his name?

   R[eply]. Joseph Süß Oppenheimer from Heidelberg.

2. How old?

   R. Between 38 and 39 years.

3. What is his profession, and what has he studied?

   R. To negotiate with powerful men and to handle them.

4. Of which religion?

R. He is a Jew by birth, but he has the religion of an honest man.

5. Whether he still to date professes the Jewish religion?

R. Yes.

6. Had he not let himself be heard to say throughout the land that he is independent of all religions?

R. Yes, he has said that, but with the intention and with this explication that he did not have a passion against any religion, therefore he is neither drawn to or away from any particular one.[80]

Over the next eleven months, the commissars rarely asked Oppenheimer for details about the life he had led before arriving in Württemberg. They showed little interest in learning more about Oppenheimer's parents and siblings, childhood and youth, education, or personal religious observance. Although frustrating for the modern historian, the commissars' general lack of interest in Oppenheimer's background is itself quite telling. In contrast to modern criminologists, Jäger and his associates were not concerned primarily with Oppenheimer's personal background or his particular motivations or thoughts. Rather, they were interested in his actions (his allegedly "atrocious crimes") and in what property he possessed.[81] This was the context of the next series of questions on the morning of March 28, which, according to Hochstetter's protocol, Oppenheimer all but completely evaded.

7. What does his property amount to?

R. He cannot know this, because his people [assistants] have been in charge of it, and he has not balanced the books within the last two years.

8. Where is his property located?

R. Partly in Frankfurt, partly in Stuttgart, he himself does not know, his people know this. He is not giving any information regarding his wealth.

9. How much property did he have before he came to this region [Württemberg]?

R. As a merchant, he is not obliged to answer that. The late duke was aware of it.

10. How much did his household cost him annually?

R. He does not know.

11. Where did he reside before he was employed locally?

R. He was received by all the princes, and he has lived many places to earn his money, largely in Frankfurt, Darmstadt, Mannheim, and Heidelberg.

12. What kind of crimes did he commit in Heidelberg, Mannheim, and those places?

R. They [the inquisitors] should tell him, he knows of none.[82]

Next came two questions about Oppenheimer's involvement in a mint-leasing contract in Darmstadt. They are of interest because, among other reasons, the Württemberg officials had no jurisdiction in the Hessian city, as Oppenheimer himself was quick to point out.

13. Whether he was already involved with the minting of coins [in Heidelberg, Mannheim, and other places]?

R. Yes, he had a mint contract in Darmstadt, which he had passed on to a subcontractor for 9,000 gulden in payment. This is public knowledge, he is not obliged to say anything about the rest.

14. What did this contract consist of, and did it only consist of the delivery of gold and silver?

R. That is stated in the contract, which the Count [in Darmstadt] has in his possession and which he will not willingly have made public.[83]

Still grasping at straws, Jäger and von Pflug next asked Oppenheimer two questions about his relationship with women, then turned to Oppenheimer's arrival in Württemberg and his status as a Jewish advisor to a Christian prince.

15. With which women has he lived in an illegal union?

R. They [the inquisitors] should make the accusers known to him.

16. What was the name then of the lady in Frankfurt,[84] who was arrested a while ago because of him?

R. They would have to ask the elector in Cologne about that, if they want to involve the same in this.

17. When did he take up his duties in Württenberg?

*R. [Various official documents] will show this. He already had dealings with the deceased duke when the same was still a prince.**

18. What did his functions and service consist of?

R. Before the reign of His Princely Highness [Carl Alexander], he had been Supreme and Military Factor and Chatoul-Administrator,† as well as agent for Her Highness, the duchess.

---

* Addition in the left-hand margin: "*addit* during the reading: he had offered the same to advance him all his appanage money and revenues, and came to an agreement with him to the effect that he really did advance it in part."

† Supreme and military factor: provider of military and other supplies to a prince. Chatoul-administrator: the person responsible for handling a prince's private money, to be distinguished from the state's.

After that he became Resident in Frankfurt, and finally Privy
Financial Councilor.*

19. What did his responsibilities consist of in the latter
functions?

 *R. As Resident, his mandate had been to bring about what His
Highness ordered him to do. Whether he had received an official
Mandate as Financial Councilor he does not know, it could be
found among his papers. But his function had been the same, to
do what His Highness ordered him to do.*

20. Whether he did not know that according to Imperial and
national [Württemberg] law no Jew can become councilor?

 *R. He was not aware of the regulations; furthermore, he be-
lieved that he was allowed to accept what the duke appointed him
to.*[85]

 Such questions notwithstanding, most of the interrogation on
the morning of March 28 revolved around very general issues that
seem to have been taken almost verbatim from the *articulos probatoriales* Jäger had composed during the Grävenitz-Würben
trial.

27. Since when has it been that nothing was allowed to happen
[at court] without him?

29. Whether he had not himself chosen and named the persons
to the Privy Cabinet?

32. Whether he had not threatened those who, in opposition to
his written or verbal orders, did not want to obey him, immediately with being fired or something else?

 * The duke's representative.

34. Had he not regularly written to public officials, provincial commissars and others in his own name concerning official business, giving orders and instructions?

39. Had he not ordered the reinstatement of an official who was earlier dismissed from the main customs office in Heidenheim, and immediately made this public?

41. Had he not arrogated to himself, quite shortly before his arrest, the right to reprimand the Princely Administrative Council?[86]

According to the interrogation's protocol, Oppenheimer's replies to the committee's interrogatory questions amounted to a complete denial of any wrongdoing. They were all variations on the same theme: "He has no recollection of any such instruction," "He had nothing to do with that," "Nobody has suggested so," "Never in his life has he used such expressions," and, "Now it is easy to say a lot, and to attribute the weight of guilt to him now."[87]

The interrogation on the morning of March 28 was indicative of much more to come. Jäger and von Pflug do not seem to have had direct knowledge of Oppenheimer's alleged crimes, nor were they familiar at this preliminary phase of the trial with other witnesses' testimonies. Hence their reliance on extremely general questions ("What kind of crimes did he commit in Heidelberg, Mannheim, and those places?" "Since when has it been that nothing was allowed to happen without him?") or outright gossip ("Had he not let himself be heard to say . . ."; "What was the name then of the lady in Frankfurt . . ."). After forty-one such questions, the first interrogation came to a close without much progress. Hochstetter reports that "[a]fter a further reading of the protocol, the above testimony was signed by Süss."[88] Jäger and von Pflug, for their part, continued the interrogation in the afternoon, then again on Friday, March 29, and the following day. According to a report Jäger later sent to the regent, he and von Pflug made little progress in their three-day preliminary interrogation of Joseph Süss Oppenheimer.[89]

Stuttgart

Having completed Oppenheimer's preliminary interrogation, Jäger remained in Hohen Neuffen. He and von Pflug took a day off on March 31 (it was a Sunday), then moved to interrogate Hallwachs and Bühler, the two councilors who had been transported to Hohen Neuffen together with Oppenheimer a week and a half earlier. The preliminary interrogations of the two councilors took place in quick succession on the morning of Monday, April 1, after which Jäger and von Pflug had a brief afternoon interrogatory session with Oppenheimer, whom they asked to respond to six final questions.[90] After that, it was all about Hallwachs and Bühler. Jäger and von Pflug interrogated Hallwachs over a period of two days (April 2–3) and Bühler over four (April 4–7).[91] At times, the two commissars took a break from the interrogations to compose and receive reports. On April 2, for instance, they authored a report to the regent, and two days later they composed a letter to their colleague Faber in Stuttgart.[92] It was during another such break that they left Hallwachs alone in the interrogation room so that he could compose a personal letter to the regent.[93] Throughout his trial, they never granted Oppenheimer the same privilege. The commissars made sure that a written version of his side of the story would always be mediated through someone else.[94]

Judging by the questions Jäger and von Pflug put to Hallwachs and Bühler in the first week of April, the two commissars were most interested at this point in what they termed Oppenheimer's *präpotenz und pouvoir*—the court Jew's alleged usurpation of power and his supposedly overwhelming (and, in the commissars' opinion, illegal) influence on the duke. On the afternoon of April 4, for instance, the question about Oppenheimer's *präpotenz* was the only one Jäger and von Pflug put to Bühler. This accusation was practically identical to the one Jäger had used against Grävenitz-Würben two years earlier. Indeed, on April 7, Jäger asked Bühler directly about Eberhard Ludwig's old mistress, and six months later, when he authored the factual part of the Relation in Oppenheimer's case, Jäger claimed the two cases showed clear continuity.[95]

With Johann Christoph Bühler, Jäger and von Pflug continued the same kind of fishing expedition they had tried earlier with Oppenheimer and with Hallwachs. They asked Bühler about Oppenheimer and the Württemberg mint; they questioned him about the court Jew's relationship with other Jews; and they interrogated him about what they called the general corruption (*Landesverderben*) Oppenheimer had supposedly brought on Württemberg. (As we have already seen, *Verderben* was a key term in the legal proceedings during the Grävenitz-Würben trial as well.) In replying to such questions, Bühler followed Oppenheimer and conceded no wrongdoing, though he employed, admittedly, a different defense strategy. Whereas Oppenheimer's recorded responses were almost always short and evasive, Bühler's were incredibly verbose. The most significant exception came toward the very end of Bühler's preliminary interrogation on the afternoon of April 7. Reaching the end of their catalogue of interrogatory questions, Jäger and von Pflug came back to the basics. They urged Bühler to explain "why he assisted the Jew in so many ways with his treacherous projects; why, indeed, he sought the

Jew's proximity like no other Württemberg princely servant." Bühler's reported response was short and decisive. Everything, he explained, was done "at the explicit order of His Highness," that is, Carl Alexander.[96]

Had Jäger and von Pflug learned much from Bühler's, Hallwachs's, or Oppenheimer's preliminary interrogations, the legal proceedings against the three would have ended quite quickly. As in the rest of the Holy Roman Empire, the criminal justice system in early modern Württemberg relied heavily on the accused's own confession as opposed to other forms of evidence. Once it was clear that Oppenheimer would not admit to any wrongdoing, the commissars had to use other and much more time-consuming means to make a case against him. This is one explanation for the staggering amount of paperwork Jäger, von Pflug, and the other members of the inquisition committee created over the next few months. These piles of paper are not only evidence of the commissars' industriousness. They are also testimony to the immense difficulties the commissars faced in finding a smoking gun in the court Jew's case.

Hallwachs's and Bühler's interrogations were similarly unfruitful. According to Hochstetter's protocol, the two arrestees told Jäger and von Pflug little that advanced the investigation. The result was that Hallwachs spent a whole decade in jail and Bühler was incarcerated in Hohen Asperg for two years and kept under house arrest for another six.[97] As in Oppenheimer's case, the significance of the two councilors' preliminary interrogations lies less in what they tell us about the defendants than in what they reveal about the inquisitors. This is especially true in Bühler's case, who singled out Jäger as the source of his predicament.

Scarcely a day after Bühler's transfer to Hohen Neuffen, his exasperated wife complained about her husband's arrest and overall treatment. Their fourteen-year-old son was left heartbroken by the separation from his father, and the family's entire livelihood was in jeopardy now that its breadwinner was in jail. Bühler, too, complained bitterly. Inspired perhaps by the outcome of the Grävenitz-Würben case, he expressed his willingness to pay "any price whatsoever" for his liberty. The conditions in jail, he explained, were "worse than death itself. My enemies locked me up like a mere beast, letting no one visit me either while I was healthy or when I got sick. . . . My enemies did such a fine job on me that I lost all memory and know not what my own defects are."[98]

Bühler considered Jäger first and foremost among his tormentors. Eight months after Oppenheimer's execution, while Bühler's own trial was unfolding, Jäger's protégé, Johann Philipp Pregizer, came to see Bühler in jail. According to Pregizer's account of their meeting, Bühler told him that Jäger had shown "a special joy regarding his [Bühler's] misfortune and had treated him so badly that he swears by his soul and salvation that [Jäger] hates him passionately and behaves toward him in the most wicked and unjust way." Pregizer further reports that Bühler, who felt "complete respect toward all the other commissars," had pleaded with him to find a way to remove Jäger (and only him) from the inquisition committee. There must have been at least some truth to Bühler's accusations, because shortly after Pregizer's return to Stuttgart, Jäger was indeed removed from Bühler's case.[99]

A day after Jäger was done with Bühler's preliminary interrogation, he traveled back to Stuttgart, followed by von Pflug a day or two later. The inquisition committee's membership had stabilized in the meantime. Bardili was still an official member, but he was sick most of the time, and Weinmann had been transferred off to a different position. This left four commissars (von Pflug, Dann, Faber, and Jäger) and three scribes (Gabler, Pregizer, and Hochstetter Sr.). The committee was working now mostly in Stuttgart, in a room in President Forstner's house. That it worked very hard in the following weeks is attested to by several sources, including the committee's logbook (kept mostly by Faber); an almost endless series of depositions, testimonies, and protocols; and external as well as internal correspondence.

During the following eight weeks, a special subcommittee began auctioning off some of Oppenheimer's property to cover the trial's expenses while the inquisition committee itself continued its work.[100] As a rule, the four commissars worked six days a week (the Sabbath was usually, although not always, observed), collecting evidence from various state agencies, conducting extensive correspondence, interrogating suspects, and taking depositions from witnesses.[101] Between April 8 and late May, the commissars showed little interest in the fate of the incarcerated Oppenheimer, who was left to fend for himself in Hohen Neuffen. Without a confession and in light of his short, evasive answers, the fallen court Jew was of little use to the committee at this point. The only exception was the issue of Oppenheimer's deteriorating health. Oppenheimer had repeatedly asked the commissars for a physician. Eventually, if somewhat reluctantly, Jäger and his associates sent one to him on April 20.[102] It was on the fifth day of the Jewish holiday of Passover.

From the earliest stages of the inquest, Regent Carl Rudolph wanted to see it quickly come to a close. The day after Jäger's appointment as commissar, the regent asked him and his colleagues to "proceed according to their obligations and with the necessary industriousness and attention to detail, but [at the same time] accelerate the thing [trial] as much as possible."[103] Two months later, it was clear that the committee, still busy with the preliminary phase of the trial, was taking its time. This was the context of a letter Carl Rudolph sent on May 16, in which he asked the commissars to proceed to the main part of the trial "without any further delays."[104]

In the following two and a half weeks, the four commissars were up to their ears in work. They continued to collect evidence against Oppenheimer through various interrogations and depositions. On the same day they received the regent's letter, for instance, Jäger, Dann, Faber, and Pregizer (the latter as secretary) conducted a long interrogation of Johann Albrecht Mez, another of Oppenheimer's alleged accomplices. A week went by, and not much had changed. On the morning of May 23, Jäger and Gabler first recorded the deposition of the forty-three-year-old court advocate, Justus Valentin Stemann, then interrogated the Jew Nathan Maram about his contacts with Oppenheimer, and finally joined von Pflug, Dann, and Faber in questioning Oppenheimer's personal treasurer, Isaac Samuel Levi.[105] It was during such activities that the commissars also reacted to Carl Rudolph's letter. On Monday, May 20, they met as usual at President Forstner's home and composed a letter to the regent in which they agreed to proceed to the main part of the trial. For the first time, they also clearly stated the overall goals of the legal proceedings, identified the main challenges that stood in their way, and devised possible solutions to these challenges.

The committee began its reply to Carl Rudolph by explaining why the preliminary part of the trial had been taking so long. The commissars had been "working tirelessly, managing the files about Süss, Hallwachs, Bühler, and Mez, reading through and analyzing the reports from the different district towns, and reading through the documents from the ducal mint." The result was a tremendous amount of information, "even a general summary of which would be far too copious" in the present context. Still, it is clear that, just as in Grävenitz-Würben's case, "in essence and substance, Süss's main crime fell under the category of treason [*crimen perduelionis*], that is, a crime committed not against a particular subject, but above all against the prince and by analogy against the country [that is, Württemberg] and the state." Süss was a traitor because of his "false council and his attacks against the laws of the land." The committee believed it had clear evidence that Oppenheimer was guilty of other crimes as well, including multiple cases of embezzlement, private usury, adultery, and the debasement of coins in the mint. The commissars were left "with no doubt" that such crimes should result "in the highest punishment": death.[106]

Despite its unfaltering faith in the final outcome of the trial, the committee acknowledged that composing a legitimate Relation in the case would take much time and effort. The commissars and their assistants had already accumulated hundreds of pages of documents, but some of them (as in the case of many depositions, for instance) had to be repeated during the main (formal) part of the trial. Jäger and his colleagues also maintained that certain matters made it mandatory to "gain special clarification by reading through various contracts and the accounting books of the mint . . . as well as to conduct more interrogations and witness confrontations."[107] That all of this could not be accomplished in just a few days went without saying.

One way of accelerating the trial was to bring both the accusers and the accused to a single place. Over the course of the preliminary stage of the trial, Oppenheimer, Bühler, and Hallwachs were kept in Hohen Neuffen, while the committee worked also at Forstner's home, in the mint, and in Oppenheimer's home in

Stuttgart. During those long weeks, the committee had no choice but to "divide the creation and reading of files among its members," because the amount of documentation in this case made it impossible for any one commissar to be familiar with "the specific details of all the materials." Working together in one location, they hoped, would alleviate the problem considerably. In this way, "while one judge records a witness deposition, another could compose the general catalogue of questions [*articulos probatoriales*] with the names of possible witnesses and an index and the whole thing would be vastly accelerated."[108]

In addition to centralizing and streamlining its work, the committee also saw a need to legitimize it. Only thus could "possible accusations against the court be avoided." In their letter of May 20, the commissars mentioned four procedures that could help this cause: the issuing of authorization and legitimation documents by the regent himself; an official swearing in of court officials; providing Oppenheimer with defense council at least pro forma; and the inclusion among the judges of two prominent jurists—Professors Schöpff and Harpprecht from Tübingen—although this was not legally required.[109]

The final obstacle the committee faced was the person of the accused himself. All early modern jurists knew that the best evidence in a criminal case was a confession by the suspect. *Confessio est regina probationum*, jurists recited for centuries: "Confession is the queen of evidence." Making Oppenheimer confess to his "enormous crimes" was very difficult, however, because "Süss, as he made clear during his first questioning, tends not to react positively to the interrogatory questions, preferring instead to discuss one topic, then another, without ever giving an adequate answer to any question."[110] The solution the commissars devised for this

challenge was simple. Should Oppenheimer persist in his obstinacy, the committee would apply the lowest of the three common
grades of judicial torture. As for the risk that being subjected to
torture might push Oppenheimer to commit suicide, this too had
a solution. The prison wardens should "keep an especially alert
eye on him and take the necessary precautions."[111]

On May 22, 1737, Carl Rudolph approved this plan. He reminded the commissars once again to do all in their power to
accelerate the trial, approved all of their requests, and issued an
order for the convening of a special criminal court (rather than a
mere inquisition committee) to deal with Joseph Süss Oppenheimer's case.[112] As the legal basis for the court's work, he named
the criminal code of the Holy Roman Empire (the so-called *Carolina* of 1532) as well as the relevant statutes and laws of the duchy
of Württemberg. Members of the court were to be von Gaisberg
as president; Professors Schöpff and Harpprecht from Tübingen;
the four members of the inquisition committee; the constantly
sick Eberhard Ludwig Bardili; and Friedrich Heinrich Georgii.
Since it fell on von Gaisberg, von Pflug, Dann, Faber, and Jäger to
run the day-to-day operations of the court, the five men were
ordered to relocate to the fortress of Hohen Asperg in the vicinity
of Ludwigsburg, where Oppenheimer and some of the other arrestees were also to be transported. Should the need arise, the
commissars had the regent's approval to use torture "without any
further request."[113]

On the afternoon of Saturday, June 1, a note written in an unidentified hand on the final page of the committee's Stuttgart logbook recorded that "the princely committee, with all its members,
has just left for Hohen Asperg." A few hours later, a different hand
began keeping a journal in the committee's new location. "The evening of June 1. The committee has arrived in [Hohen] Asperg."[114]

Hohen Asperg

For the next two and a half months, Jäger was in Hohen Asperg, extremely hard at work. We know this because the protocols name the officials who were present at each interrogation and the commissars always signed their names on the letters they composed and sent. Add to this the meticulous entries in the Hohen Asperg logbook and the result is an extraordinary documentation of where all the court officials were and what all of them were doing on practically every day in the summer of 1737. Philipp Friedrich Jäger's name appears in this massive documentation more frequently than that of any other court official.

The reason Jäger's name pops up so often in the Hohen Asperg records is related to the ongoing division of labor between the members of the criminal court. As had been the case during his twelve-day visit to Hohen Neuffen in late March and early April, in June Jäger was once again assigned to the interrogation of Oppenheimer himself. In contrast to the early spring, however, he was now surrounded by a changing cast of characters. If one includes the preliminary interrogation in Hohen Neuffen, Jäger interrogated Oppenheimer for exactly forty-five days between March and mid-August 1737, compared to von Gaisberg's thirty, von Pflug's twenty-two, Dann's twenty, Harpprecht and Schöpff's six (always together), and the sickly Bardili's zero. Indeed, Jäger missed only two interrogation days during the main part of Oppenheimer's trial. During this summer—indeed, during the entire trial—he logged more hours with Oppenheimer than anyone else.

As in the case of so many other documents stemming from Oppenheimer's trial, the specific details the Hohen Asperg protocols describe should be taken with a grain of salt. To the usual caveats of using such sources, one should also add Secretary Gabler's documented mental health issues from a few years later and the fact that we already see during this summer that the interrogation protocols were "prepared" (*preparirt*), that is, copied anew by a scribe, who also took excerpts from them for the benefit of various state agencies and the future Relation (the *extractus actorum*).[115] What we have in front of us is not a faithful transcription of the exchanges between the inquisitors and their prisoner, let alone a truthful representation of Oppenheimer's alleged crimes. We find ourselves twice removed from the truth here: first by the witnesses themselves, whose statements may or may not be truthful, and second by the court documents through which these testimonies are transmitted to us, whether faithfully or not.

According to the protocols, Jäger was joined at first by the three other veterans of the pretrial stage: von Pflug, Dann, and Faber. The records continue to call the four men "commissars," in distinction from the other members of the criminal court. The four men began the main inquisition on June 4 with the usual standard questions, then moved on to a few questions about Oppenheimer's life before arriving in Württemberg (*vita ante acta*). Over the next few days, the commissars concentrated on questions of *präpotenz* and *pouvoir*. "What, exactly, was his [that is, Oppenheimer's] role at court?" "Was he trying to make the duke ennoble him?" "Why did he make all local councilors so hated by the duke?" "Why had he acted against the Württemberg constitution?" Sometimes the commissars brought documents from a nearby room, placed them before Oppenheimer, and waited to see his reaction. They were clearly left unsatisfied by Oppenheimer's responses and his overall demeanor.[116]

For a whole week, between the afternoons of Friday, June 14, and the following Thursday, Harpprecht and Schöpff were present in the interrogation room.[117] The reason the two law professors were invited to Hohen Asperg is not documented, but the circumstantial evidence for it is overwhelming. Carl Rudolph had already given the commissars carte blanche for judicial torture, but it was the legal custom in Württemberg (as in the rest of the Holy Roman Empire) to have two jurists formally approve the use of such legal means. The four commissars were quite concerned about their work's legality. They consequently called on Harpprecht and Schöpff to join them. Together with President von Gaisberg, the court was therefore seven men strong now: the four commissars, von Gaisberg, Schöpff, and Harpprecht.

The protocols describe how the seven men began their first joint interrogatory session by covering a wide range of issues in quick succession: Oppenheimer's relationship with women, various monetary transactions, and the appointment of allegedly unworthy candidates to state offices. The court took Sunday off, but when it resumed its work on Monday, Gabler added in the protocol that "this afternoon, the suspect has proven so obstinate and evasive in his answers that he was transferred to, then locked up in, another room, with strong bars."[118] Although they were not required to do so, the judges also had Gabler draw up a letter to Carl Rudolph with a report on their actions. "Despite our patience and our best efforts, we cannot allow the Jew Süss to continue with his obstinate, evasive ways. . . . We have consequently decided to make one last attempt with him this morning and tell him that if he continues in his usual ways we shall have to proceed differently." When this obvious threat did not work and Oppenheimer persisted in his "obstinacy, ramblings, and lies," the judges ordered his transfer to a different cell, reduced his diet to bread and water, and even used the first grade of torture, whereby "the right arm is tied to the leg for a long time." The inquisitors concluded their report to Carl Rudolph cautiously. "We shall see tomorrow if these remedies have had any effect."[119]

Indeed they had. According to Gabler's report from the following day, Oppenheimer came back in the morning much subdued, excused himself for his past behavior, and began to answer the interrogatory questions in more detail.[120] During the first inquisition session after he had been subjected to torture, only von Pflug, Dann, and Jäger were present, but in the afternoon, the two Tübingen law professors joined in too. Because extracting information from a suspect through torture was considered valid only if he or she then repeated the testimony later without physical coercion, Harpprecht and Schöpff were not expected to join the inquisitors right away. Only once it became clear that Oppenheimer was, indeed, cooperative, did the two jurists enter the room. After that special session, they were no longer needed. They left Hohen Asperg the following day and would not rejoin the criminal court until November, during the verdict deliberations in Stuttgart.

On the same day the two law professors left Hohen Asperg, the inquisitors regrouped. Oppenheimer's resistance seemed largely broken, but he was still not providing all of the information the inquisitors wanted. The latter consequently split into two teams. Dann and Faber began with the questioning of Bühler and Hallwachs, while Jäger and von Gaisberg were assigned exclusively to Oppenheimer's case. Von Pflug, when he was present, joined one group or the other. The topics covered in the interrogation were the usual ones. In Oppenheimer's inquisition, for instance, Jäger and von Gaisberg proceeded quite methodically, moving every few days from one topic to the next. Only very late in the Hohen Asperg period did Jäger and von Gaisberg interrogate Oppenheimer at length about those issues that came to be associated most strongly with Oppenheimer's case after the trial: his assisting other Jews to settle in Württemberg (July 23); his alleged attempt to make the Ehrbarkeit hateful to the duke (July 26); the debasement of coins in the mint (July 27); and his sexual relations with women (not before August 2). Very tellingly, they also never used classical blood-libel accusations against Oppenheimer, such as ritual killing or host desecration.

It is easy to see why Oppenheimer's answers during this phase of his trial cannot be taken at face value. Not only were his responses forcefully extracted from him, but they were also recorded by a possibly mentally unstable secretary before being "prepared" for later use. Similar issues affect the interrogation protocols of Hallwachs, Bühler, and the close to two hundred witnesses the inquisitors interrogated in Hohen Asperg during the summer and in Stuttgart in the fall. Using the same documents to shed light on Jäger and the other inquisitors, on the other hand, is quite revealing.

In some respects, we see here the already familiar Jäger. He has a preconceived notion of what Oppenheimer had done, which he draws directly from the Grävenitz-Würben case. He is industrious almost beyond measure. He is severe, sending both Oppenheimer and Bühler to dark rooms and applying torture in the former's case. Most of all, however, Jäger appears as a faithful representative of his social milieu. In the *species facti* he later composed, Jäger writes that Oppenheimer "treated all members of the Swabian Nation [that is, all honorable Württembergers] as if they amounted to nothing, and used every opportunity to belittle them" in the eyes of the duke.[121] This damaged sense of pride is also present in the trial's protocols. On July 12, 1737, for instance, after discussing the introduction of many foreigners to Carl Alexander's state administration, Jäger simply asked, "What would he [Süss] feel if all these things were done to him?"[122]

At times, distant echoes of Jäger's upbringing become audible. As a ten-year-old boy, Jäger had delivered a speech from the balcony of Schorndorf's town hall, explaining to the assembled townspeople that "we are all conceived and born in sin, already full of lust and desire in our mothers' wombs."[123] Now, as a thirty-year-old man, he expressed similar sentiments. In the early stages of the trial, it had been Faber, Dann, and the ducal commissioner in Stuttgart who dealt with the question of Oppenheimer's alleged sexual relationships with non-Jewish women, including the court Jew's young partner, a nineteen-year-old local girl by the name of Luciana Fischerin. By early August, Jäger too started showing interest in the history of Oppenheimer's sexual exploits.

Jäger's relentless exploration of sexual issues in the later stages of Oppenheimer's trial is evident in several interrogation sessions in early August, but it becomes especially pronounced two months later, when the verdict deliberations in Stuttgart are only a few weeks away. On October 19, 1737, Jäger went by himself to the home of the government secretary Johann Friedrich Faber (no relation of the commissar) in order to take a deposition from the secretary's wife, Christina Dorothea Faberin. Both the place— a private person's home—and the absence of a scribe were highly unusual. For the first and only time in the trial, Jäger served as both inquisitor and scribe. His impatience, drive, covert threats, and fascination for details of sexual intercourse all come into clear focus in his report from that day.

The report begins with only one of the usual standard questions, and follows immediately with two specific queries:

1. How old is she?
   R. 23 years.

2. Whether she did not often go to see Süss in private and he, on his part, came to see her?
   R. She went to see him twice on behalf of her mother . . . and when he [Süss] came to her house it was only to visit the Countess von Sponek.[124]

3. Whether Süss has ever asked her for anything unbecoming?

   R. No, she has never been so naïve as to go to him by herself.[125]

Having made no progress with the first three questions, Jäger then changed his tone. According to his own report, he dropped the clear rules of the question-response format and switched to a much freer interrogatory style. He told Faberin that she should "not keep anything from him, the issue of her relation with Süss is not only a matter of gossip, Süss himself had admitted that he had done many unbecoming things to her." Though Jäger provided no evidence to this last claim, Faberin broke down, at least according to Jäger. "She cannot deny that she had been with him [Süss] alone many times; at one point, he threw her on the bed and tried to take her clothes off. Finally, he got naked but despite all the violence he accomplished nothing." Even this was not enough for Jäger, however; he wanted more. "After three more questions [by me, that is, Jäger], she finally admits that he had intercourse with her and after another [question] that he had put his penis in her but she did not feel the semen in her body. It was an evening in late 1734, after that he tried to do so again several times, but could only push her on the bed, nothing more."[126]

Such a report is obviously extremely problematic as a source about Oppenheimer's or Faberin's past. What Oppenheimer and Faberin did or did not do we simply cannot tell. What is clear are Jäger's actions: conducting an interrogation at a woman's house without a scribe or any other witness present, all the time pressing her to confess to things she would not voluntarily admit. There is reason to believe that even Jäger knew he was crossing a line here. Despite this supposedly clear testimony, he would not mention Faberin's story in the part of the Relation he prepared only a few weeks later.

There are two final pieces of evidence about Jäger's working methods that are quite telling. The first is circumstantial. As we saw, in May 1737, Carl Rudolph approved the committee's proposal to appoint an attorney to help in Oppenheimer's defense at least pro forma. The choice fell on the Tübingen attorney Michael Andreas Mögling. Oppenheimer biographers have repeatedly pointed out that Mögling, if he ever seriously tried to help Oppenheimer (which is doubtful), was all but completely ignored by the criminal court. The crucial piece of evidence in this respect is a long document Mögling composed in Oppenheimer's defense, which he submitted to the court in early November. Despite the effort Mögling had clearly put into crafting it, this document was not quoted extensively in the Relation and, according to at least two historians, was read by very few people, if any at all.[127]

Following Jäger's activities during the main stage of Oppenheimer's trial corroborates the same conclusion from a different angle. After his lengthy interrogation by Jäger and von Gaisberg, Oppenheimer was allowed to undergo an interrogation by his own attorney. This so-called *Gütliches Verhör* was the closest the criminal justice system of early modern Württemberg got to a modern-style cross-examination by the defense. It was supposed to take place in the presence of the defense attorney, two of the judges, and a scribe. Before this cross-examination, Jäger had missed only two interrogation sessions with Oppenheimer, but during the main part of the Gütliches Verhör, he was completely absent. He appeared in the room only toward the very end of the final interrogation on September 3.[128]

Jäger's absence during Oppenheimer's Gütliches Verhör seems to have been no mere coincidence. From the very beginning of the trial, Jäger engaged in a type of logical reverse engineering. Instead of drawing conclusions from evidence, he was drawing "facts" from a predetermined conclusion. This is why, when confronted with statements that contradicted his preconceived story, he either reacted with violence and threats (such as against Oppenheimer, Bühler, and Faberin, for instance) or ignored it altogether (Mögling's defense). Similarly problematic was Jäger's treatment of evidence that only partly corroborated his preconceived narrative. He edited, amplified, and dramatized it almost beyond recognition. This was the case, for instance, in his treatment of the documents that came during the trial from his hometown of Schorndorf.

In the immediate aftermath of Oppenheimer's arrest, Regent Carl Rudolph asked ducal commissioners across Württemberg to provide the inquisition committee with evidence against Oppenheimer. The yield from Schorndorf was extremely meager. Philipp Heinrich Andler, the local commissioner and an old acquaintance of Jäger and his father, reported in a letter of April 6 that Oppenheimer "is not especially known in this town." When it came to Oppenheimer's activities, Andler could only cite a claim about overtaxation of an inheritance in a nearby village and the redrawing of district boundaries that left one village outside Schorndorf's jurisdiction. Later in the month, pressed by Jäger to provide more evidence against Oppenheimer, Commissioner Andler added that "the Jew Süss wrote to me only on a few occasions," and "without any hint of threats [*nichts bedrohliches*]." Finally, when asked one last time in early June to say something against Oppenheimer, Andler resorted to extremely general statements about the burden of quartering soldiers, maintaining the town's fortifications, and state monopolies—anything more specific against Oppenheimer he simply did not seem to have.[129]

Jäger seemed undeterred. Of the almost 2,000 questions he put to Oppenheimer during the spring and summer of 1737, only one was related to Schorndorf. (It was about the district's boundaries.[130]) Nevertheless, when it came to composing his part of the Relation, Jäger did not hesitate to rely on Schorndorf to make his case. He did not mention the correspondence with Andler or that in a district of several thousand people, only one inheritance taxation dispute might have been related to Oppenheimer's *pouvoir*. He also did not note that Oppenheimer was never asked to respond to this particular allegation against him. Rather, in his part of the Relation, Jäger amplified the inheritance taxation dispute in his hometown district and presented it as indisputable, dramatic evidence against Oppenheimer. "Sind sogar die Verstorbene unter der Erden nicht sicher [von Oppeheimer] gewesen," he wrote—"Even the dead under the earth were not safe from Oppenheimer."[131]

Modus Procedendi

After the conclusion of the Gütliches Verhör, Jäger moved back to Stuttgart. Starting on September 16, he, Faber, and Dann spent almost a month recording depositions from over a hundred local witnesses. One such witness was the Jew Mordechai Schloss, a man who had already been interrogated during the Grävenitz-Würben trial and the main character of a later chapter in this book.

A month later, in mid-October 1737, Jäger, Dann, and Faber felt it was time to slowly bring the trial to a close. In a letter the three commissars sent to the regent on October 14, they called for the entire criminal court to convene in Stuttgart, where they would tackle one accusation at a time (*puncta zu puncta*), collect relevant facts for each one, and consult collectively over the verdict. A few issues still stood in the way, though. The court had yet to receive all the protocols from the witness depositions in the district towns, and its members hadn't had the opportunity to interrogate several persons of interest. Further complicating the picture was the need to find a replacement for Friedrich Heinrich Georgii, a member of the criminal court who earlier in the fall had decided to resign from his post due to personal circumstances.[132]

Carl Rudolph's reply came on October 16 in the form of two separate documents. The first was a decree that replaced Georgii with Government Councilor Günther Albrecht Renz, then summoned the entire criminal court to Stuttgart on November 5. Once in Stuttgart, the judges were to each read through the files separately and write down their individual opinions in the case (*vota*). Then they were to proceed to discuss the case together, compose the verdict, and send one copy of it "to our privy council for ratification."[133] In addition to the official decree, Carl Rudolph also composed a personal note to the three commissars, which he added as a rescript to the original request letter. He ordered them to "compose the final verdict without any overly long Relation, to include only the main points of the verdict, then to attach the individual votes and the protocols of [your] meetings."[134] The whole process was to be straightforward and swift.

On October 22, Jäger and Faber composed yet another letter to Carl Rudolph. The two jurists were of course "the regent's most humble servants" and they were "deeply obliged to follow his orders to the letter." If the regent insisted on his instructions, they would indeed start the verdict consultations by having each judge read the files individually before proceeding to a plenary session. Perhaps, however, the regent would be willing to consider an alternative they and Dann had already raised in their original request? "The complex nature of the investigations in this case made it unavoidable that the members of the inquisition team would divide the work among themselves." The result was such a mountain of paperwork that "not a single member of the inquisition committee has read all the files, and those documents the committee members did read they now have to read anew."[135] The predicament of those judges who had not participated personally in the creation or collection of the evidence was even worse. Each of them would need an extended period of time to master the material, and because each document could be read by only one person at a time, the whole process was bound to be extraordinarily time-consuming.

Jäger and Faber had a different suggestion. What the members of the criminal court lacked individually they possessed as a group. By definition, every document in the trial had been created or collected by one or more members of the court, so collectively, if never individually, the judges had already mastered the whole body of evidence in the case. The court should consequently meet in plenum right away, tackle the main points of the accusation one at a time with the judges, "one looking in the protocols of Oppenheimer's own interrogations, another in witness depositions, a third in [Mögling's] defense and other relevant documents, and so forth."[136] After the secretary recorded all the relevant information in the protocol, the discussion could move to the next item on the agenda until all the bases have been covered. Finally, the time would come for the judges to cast their votes and reach the verdict.

There is reason to believe that Jäger and Faber's suggestion to streamline the verdict consultations was more than just a procedural solution to a bureaucratic problem. According to Jäger and Faber's own assessment, had Carl Rudolph's original procedure been followed, the court would have required a long time to reach a verdict. What consequences such a state of affairs would have had no one can tell with certainty, but in one far-fetched scenario it might have even saved Oppenheimer's life. If Oppenheimer's case taught anyone anything, it was that the political situation in Württemberg was so volatile that what seemed inevitable one moment became obsolete the next. A contemporary eyewitness described this situation in cosmological terms. Württemberg had undergone "a great change, which since March 12, 1737, not only caused a total eclipse of Württemberg's sun [Carl Alexander], but also made some of the stars fall to earth."[137] Who could vouchsafe, in autumn 1737, that this scenario would not repeat itself?

The specific procedure Faber and Jäger suggested in late October 1737 should be taken seriously for a second reason. Power is often inscribed in procedure. Social scientists have long insisted that when a group of people proceeds to make a collective decision, the private opinions of its members are only part of the equation. Also of relevance are procedural issues such as who presides over the deliberations, who is allowed to voice an opinion and when, whether the decision-making process is public or private, and how much access group members have to relevant information before and during the deliberations. Consider the case of jury deliberations in the American criminal justice system, for instance. One does not need to be a social psychologist to realize that it matters a great deal that juries deliberate behind closed doors and not in public, that they do so orally and not in writing, and that they are instructed to refrain from discussing the case with any nonjurors or, until the deliberations begin, even with their peers. Similar arguments can be made about decision-making processes in many different types of organizations. What we decide often depends on how we decide.

Jäger and Faber had of course no background in modern social science, but they seem to have intuitively grasped that the criminal court was much more likely to reach a quick and unanimous decision if it worked together from the start. Moreover, the kind of procedure they envisioned would give them a built-in advantage over the other judges. Because it was the commissars who had created and collected the trial documents in the first place, they knew where to look for evidence that supported their particular position on any given point. On October 24, 1737, without any explanation, Carl Rudolph approved this scheme.[138]

Deliberations in Stuttgart

Although Carl Rudolph's original plan was to convene the criminal court on Tuesday, November 5, the court's deliberations had to be pushed back to the following Tuesday. The delay had more than one cause, but it was at least partly because of Georg Friedrich Harpprecht. The Tübingen law professor received the official order to come to Stuttgart only on the evening of November 2. In a letter he sent to Carl Rudolph the following day, Harpprecht told the regent that he had just recovered from an illness and that his physician forbade him to undertake the trip. For an undisclosed reason, Jäger, Dann, and Faber received this news with alarm and urged Carl Rudolph to order the law professor to travel to Stuttgart no matter what. When the regent did so, Harpprecht had no choice but to comply, but the proceedings were delayed to accommodate him. Thus, on November 12, 1737, he was indeed present at the first meeting of the court's verdict deliberations.[139]

The court met in the upper heated room (*Obere Stube*) of Stuttgart's town hall, a four-story Renaissance-style building overlooking the city's main marketplace. From there, it was only a short walk to the house in which Jäger had lived while attending the Stuttgart gymnasium fifteen years earlier. Jäger's future resting place, the cemetery of the Spitalkirche, was also only a short walk away. Present at the meeting were all but one of the court's nine members: von Gaisberg, von Pflug, Faber, Dann, Jäger, Renz, Harpprecht, and Schöpff. The only member missing that day was Bardili. As secretary (*actuarius*), the court retained Christoph Ludwig Gabler.[140]

The official decree that called the criminal court into existence had been issued eight days before the opening session. It stipulated that the president, judges, and actuarius would be sworn in by the president of the regent's privy council. The texts of the three oaths—one for President von Gaisberg, an almost identical one for the judges, and a third for Gabler—were laid down in the Carolina, the criminal legal code of the Holy Roman Empire. Carl Rudolph's decree also specified that the Carolina would serve as the legal basis for the deliberations together with Württemberg's penal code of 1735 and the procedure (*modus procedendi*) that Faber and Jäger had sketched in their letter of October 22.[141] Several days before the session began, Christian Friedrich Sattler, the head archivist of Carl Rudolph's administration, had transferred the main trial documents to the care of Jäger and his colleagues in the town hall, and eleven days before the deliberations began, Mögling also sent the written statement of the defense.[142] Everything was ready; the court could finally begin its verdict deliberations.

In the four weeks following its opening session, the special criminal court deliberated on Oppenheimer's case six days a week, almost always both before and after midday. The deliberations were held behind closed doors, but their location in Stuttgart's town hall was so central that the population could not but be aware of them. Gabler wrote down the protocols of all thirty-nine sessions, and three other members—Jäger and his two old mentors Harpprecht and Schöpff—also never missed a session.

Other members of the court had to excuse themselves from time to time. Dann and Renz missed one session each, Faber three, and Bardili eight. The elderly von Gaisberg, who would die the following year, had to miss the entire last week of deliberations. The record holder, however, was von Pflug. Of the thirty-nine sessions, he attended only seventeen.

Judging by Gabler's meticulous protocols, the judges indeed worked their way point by point and in plenum, just as Jäger and Faber had envisioned. At times, a session would be devoted mostly or even solely to Jäger or other member of the court reading aloud extracts from the trial documents to the other judges. That was the case on the morning of November 15, for instance, and for the entire days of November 23, 25, 27, 28, and 29. On other days, all participants seemed to work together, collecting the necessary references from the files for each accusation point, then dictating their findings to Gabler.

First on the agenda was the issue of Oppenheimer's various crimes before arriving in Württemberg. The court discussed materials relevant to this topic very briefly during its first two sessions, in the morning and afternoon of November 12. Later in the afternoon of the 12th, the court proceeded to the second point, relating to Oppenheimer's *präpotenz*. The court continued to discuss this topic for a whole week. Deliberations on the other charges ensued in the following three weeks. Between November 19 and December 2 and then again between December 4 and 6, the criminal court collected materials regarding monetary issues. In scope and detail, these items outweighed all others by a large margin. They were addressed during twenty-three of the court's thirty-nine sessions and account for over seventy percent of the entries in Gabler's protocol, just as in the Grävenitz-Würben case. Finally, the court also discussed very briefly three other topics:

Oppenheimer's alleged abuse of the limited right of Jews to settle in Württemberg (afternoon of December 2); his alleged advice to Carl Alexander against the Württemberg estates (morning of December 3); and his private life, including the sexual allegations (very briefly on the morning of December 6).

What was the purpose of these detailed deliberations? After all, the inquisition committee had been extremely prejudiced against Oppenheimer from the start, Carl Rudolph had explicitly asked for no "overly long Relation" in this case, and the public at large was never supposed to read a detailed verdict, let alone have access to Gabler's protocols. Was not the whole trial, as Hellmut Haasis passionately argued, simply a farce?[143]

The sources suggest at least two intriguing explanations for the extensive deliberations of November and early December 1737. The first has to do with the legitimacy of the legal proceedings against Oppenheimer. As we saw, this issue was of concern to Jäger and his associates already in May 1737 and again in June when the question of judicial torture was brought up. As the trial unfolded, its legitimacy seems to have acquired even more urgency. In a sermon delivered two days before Oppenheimer's execution, Georg Konrad Rieger, vicar of St. Leonhard's church (and Jäger's former teacher in the Stuttgart gymnasium) acknowledged this state of affairs. He addressed directly the many Württembergers in the audience he believed did not see the reason for the fallen court Jew's harsh treatment, asking them to reconsider their position. Others, including Schöpff, Carl Eugen (Carl Alexander's son), and perhaps even Harpprecht himself, while not necessarily sympathetic to Oppenheimer, were nonetheless unsure about the legality of the criminal procedures. Carl Eugen openly called the entire affair "judicial murder" when he finally ascended to the throne in 1744; Schöpff explicitly stated his misgivings on December 13 during the final verdict deliberations; and there are some indications that Harpprecht too felt some unease about the whole affair.[144] Perhaps this, and not health issues, was the reason behind his reluctance to travel to Stuttgart in early November to join the criminal court.

The uneasiness about the legitimacy of the proceedings against Oppenheimer suggests one possible explanation for the length of the verdict deliberations. The four weeks of labor-intensive discussions were not meant to satisfy Jäger and the other core members of the criminal court, who had long before made up their minds about Oppenheimer's guilt. Rather, they were meant to convince Harpprecht and Schöpff of the legality of the proceedings and, through the two jurists' stamp of approval, sway the higher echelons of the state administration and perhaps even the public at large as well. This hypothesis goes some way toward explaining why Jäger and his colleagues strongly insisted on Harpprecht's participation in the deliberations despite the latter's alleged bad health and why it was important to the members of the inquisition committee that Harpprecht and Schöpff be present not only at the inquisition sessions immediately before and after Oppenheimer's torture but also at every single one of the sessions where they deliberated over the verdict. Unlike the commissars, Harpprecht, Schöpff, and some in the Württemberg population at large still had to be convinced of Oppenheimer's guilt in December 1737.

The sources also suggest a second explanation for the long verdict deliberations. A close examination of Gabler's protocols shows that the court paid surprisingly little attention to some of the components of a typical Jew Süss story. It devoted only one of its thirty-nine sessions to discussing Oppenheimer's supposedly promiscuous private life and only one session, too, to the alleged infractions against the prohibition against Jews to settling in Württemberg. What kept the court busy during the first week of deliberations was the issue of *präpotenz*—that is, Oppenheimer's treatment of the duke and his disrespect toward other Württemberg officials. This was clearly related to the personal honor of the commissars themselves, Jäger included. The second major topic of deliberations, accounting for over seventy percent of the court's time, was Oppenheimer's finances: the whereabouts of his remaining money and property, the sums of money he owed, and the money others owed to him. Even if the verdict itself had been a foregone conclusion by December 1737, the court had good reason to read the trial's records carefully. Legitimizing the legal proceedings against Oppenheimer, asserting the commissars' own personal sense of honor, and locating Oppenheimer's remaining money and property: these three issues seem to have been the primary motivations behind the prolonged verdict deliberations of November and December 1737.

Species Facti

By the second week of December, the stage was finally set for the composition of the document detailing the judicial "facts" leading to the death sentence.

The court's deliberations ended on December 7, after which Jäger had a few days to compose the *species facti*. This eighty-page document formed part of the Relation, alongside excerpts Gabler copied from the interrogation protocols (*extractus actorum*), a draft verdict (*Urthel*), and von Pflug's legal reasoning for the court's death sentence (*rationes decidendi*).[145] On December 13, the criminal court assembled one last time in the upper heated room of the Stuttgart town hall, approved the Relation with only Schöpff "[informally] asking himself whether [Oppenheimer] deserves the death penalty," then sent the Relation to the administrative council and the regent for final approval.[146]

Jäger's *species facti* is an important but also profoundly misleading document. In it, the Schorndorf native selectively chose from the many thousands of documents the court had assembled since March to support a preconceived image of Oppenheimer as the antithesis for everything the Ehrbarkeit supposedly stood for. By creating an extensive list of "facts" pertaining to the court Jew's life, Jäger was clearly ignoring Carl Rudolph's explicit order not to compose an "overly long Relation in this case." The document's length and many convoluted details served a double purpose, though. They camouflaged the *species facti's* extreme tendentiousness, and they helped hide the very personal stakes Jäger had in its composition.

From the first pages of Jäger's *species facti*, the document's many prejudices are abundantly evident. That before he came to Württemberg, Oppenheimer had worked in Darmstadt and participated in the creation of a stamp duty on behalf of the local prince is well documented. But that "[a]fter 3 months, the business was taken away from him and Süss lost all his means and credit, going bankrupt by 100,000 gulden," is manifestly false.[147] Even more important are Jäger's claims that "[t]he notorious Jew Joseph Süss Oppenheimer was the natural son of the famous general von Heitersdorf in Heidelberg."[148] This statement, which the jurist presented matter-of-factly, was in fact denied by Oppenheimer himself and, as the entry in Zedler's lexicon quoted in this book's introduction put it a few years later, by "most learned people" as well.[149] The logic behind Jäger's statement was clear, however: Oppenheimer was the offspring of a Jew (his mother) and a Catholic prince (von Heitersdorf); he was a creature of the unholy matrimony between Jews and Papish princes.

As far as Oppenheimer's character was concerned, Jäger saw what his old gymnasium teacher, Georg Konrad Rieger, described later as "a possible mirror image of [one's] own happiness."[150] Jäger's Süss was a man of a conniving, treacherous, and extremely greedy nature. "Four months before Carl Alexander ascended to the Württemberg throne, the Jew Simon Isaac from Landau introduced the late duke to Süss. The latter, because of his impertinence and pride and although he himself had neither money nor credit, managed to negotiate with Carl Alexander that he would give him his future revenues in advance in exchange for his nomination to the position of the prince's personal military supplier and personal banker [*Lieferant, Chatoul-Administrator*]."[151] As it turned out, calling Oppenheimer impertinent and proud was only the tip of the iceberg. Süss "had an unbearably arrogant air about him and he showed no respect to great lords or the late duke, let alone to the latter's councils and councilors. The least amount of consideration, however, he reserved to the oppressed and to people in need, always thinking about new ways to extort money and property from them, bringing everything into a great confusion, and mocking all good order."[152]

According to Jäger, Süss had developed a simple but effective way of accomplishing his schemes. He pushed the prince's old councilors aside, then shored up his own power by creating special administrative bodies under his direct supervision. Jäger wrote of Oppenheimer that "[h]e made the duke's loyal councilors leave their old jobs so that he would have no opposition to his pernicious projects" and that he had "published a statute giving to himself the right to cite and order administrators at will."[153] Then, with the old councilors sidelined, "Süss created a secret cabinet whose members he himself had advanced despite their notorious characters."[154]

These allegations should give us pause. Jäger came from a long line of civil servants, and his career advancement, meteoric at first, had ground to a halt in the early 1730s. At one point in his *species facti*, Jäger singled out administrators like himself as the worst affected of all of Oppenheimer's victims.[155] What he described in the *species facti* was not necessarily the real "Jew Süss"; it was, rather, a shadowy agent, the real cause of Jäger's own stalling career.

One can develop this argument further. Jäger had served as Fiskal in the Grävenitz-Würben case but failed to secure a conviction in it in 1735 all because of the financial settlement Oppenheimer brokered between Grävenitz-Würben and Carl Alexander. In the *species facti* of December 1737, Jäger returned to this issue by describing it in general, rather than personal, terms. He narrated how Oppenheimer managed to squeeze money from people by manipulating state agencies like the office of the Fiskal. Oppenheimer's actions, Jäger wrote with great hyperbole, were "not dissimilar to [those of] the Spanish Inquisition."[156] The Jew was so intent on punishing people "not according to their crimes, but according to their property," that "[t]here was no case *in causis civilibus, criminalibus, ecclesiasticis, militaribus, matrimonialibus, politicis et oeconomicis*," that was left unaffected.[157] Jäger said not a single word here about his documented involvement in these matters. The *species facti* was Jäger's own story of victimization (as he saw it), told by concentrating only on the alleged victimizer and by erasing completely the name of the victim-turned-inquisitor.

According to Jäger, what Oppenheimer did not manage to do through the office of the Fiskal he accomplished through other state agencies as well as, even more important, through treacherous assistants like Hallwachs, Bühler, and several Jewish helpers. Indeed, the Jew's conspiracies knew no bounds. He cheated the

Württemberg estates by transferring moneys belonging to them to the duke, and from there to his own pocket; he transferred wills to his own name (hence the lines from Schorndorf about how "even the dead, buried under the earth, had no peace from him");[158] and his work in the mint was thievery pure and simple. "It is impossible to describe what kinds of punishable acts the Jew practiced there," Jäger commented, without noticing the irony of his own statement.[159]

Jäger's construction of Jew Süss reaches its rhetorical culmination and conclusion in the last paragraph of the *species facti*. Although he expressed his views on Oppenheimer throughout this long document, it is here that we see Jäger's Jew Süss in all of his malignant, and indeed devilish, notoriety. One cannot emphasize the point enough: this is not a faithful description of the historical Joseph Süss Oppenheimer. Based on rumors, gossip, outright lies, and (at best) half-truths, it is one of the most radical and fictive versions of Jew Süss ever written. "As for [Süss's] personal life, it is unnecessary to say too much about it. It is known to all that he considered himself independent of all religions. He was without any religion at all, without conscience, without honor, without culture, without loyalty, and without faith. He nourished himself only on robbery and treachery, and indeed often made it known throughout the land how he lived almost like a prince, engaging in prostitution, fornication, and possibly also incest, all extremely insolently, and sometimes even with Christian women. This is the summary of Süss's treacherous machinations, a full account of which would be even more vile but also too long." [160]

Epilogue

Eight years later, in the Spitalkirche in Stuttgart, we can see many of them, gathered to pay their last respects to Philipp Friedrich

Jäger. Here again are Faber, Dann, and Günther Albrecht Renz, professors Harpprecht and Schöpff, ducal archivist Sattler, Pregizer the scribe, and Schorndorf's ducal commissioner, Philipp Heinrich Andler. In attendance as well are people who helped Jäger in pivotal stages of his career: his old Schorndorf teacher Wisshack, for instance, and representatives of the Stuttgart gymnasium, the university in Tübingen, Württemberg's Hofgericht, and the administrative council and other governmental bodies the deceased joined after Oppenheimer's trial. Last but not least are members of Jäger's immediate and extended family: the elderly mother, the siblings and their spouses, and the orphaned girls. Little Maria Rosine is eight years old now, her age practically identical to the amount of time that has passed since the opening of Oppenheimer's trial. She is accompanied by her two older sisters but also by a younger one, Justina Elisabetha, born in 1741.

Many of the people assembled in the Spitalkirche on August 5, 1745, had firsthand knowledge of Jäger's role in Oppenheimer's trial. Always the hardworking representative of his social group, Jäger helped to develop the list of accusations against Oppenheimer, assisted in collecting the evidence, served as the prisoner's most frequent inquisitor, laid down the procedures for the criminal court's deliberations, and composed the document that summed up the court's views on the factual circumstances of Oppenheimer's alleged crimes. Important though he was as a jurist, Jäger was not a powerful political figure during the trial. Unlike von Gaisberg and von Pflug, he was not a nobleman; unlike Dann and Faber, he was not yet a state councilor; and unlike Harpprecht and Schöpff, he was not a distinguished law professor or a judge on the bench of Württemberg's Hofgericht, at least not yet. Once he successfully fulfilled his role as commissar, Jäger was pushed aside, yielding the spotlight in the final act of Oppenheimer's life to more powerful people than himself.

Jäger's marginalization is already discernible during the court's final work meeting, on December 13, 1737. In the hierarchical world of early modern Württemberg, questions of precedence were a constant source of contestation because they were understood to reflect and at times even to constitute participants' social positions. That during the vote on Oppenheimer's death sentence Jäger's turn came second-to-last (followed only by Bardili's) is therefore quite telling.[161] In the following weeks, while the administrative council and the regent discussed the Relation, Jäger's name also appeared less and less frequently in the trial records. The modern historian cannot but regret this diminished visibility. Gone are the types of documents that allowed us to reconstruct Jäger's whereabouts and actions earlier in the trial almost on an hourly basis. Still, Jäger clearly remained active in the events of the last month and a half of Oppenheimer's life: he personally approved the list of visitors who came to see Oppenheimer in jail (more about these visitors in later chapters of this book), and he personally participated in the events of February 4, 1738, Oppenheimer's day of judgment. After the prisoner heard his verdict in the upper hall of the Herrenhaus in Stuttgart (see figure 6), he was led in a long procession toward the execution site, just north of the city. At this point, both contemporary eyewitnesses and modern historians direct their gaze at the accused. For us, who in this chapter have been interested above all in Jäger, this is not a small problem. All the trial documents afford us now is a receipt by the coachman who drove Jäger together with Faber and Dann to the execution site.[162] How the three commissars came back to the city afterward we simply cannot tell.

* * *

To follow Jäger and his colleagues closely, as we have done here, is to see them for the first time as three-dimensional figures. These men were certainly not psychopaths; nor did they leave any record of Jew-baiting before Oppenheimer's trial. What bound them together was the tight-knit nature of their social milieu, their close educational and professional ties, and their common failure in the legal proceedings against Grävenitz-Würben. The latter point is especially significant as background for Oppenheimer's ordeal. The ideological and personal ties between the two political trials shed light on the ready-made nature of the accusations against Oppenheimer; they explain at least in part the vehemence with which Jäger and his colleagues prosecuted their old adversary; and they highlight how, despite the obvious anti-Jewish sentiments of some members of the court, one cannot reduce Oppenheimer's case to Judeophobia alone. After all, as Fiskal in 1735, Jäger accused Grävenitz-Würben of crimes against Jews and not the other way around.

Jäger's story is important for other reasons as well. By reconstructing the way the court assembled the evidence against Oppenheimer, we can see how the enormous extent of the trial documents, the basis for so many later interpretations of Oppenheimer's case, is not only a problem for the modern historian but also a clue. It seems to be above all a testimony to the difficulties Jäger and his colleagues were facing in amassing concrete evidence against their prisoner. It also helps us to better characterize the nature of the accusations Jäger advanced against Oppenheimer. Oppenheimer's court records closely resemble the ones from the Grävenitz-Würben case in that they lack explicit theological arguments. Jäger's Jew Süss is no Christ-killer or host desecrator. He is rather a libertine, a foreigner, and the good administrator's worst nightmare. He "sucked the money out of the prince, the country, and the people," rather than sucking the blood of defenseless Christian children.[163] Despite the occasional religious overtones, Jäger's *species facti* was primarily about administration and politics, and only indirectly about religion or ethnicity.

All of this leads us back to 1745 and to the starting point of our story, Jäger's funeral in Stuttgart's Spitalkirche. Much like the *species facti* Jäger composed in Oppenheimer's case, the evidence from Jäger's funeral cannot be considered a faithful description of who the Schorndorf native "really was." The importance of the two documents lies in the cultural code they contain rather than in the historical reality they purportedly depict. Cleß constructed his eulogy as an almost complete mirror image of Jäger's portrayal of Oppenheimer eight years earlier. Whereas Oppenheimer had been quite literally a man *without* ("without religion, without conscience, without honor, without culture, without loyalty, without faith"), the Württemberg jurist was in Cleß's eyes a paragon of the good community member and administrator. He was "talented, industrious, honest, and a lover of truth and justice." These binary oppositions were part of the same code through which members of the Ehrbarkeit interpreted their social world, reducing its extraordinary complexity to a manageable, sensible system. It is the inevitable but also often tragic outcome of such a reduction that it not only describes the world, but also constantly creates it anew, and in its own image at that.

Second Conversation

READER: I must say that this last paragraph is quite cryptic. Before I continue reading, though, may I ask a methodological question that really bothers me?

AUTHOR: Please do.

READER: I just don't see why all the historical reconstruction you undertake with such flair and circumspection in Jäger's case can't be applied to Oppenheimer himself. Is there really a major difference in kind in the intellectual exercise? Why do you pretend that what you write about Jäger is somehow "truer" or of a different order from what previous historians wrote about Oppenheimer?

AUTHOR: This is a crucial question that really brings into focus the methodological stakes here. In reconstructing any historical event, it matters a great deal who is reporting what. Oppenheimer was never allowed to write down his own side of the story. His speech was always mediated and controlled, and by his professed enemies at that. This is the main source of my skepticism of any attempt to reconstruct events based on his recorded speech. Jäger's case is very different. He personally supervised the court scribes (Pregizer even lived in his home for four years), and the protocols of his interrogation of Faberin, much of his correspondence, and the entire text of the *species facti* were all written in his own hand. I don't think that what he reports is always true—far from it—but I do believe that even when he lies it is his voice that we hear.

READER: So in the ongoing exchange between Oppenheimer and his main inquisitor, you think we can hear the latter's voice but not the former's?

AUTHOR: Yes. Exploring the relationship between Jäger and Oppenheimer is like trying to reconstruct a whole phone conversation based on only one side of it, or even better, it's like figuring out an entire chess game from the moves of only the white pieces. Sociologists call this method "second-order observation." We can't observe Oppenheimer, but we can observe his observer quite closely.

READER: An intriguing thought. Where does it leave us?

AUTHOR: A little patience, my friend. I was only just getting started.

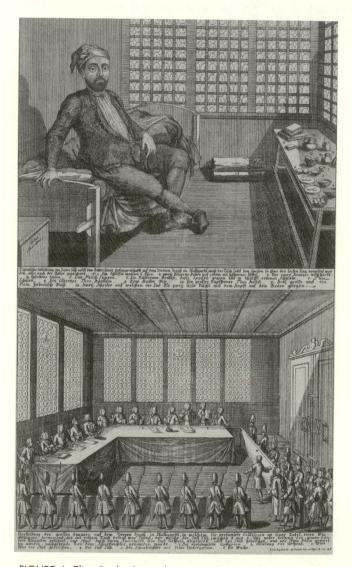

FIGURE 6. Elias Beck. Oppenheimer in the Herrenhaus and the reading of his verdict, 1738. *Source*: WLB, Grafische Sammlung.

CHAPTER 2

A Convert's Tale

And as Samuel turned about to go away, he
laid hold upon the skirt of his mantle, and it rent.
And Samuel said unto him, The Lord hath rent
the kingdom of Israel from thee this day, and
hath given it to a neighbour of thine, that is
better than thou.
—1 Samuel 15:27–28

A few weeks after Oppenheimer's execution, University of Tübingen lecturer Christoph David Bernard wrote an account of his first visit with the condemned man. They had met on Saturday, February 1, 1738, three days before the public hanging. Also present in the room were the court secretary Johann Philipp Pregizer and a prominent member of the small Jewish community in Stuttgart, Marx Nathan (also known as Mordechai Schloss).

Bernard later reported that even before their meeting, he had formed a very negative opinion about Oppenheimer. As he stepped into the room, he contemplated several biblical passages he found fitting to the case of this evil man: "He shall not be rich, neither shall his substance continue," for example, and "The flame shall dry up his branches" (Job 15:29–30).[1] Nevertheless, when he came face to face with Oppenheimer he was horrified, almost despite himself.

> It is almost beyond belief how dreadful was the first sight of this suffering man. The person I saw before me seemed to have little in common with the eminent, splendid man of the past. He was little more than a walking corpse, so brittle that he threatened to crumble if you touched him. Pain and fear ate away at his flesh like worms at a real dead body, and his face, already unpleasant before, became outright disgusting, covered as it now was with a thick black beard resembling moss on a gravestone.[2]

Oppenheimer's reaction upon Bernard's entry into the room is also of note, not least because—if we choose to believe Bernard—it switched very quickly from puzzlement to joy to horror. Bernard was the only member of the three-man delegation that Oppenheimer did not immediately recognize, hence the puzzlement. But when Pregizer introduced the lecturer, Oppenheimer immediately recalled a crucial fact about Bernard: he was a convert from Judaism. "Ha, ha," Bernard reported Oppenheimer as saying, "I already know who he is. The gentleman knows Hebrew as much as I do, or even better. He is welcome here." And then another radical change in mood: almost immediately after the "ha, ha" of recognition came a series of cries in a shrieking voice, "Shema Isroel, Odonoi Elohenu, Odonoi Echod, Odonoi Hu Elohim, Odonoi Hu Elohim."[3] Oppenheimer repeated this Jewish confession of faith seven times with such force that Bernard feared he would lose his breath and faint.

According to Bernard's account, he stayed with Oppenheimer for a long time that day, engaging the prisoner in a detailed and highly emotional conversation (figure 6). They spoke about God, about the relationship between fathers and sons, and about Jewish customs and prayers. They addressed questions about Oppenheimer's past life, his real or supposed crimes, and his relationships with other Jews as well as women. And they discussed his chances to still save himself even after the judges had declared their verdict. Oppenheimer often cried and yelled during the conversation though at other points he seemed a bit more composed. Bernard later recalled how bewildered he had been at the prisoner's "mixture of madness, rage, and suffering" and the man's complete inability "to have any kind of serious, reasonable conversation about important and useful things."[4] Promising to return again one more time before the execution, at which point he would be a witness to Oppenheimer's last will and testament, Bernard then left the room. His account of the meeting—if we choose to believe its details—is the most psychologically revealing of the many contemporary eyewitness accounts of Jew Süss.

Historians of Oppenheimer's case tend to take Bernard's narrative account at face value. Although they often recognize that Bernard's status as a convert might have influenced the tone of his account, they all use the account itself as if it were a fairly accurate description of Oppenheimer's deteriorating health, his state of mind, and even his actual voice just a few days before his execution.[5] As the present chapter will make abundantly clear, there are good reasons to doubt the veracity of many aspects of Bernard's account of his meetings with Oppenheimer. The Tübingen lecturer wrote it in a highly stylized manner, and his main purpose was not to tell the truth, the whole truth, and nothing but the truth, but to make a claim about himself (Bernard) and his relationship with the wider society around him. While reading this as well as other documents produced during Oppenheimer's trial, it can be very misleading to follow the suggestion of a recent book and simply "let the sources speak for themselves."[6] Bernard's account was anything but an uncomplicated representation of reality. It was an attempt to act in the world and not simply, or primarily, to describe it. As such, but only as such, it was revealing, moving, and indeed profound.

Who, then, was this Christoph David Bernard? What can we know about his life? Why should we view his account of the meeting in the Herrenhaus with a big dose of skepticism, and why is it nonetheless so telling? In the following pages, these questions will lead us through several crucial moments in Bernard's life both before and during Oppenheimer's trial. Among such moments, Bernard's conversion to Lutheranism in 1713 must serve as the starting point.[7]

The Baptized Jew

Only twice during his almost forty-year stay in Württemberg did Bernard refer in print to his preconversion life. The first time came in 1722, in the introduction to his first book, a Hebrew grammar. There, Bernard mentioned briefly that ten years earlier he'd had a conversation with the Lutheran priest Johann Philip Storr in Langenschwalbach, a town about a day's walk north of Mainz. It was then and there that his eyes were opened to the "true faith." "I felt esteem and love toward Storr's qualities," Bernard wrote in a sentence that sounds as awkward in the original German as it does in modern English translation, "and these brought me to pay special attention to [Storr's] words." Then, after some "further reflection and through the grace of God, I turned from a blind Jew into a Christian."[8]

Bernard kept a publishing silence about his Jewish past for sixteen more years before making another comment about it in print. Only in 1738, in a side comment while describing his first meeting with Oppenheimer in the Herrenhaus, did he return to the topic. Some of Oppenheimer's contemporaries (including, as we saw, Philipp Friedrich Jäger) believed that Oppenheimer was the son of a Christian man rather than of Issachar Süsskind, the first husband of Michal Oppenheimer. Bernard disagreed. Back in 1712, he had traveled to Langenschwalbach from England, and during his trip he had met "a troupe of poor Jews who tried to collect alms by singing to both Christians and Jews."[9] The troupe's lead singer was one Süsskind, the son-in-law of the famous Frankfurt cantor Selmele Chazan. It was this Süsskind and his wife (the cantor's daughter) that Bernard identified as Oppenheimer's parents, so Oppenheimer's father was Jewish after all. Like much else in his account, the supposed meeting with Oppenheimer's father in 1712 must be considered a figment of Bernard's imagination: Issachar Süsskind Oppenheimer had already been dead for five years in 1712, and unlike his father-in-law, he was certainly no singer, but a tax collector.[10] Be that as it may, this is all Bernard ever committed to print about his preconversion life.

While Bernard's books are almost completely silent about his Jewish past, other sources are much more forthcoming about it. This is primarily a result of the conversion process itself, which, apart from leaving its own paper trail, also required the proselyte-to-be to provide church authorities with at least some information about his former life. Thus we learn from Bernard's Württemberg church records that he was born on March 6, 1682, that his parents' names were Baruch and Esther, that he was originally from Lemberg (Lviv in present-day Ukraine), that his original name was Moses, and that he had received religious education that allowed him to become a rabbi in the city of Bar, about 200 miles east of Lemberg.[11] What was his life like in its first thirty years? What was his father's occupation? Did he have any siblings? Had he ever been married or had children? Why did he leave Bar and travel to England and later to Germany? Why, indeed, did he find himself in the distant town of Langenschwalbach in 1712, where he met Storr? These and many other questions remain open.

A second group of church documents outlines Bernard's conversion process itself, though here, too, the gaps in the historical record are often substantial. What Bernard did between his meeting with Storr in 1712 and the summer of the following year is unknown. But in early July 1713, we find him in Stuttgart and events start to heat up. First, he seeks help from the Württemberg Consistory (the state organ responsible for religious affairs) to receive instruction in the Christian religion and financial support before conversion.[12] On July 11, 1713, his request is granted, a deacon is assigned to instruct him in the catechism, and he is given a bed at the Geistliche Herberge, a church-owned hostel across the street from the Collegiate church in the center of town.[13] Hardly a month goes by, and Moses already feels ready. "The Jewish proselyte Moses Bernard," the Consistory recorded in its books on August 25, "asks for a baptismal garment as well as assistance in gaining permission to remain in Württemberg."[14] Finally, two weeks later, on September 11, 1713, he is baptized in Stuttgart's Collegiate church as Christoph David Bernard, surrounded, as was then the custom, by seven prominent godparents, including Christian Zeller, an important Tübingen theologian, and Duchess Johanna Elisabetha, Duke Eberhard Ludwig's estranged wife.[15]

Not all historical sources are created equal, and the ones that shed light on Bernard's early life are a case in point. The closer one gets to Bernard's moment of conversion, the more reliable and numerous the relevant records become. They are written down as the events they describe are unfolding and by people who all corroborate the same basic story. The same cannot be said about the details of Bernard's life before his arrival in Germany. The problem here is not only Bernard's silence vis-à-vis his Jewish past, but also the absence of any archival footprints about Bernard from outside Württemberg as well as what we now know about converts from Judaism in early modern Germany. If Bernard had indeed come from Lemberg, it is very unlikely that he would have used the surname Bernard there. As a rule, Polish Jews did not take family names until the late eighteenth century, and the name Bernard is also extremely rare in those parts of central Europe. Why and when Bernard chose this particular surname and when he used it for the first time are parts of a story that has probably been lost forever. Furthermore, even if one tries to locate the preconversion Bernard in Polish and Ukrainian archives by using different versions of his and his father's names, the result is disappointing: a paper trail for Moses from Lemberg, son of Baruch and Esther and later a rabbi in Bar, is nowhere to be found.[16] The case of Bernard's alleged sojourn in England is similar. Ashkenazi Jews, who started immigrating to England in the late seventeenth century, usually came from very modest backgrounds and therefore left few, if any, traces in the historical record. This holds true for newspapers, trade directories, and other types of civil and public documents. Even synagogue records are unlikely to mention them unless they were born or got married in England. It is consequently impossible to know whether Bernard had in fact been in England, and if so, why, where, and for how long.

There is one final and very important reason not to take at face value the little Bernard had to say about his preconversion life. As the historian Elisheva Carlebach showed in a book about converts from Judaism in early modern Germany, the stories many converts told about their previous lives were highly dubious. In some cases, converts left their old religion for material reasons and even invented completely imaginary pasts for themselves in order to gain access to academic posts—usually as teachers of Hebrew. We even know of cases of deceptive baptisms in which, when faced with the harsh reality that Christians tended to care about them more before their conversions than afterward, Jews converted over and over again, each time in a different city and under a different name.[17] These might have been extreme cases. But even if Bernard's case was not that of a "serial convert," the few facts he does mention about his preconversion life must be taken with a grain of salt. This is the case not only with Bernard's supposed meeting with Issachar Süsskind Oppenheimer in 1712, but also with his suspiciously accurate date of birth and his claim that he had been a rabbi in Bar. Especially this last point should make us wary: how could anyone corroborate such a claim in distant Württemberg? Was there not something suspicious about Bernard serving as a rabbi in Bar (200 miles east of Lemberg) and not in a closer or better-known place? Is this story not a bit too conveniently inconvenient? The Stuttgart Consistory certainly felt this way, at least at first. Three months after Bernard's conversion, it found the necessary "scope of knowledge of rabbinical literature not achievable" in his case.[18]

It is easy to become disoriented vis-à-vis the limited and often contradictory record of Bernard's preconversion life, easy to lose sight of what about it was important for contemporaries and what in it is most relevant for us today. Bernard's contemporaries seem to have known little about the exact identity of Bernard's parents, his reasons for leaving Bar and going to England (and whether he had actually been to these two places at all), or his motivation for traveling to Langenschwalbach in 1712. What was important for them was that Bernard was a convert, a proselyte. As such, though he could be useful for certain things, he was also often disrespected and almost always under suspicion of not telling the truth.[19] In 1732, when a Jew whom Bernard himself helped to convert was baptized in Ludwigsburg, the preacher beseeched his flock to refrain from passing judgment on converts with the usual "disrespect, carelessness, and hate."[20] In one of his books, Bernard echoed the same sentiment, claiming that it was common for Christians to distrust converts, to use "abusive, malicious, and curse words to describe Jewish converts to Christianity" and indeed that "some do not consider [the converts] to be Christian at all."[21]

While Bernard himself kept a publishing silence about his Jewish past, some of his contemporaries never ceased to write about it. Were not these two facts perhaps related? They called him "a proselyte" immediately after his conversion in 1713, and he was still a "Proselyte from Judaism" in the entry about his death in 1751.[22] They called him a proselyte in Stuttgart and in Tübingen and during a brief sojourn in Jena in northern Germany; proselyte in state, town, university, and church records; proselyte when former students came to visit him at the university, and proselyte when others wrote about him, and once (though very early, and only once), he called himself proselyte when he introduced himself in one of his books.[23] Things didn't stop there. In the same year he met Oppenheimer, Bernard also wrote a letter to the authorities in Stuttgart, complaining that despite his academic position, he was seated in church behind everyone "from the university or from the town" simply because of his past.[24] A few years later, he protested to a local official about a young schoolboy by the name of Häfelin. Bernard reported that Häfelin liked to stand outside his (Bernard's) house, make foul gestures toward him, abuse him verbally, stick his tongue out at him, and even spit on him whenever he walked by, all the while calling him, a Christian university professor close to sixty years of age, "ein verfluchter Jude" (a damned Jew).[25]

All of this is important in and for itself but also because it helps us understand the complexity of Bernard's social position in Württemberg and, with it, the difficulty of assessing the reliability of the account of his meetings with Oppenheimer. As the case of the supposed meeting with Oppenheimer's father demonstrated, Bernard did not always stick to the truth. At the same time, had Bernard lied outright about the details of his meetings with Oppenheimer and had his lies been exposed (and remember that Johann Philip Pregizer, the clerk of the judicial committee, was also present in the room), he could have lost everything he had worked to create for himself since his conversion in 1713. As a convert who often faced very hostile prejudices about his true beliefs, Bernard was dependent on his claim of being a sincere and truthful person. Hence a paradox: Precisely because so many people entertained doubts about who Bernard really was, there is room to believe that his account did contain many truthful elements about Oppenheimer and not only prevarications.

Move to Tübingen

In the autumn of 1713, Bernard's life seemed promising. Six days before his baptism, the Württemberg Consistory decided to send him afterward to the theological seminary in Tübingen for a test period of three months.[26] He remained in Stuttgart for eleven days after his baptism and left the Geistliche Herberge, the hostel where he had been staying since July, on September 22. Perhaps the symbolism didn't escape Bernard himself: that year, September 22 was the second day of Rosh Hashana, a traditional time in the Jewish calendar for reflecting on one's transgressions against man and God, the Lord's wrath and forgiveness, the past and the future. (According to Jewish tradition, Rosh Hashana marks the beginning of a ten-day period in which God inscribes people's fate in a Book of Life. The book is sealed on Yom Kippur.) A quarter century later, one of the things Bernard recalled about his first meeting with Oppenheimer was how he had called on the prisoner to meditate on this aspect of the Jewish calendar; whatever God had in store for him (Bernard told Oppenheimer), this fate had already been sealed.[27] In September 1713, on his way to Tübingen from Stuttgart, Bernard might have been meditating on this aspect of the Jewish calendar himself.

The seminary Bernard was sent to in September 1713 was located on the southern edge of Tübingen, the external wall of its southern wing protruding beyond the town's medieval fortifications.[28] Built as an Augustinian monastery in the thirteenth century, the seminary had long served as a preparatory school for Lutheran priests. Its architecture was simple. Surrounding a small inner courtyard (the original cloister) were four wings. On the eastern (entrance) side were storage areas, and on the opposite side was the kitchen. To the south was the long building of the refectory with several residential floors above it, and to the north was the so-called Old Building. The latter contained more residential rooms and some offices, all lying heavily on top of the old, neglected monastic chapel, which in the early eighteenth century still showed some faded frescoes of Catholic saints.

The heart and soul of the seminary were its students, numbering exactly 333 in 1713.[29] They were divided into different cohorts. The novices were students who had not yet obtained an academic degree, the baccalaurei had only bachelor's degrees, the magisters already had master's degrees but still studied theology, and the so-called repetitioners were those students who had finished their studies but stayed on at the seminary as study section leaders for the younger cohorts. (One of the repetitioners in 1713 was Georg Konrad Rieger, Jäger's future gymnasium teacher and a man who would come to play a small but important role in Oppenheimer's trial.) The different cohorts of the seminary had their separate tables in the dining hall. We know that, at least at first, Bernard sat with the magisters, at the eastern end of the refectory. This was right below the elevated platform reserved for the seminary's three directors, one of whom was the same Christian Zeller who had attended Bernard's baptism in Stuttgart. We know the names of Bernard's table companions; we know when he took his meals and even what he ate and drank on a typical day.[30]

Bernard must have been somewhat of an odd bird at the seminary. About thirty years old when he arrived in the fall of 1713, he was now surrounded by teenagers, and as a foreigner he must have spoken imperfect German (this is evident in his early published works). If the experience of a later convert in the same area is any indication, Bernard was also asked "innumerable times" about his Jewish background and his decision to convert.[31] Even Bernard's sleeping room had something to do with his past. The seminary's convert-guests—predominantly former Catholics, but also a handful of converts from Judaism—had traditionally inhabited a separate chamber at the seminary, the so-called convert's room (*Convertitenstube*), on the third floor of the Old Building.[32] A few years before Bernard's arrival, however, the seminary had forbidden converts from living together, although their old room kept its name. It seems that some of the converts had not taken the institution and its rules very seriously: a former Jesuit had to be expelled after trying to convince his fellow students to follow Calvinist principles (the seminary, like Württemberg as a whole, was Lutheran); an ex-advocate general of the Franciscan Order was shown the door after repeatedly disobeying the seminary's regulations; and one, Thomas Gruber, was thrown out after pursuing the fourteen-year-old daughter of the seminary's washerwoman, "putting her on his lap, kissing and pressing against her."[33]

Thus, in 1713, Bernard did not sleep in the converts' room. After daytimes spent in the university's lecture halls and in the seminary's chapel, dining hall, small library, or study rooms, he would have gone to one of the other ten heated rooms (*Schlafstuben*), where several students lived together in such close proximity that, in the words of one eighteenth-century report, "a student couldn't write down even a letter without his neighbor peeking over his shoulder."[34] It is perhaps this fact that prevented Bernard from writing his life story at this point, which was the norm among converts at the time. We consequently know where Bernard spent his days and where, when, and with whom he ate; we even have a sense of what his nights must have looked like. But while it is possible to learn a great deal about the physical environment in which Bernard lived in the fall and winter of 1713, we are at a complete loss when it comes to his feelings and state of mind. Now, as then, what Bernard really thought and felt about Judaism and Jews is shrouded in mystery.

Education

The reason the Consistory sent Bernard to the seminary in the first place was to see how "versed he [was] in rabbinical literature" and whether he could eventually teach Hebrew and Aramaic to the other seminary students as a repetitioner and perhaps, in the more distant future, as a university lecturer.[35] The beginning did not bode well. His knowledge of rabbinical literature proved so poor that the Consistory decided to send Bernard away after the initial three-month period of probation; he was given, however, a second chance.[36] Then, in early 1714, Bernard failed a major exam and was dismissed from the seminary before, once again, receiving a dispensation from the Consistory.[37] Although Bernard was not immediately successful in his studies, he seems to have worked hard and clearly made some powerful friends. Reading the sources today, one gets a darkly comic picture of him at this point in his life, anxiously working to recall childhood Hebrew and Bible lessons in order to impress his superiors and gain the reputation of a former rabbi. Be that as it may, it is clear that after the initial difficulties, Bernard did prove his ability to teach Hebrew, Aramaic, and rabbinical literature on the one hand, and displayed a command of the primary methods of Christian scholarship and polemics on the other hand. Without the former, there would have been no reason for the Consistory to continue paying his expenses at the seminary; without the latter, one couldn't have trusted him (that word again: trust) to instruct other students in these subjects.

It is worth elaborating on these last two points because they are decisive for any interpretation of Bernard's involvement in Oppenheimer's trial. Interest in the Hebrew Bible, post-biblical rabbinical texts, and Jewish mysticism (Kabbalah) was widespread in early modern Europe. Long before Bernard's time, observant Jews taught Hebrew to Christian scholars, while converts from Judaism used their knowledge of the holy tongue to gain academic positions at schools and universities, publish polemical literature against their former coreligionists, and even participate in public disputations with them. Bernard also belonged to this double tradition. His entire professional raison d'être was to serve as a specialist on all matters Jewish. His job was to teach, translate, and comment on Hebrew and Aramaic texts, uncover their original meaning, and, if needed, expose their falsity. As we shall see in detail later, this is how Bernard got involved in Oppenheimer's case even before his first rendezvous with the prisoner.

The second crucial point about Bernard's education at the seminary relates to his immersion in methods of Christian polemics. What kind of education Bernard received before his conversion we simply do not know. Perhaps he had already been immersed in the old ways of studying the Talmud, the hairsplitting *pilpul*, one method of which is the practice of taking one's opponent's perspective as one's own only to show that it leads to the exact opposite conclusions from what the opponent had suggested—a method known in Aramaic as *ipcha mistabra*, "on the contrary." Some of Bernard's contemporaries viewed his argumentative nature in this light. Stephan Schultz, an important Lutheran missionary who had lunch with Bernard in 1741 while visiting Tübingen from northern Germany, felt that the lecturer's conversion had perhaps been sincere, but he accused Bernard nonetheless of "Jewish pride" and a proclivity to seek out verbal arguments with others. Similarly, in 1747, a fellow Tübingen resident claimed that Bernard still had some "oriental trickery" about him when it came to arguing with others.[38]

More convincing than the argument about Bernard's supposed "oriental" methods is the issue of his education at the seminary. Bernard certainly read quite a few books there, including the Church Fathers and St. Augustine in particular. Next to reading, Bernard's education consisted of theological disputations—academic exercises in which students debated a given argument. There were different types of disputations in early modern German universities, depending on the occasion (ceremonial, public, private, and so on), the discipline (law, the liberal arts, theology), and the statutes or rules of any given university.[39] In principle, however, disputations followed similar rules. Presided over by a professor, the disputation took place between two sides: a respondent, who defended an argument, and one or more opponents, who attacked it. Everyone had a prescribed place here, literally and figuratively. The professor presided over the verbal exchange from an elevated platform, while the respondent stood just beneath him, both turning in the same direction, toward the opponents in the room (and the audience, too, if such existed). Days in advance, the argument had already been made public, so the disputation itself began immediately with an attack on the argument, followed by a rebuttal by the respondent. The disputation then continued as the two sides took turns attacking each other, always following the prescribed course and disputational rules. It was not permissible, for instance, to ask your opponent a direct question, but it was acceptable to start an argument from the assumptions of one's opponent only to draw the exact opposite logical conclusions from them.[40] In a university disputation—just as in a Talmudic *pilpul*—looking at an issue from opposite sides was a crucial part of the intellectual exercise; there was nothing necessarily "Jewish" or "oriental" about it.[41]

That Bernard was deeply versed in the disputational method is clear both because of circumstantial evidence (that is, the important role of disputations in the education of any seminary student) and in more direct ways. In the same year that Oppenheimer was executed, a journal article described Bernard as a man with the uncanny ability to "refute the views of blind Jews by using the very principles of their religion."[42] "Whenever I dispute with a Jew," Bernard himself wrote at the time, "I first show him the absurdity of the Talmud and all other rabbinical literature . . .

which are held by the Jews to be higher than God's own words. . . . Then, when [the Jew] becomes defenseless [against my arguments], I find it easy to convince him of the true nature of the Christian faith."[43] A few years earlier, Bernard had led a *collegium anti Judaicum* at the university in which the disputational method must have been central,[44] and once, as we shall see, he even tried to stage a public disputation with the Jews of Karlsruhe. Perhaps related to his university colloquium is a manuscript from 1734, kept today at the Württemberg State Library in Stuttgart, which Bernard copied in his own hand and to which he added a few lines on the very last page. The book was the fifteenth-century *Sefer ha-ʿIkkarim* ("The Book of Principles"), a work dedicated to the fundamental principles of Judaism and written by the Spanish Jewish rabbi Joseph Albo (ca. 1380–1444). Albo was a participant in the major Christian-Jewish disputation in Tortosa, Spain, in 1413–1414, and his book was an attempt to lay down the basic fundamentals of Judaism for use in later disputations in defense of Judaism. For that very reason, however, *Sefer ha-ʿIkkarim* could also be useful in preparing for a disputation against Judaism: it revealed in advance some of the arguments a Jewish opponent might raise during the verbal exchange.[45]

It was on the last page of Albo's book that Bernard scribbled a few short lines in Hebrew about himself, the copyist.

Blessed be He, who has never ceased to show His grace to me

And has given me strength and vigor to complete my task

Of copying this Book of Principles in my own hand.

My name is Christoph David Bernard and in Tübingen I lived

And in Lemberg, the great city among the nations, I was born.

It is twenty-two years since I concluded my covenant

With Jesus the Nazarene, in whose salvation I trusted,

And He shall be my true haven in my life and in my death.[46]

There are several reasons why Bernard's mastery of the disputational method is relevant to any understanding of the meeting with Oppenheimer. First, it sheds light on a perplexing paradox. In his account of their meetings, Bernard agreed with many of Oppenheimer's assumptions—which seems to show at least some empathy with the prisoner—while also portraying his arguments as logical absurdities—which seems very negative. If we think about the text of the meeting as a disputation, the contradiction disappears: here are two sides of the disputational method rather than a contradiction. Indeed, in his 1738 account, Bernard refers to the first meeting with Oppenheimer both implicitly and explicitly as a kind of disputation. He was trying, he writes, "to convince [Oppenheimer] by using the principles of his own religion and to entangle him in his own web, as it were."[47] If we believe Bernard, Oppenheimer too understood what was afoot. Earlier in their conversation, he resisted Bernard's conversion attempts by stating not only that "the gentleman [Bernard] should know that I have resolved to die as a Jew," but also that he, Oppenheimer, "was in no state to have a scholarly disputation."[48]

A second pertinent point has to do with the reliability of Bernard's account. Because of the nature of Oppenheimer's trial and the high stakes many people had (and still have) in it, it is very difficult to determine which of the many contradictory eyewitness accounts one might believe. In the case of the retelling of a long conversation several weeks after the fact, the problem might be not only malicious intent but also the natural failing of human memory. Even if Bernard had wanted to tell only the truth about his meetings with Oppenheimer, how many of the details could he have possibly remembered accurately several weeks later?

Bernard's immersion in the disputational method can be seen alternately as a problem or a solution here. It is a problem if we assume that Bernard tried to fit his account into the constraints of a disputational structure after the fact, editing, transforming, and perhaps even inventing some of its contents in the process in order to impress his audience. As we shall see later, there is much to be said for such an interpretation, because there are certain passages in Bernard's account of his exchanges with Oppenheimer that almost certainly underwent such later editing. But the disputational method Bernard had mastered in the seminary can also support the opposite view: much in the same way that disputations had to follow a clear and predetermined logical order and be prepared in advance, so too Bernard's conversations with Oppenheimer might have followed common disputational rules even as they were unfolding and not only in retrospect. According to this scenario, the disputational structure of the conversations as reported by Bernard is not necessarily a later construct imposed on reality but may actually reflect an a priori script for it, especially because Bernard had been preparing to dispute with Jews long before his meeting with Oppenheimer in 1738. In short, recalling the overall contours and even specific details of their conversations later might have proved much easier for Bernard than one would perhaps assume.

And then there is the issue of Bernard's self-description in *Sefer ha-'Ikkarim*. Whom did Bernard write this short text for? It was unusual for Bernard to put in writing anything about his past, but here he wrote the self-description in Hebrew, and he used the past tense rather than the more appropriate present tense in crucial places. ("I lived in Tübingen," he writes while still living in Tübingen, and "In Jesus the Nazarene I believed.") It is as if Bernard had been writing posthumously to Hebrew-speaking readers of this copy of Albo's book. This is an important point: in *Sefer ha-ʿIkkarim* and in all likelihood also in the account of his meeting with Oppenheimer, Bernard was not a mere chronicler; he was actively trying to influence his own legacy. Copying and teaching Albo and writing about Oppenheimer were highly personal issues for him. He was using them to make a statement about what or who he was not, which is of course another way of suggesting who he really was.

Lecturer Bernard

Bernard did not live in the seminary for long. The records show that by May 1714, he was living in an apartment in the town itself, though its exact location is unspecified. What is clear is that Bernard, facing some financial duress, applied to the Consistory in Stuttgart to allow him to distill schnapps in his house while also continuing his studies at the university.[49] This is not an insignificant detail: Polish Jews were known as excellent schnapps distillers and tavern keepers in the early modern period and well into the nineteenth century.[50] Just as with his Jewish education (however much of it he actually possessed), Bernard was using his past to his advantage; he was by no means only its victim.

Bernard's exact whereabouts in the years before the publication of his first book in 1722 are somewhat unclear. Although he never received any official degree from the university at Tübingen, he spent some time teaching privately at faraway Jena and by March 1718 returned to teach Hebrew and Aramaic regularly at the seminary.[51] By the early 1720s, Bernard's life seems to have finally stabilized and the archival paper trail that allows us to get closer to him reappears. One series of documented changes occurred in Bernard's professional life. In 1722, he published his first book, a Hebrew grammar called "David's Tabernacle." This corresponded to his role as a Hebrew teacher at the seminary. But Bernard did not stop there. In 1724, he published a long commentary on Isaiah 7 titled "The First Words of David"; in 1728, during a general debate on the topic, a text on the question, "To what extent could one trust a Jew's testimony in court?" (answer: quite a bit, but only if certain conditions are met); and in 1730, a polemical text against rabbinical literature in general called "David's Rod."[52] The relevance of these books to the present story is twofold. First, we see here a clear progression in Bernard's academic interests. With each successive book, Bernard claimed more scholarly territory as his own, moving from a seminary teacher of Hebrew and Aramaic (the grammar), to a commentator on the Bible (Isaiah 7), to an expert on all things Jewish (including legal oaths), to finally a professional polemicist. This progression corresponds exactly with Bernard's scholarly career. In 1718, he taught only Hebrew and Aramaic at the seminary (and before that, privately, at Jena), but by 1723 he was already considered a regular faculty member at the university. In 1726, we find him delivering lectures on all aspects of the Old Testament, and finally, by the mid-1730s, he was a university lecturer (*Lektor*) of Hebrew, Aramaic, and rabbinical literature who also directed a colloquium about anti-Jewish polemics and disputation. Thus, in the winter semester of 1737–1738, while Oppenheimer's trial was unfolding, Bernard was finishing a series of lectures on the Psalms and was about to offer a lecture course on the Minor Prophets and a colloquium on the Talmud and rabbinical literature.[53]

The second pertinent point here relates to Bernard's decision to use his Christian name David in the titles of all his early books and indeed to be christened Christoph David in the first place. Since at least the time of St. Augustine, Christian theologians had seen King David as an exceptional figure. According to two of the Gospels, Jesus was the direct descendant of King David, but Augustine saw the Jewish king as a precursor of Christ more broadly. In his famous commentary on Psalm 51, for instance, Augustine claims that King David was a precursor of Jesus both in spirit and in the flesh. David is a figure, Augustine writes, in which "God was foreshadowing a reign of eternal salvation, and he chose David to abide for ever in his posterity. Our King, the King of ages, with whom we shall reign eternally, was descended from David according to the flesh."[54] Augustine's interpretation of David had never been forgotten, but during the Reformation it became especially prominent and widespread. Martin Luther saw in David a model for the reformed movement in general, while John Calvin identified with David directly.[55] Bernard's decision to keep evoking the name David throughout his works had therefore potentially very powerful theological overtones, especially for someone like himself who, just like David, had been born a Jew. Indeed, in 1722, Bernard made this point explicitly in his first book.[56] We will soon come to see the full implications of all of this for Bernard's meeting with Oppenheimer in the Herrenhaus. The most profound message of Bernard's account of the Herrenhaus meeting is in all likelihood undecipherable without reference to King David's life story.

Not everything in Bernard's life in the 1720s and 1730s was purely intellectual, of course. Apart from his academic work, sur-

viving sources document Bernard's continued interest in two
other activities. The first was the distillation of schnapps. Even
when his financial situation improved following his first marriage (more about that in a minute), Bernard continued to look
for ways to make ends meet. His modest academic salary was
partially paid to him in kegs of local wine and bales of hay.[57]
Producing the fruit-flavored liqueur in his house was supposed
to alleviate his financial difficulties at least to some extent. That
Bernard ever really succeeded in this endeavor is highly doubtful. His neighbors complained about the distillation activities in
Bernard's little kitchen (*Küchlein*) not long after the lecturer
moved into his first wife's house.[58] In a town where practically all
the houses had wooden frames, lighting an unsupervised fire in
one's home was a cause for great concern, so the local magistrates
asked Bernard twice to desist from doing so. (Indeed, this part of
town, including Bernard's own house, did burn down in 1789.[59])
This schnapps business is not irrelevant to Bernard's involvement with Oppenheimer. Beside the obvious religious differences between the two men, there was also a huge socioeconomic
divide. Though he was by no means impoverished, Bernard lived
on a modest salary and he constantly struggled to make ends
meet (and complained about it).[60] His most prized possession
was his first wife's house, which was worth about 300 gulden in
1728.[61] Oppenheimer's case was strikingly different. By the time
of his arrest in 1737, his house in Stuttgart was worth approximately 15,000 reichsthaler (30,000 gulden), an unimaginable
sum to Bernard. Even after nearly all of his property had been
confiscated by Württemberg and Frankfurt officials, Oppenheimer still had 3,000 reichsthaler (6,000 gulden) in his possession in prison.[62] This was twenty times what Bernard's whole
house was worth.

The second nonacademic activity Bernard was interested in was the actual conversion of Jews. We already saw that, as he was expanding his academic activities from the early 1720s onward, Bernard began to argue with Jews in his books and even led a colloquium on anti-Jewish polemics at the university. But Bernard clearly wanted to engage Jews in person and not only through his writing. He had limited success with this. On January 14, 1721, the Stuttgart Consistory asked him to instruct the Jew Jakob Daniel, a would-be convert from Cracow, in the fundamentals of the Christian faith, and in 1732 he even succeeded in proselytizing one Chaijm (Haim) David from Mühringen after the latter tried to persuade him (Bernard) to return to Judaism.[63] The best-documented conversion episode involving Bernard, however, comes from outside Württemberg. In November 1730, Bernard sent his latest book to the Baden authorities in Karlsruhe with the request that they allow him to enter the land and convince the Jews there "of the truth of our Christian religion" and the "errors of theirs."[64] His request granted, Bernard wrote another letter on January 18, 1731 (he was already in Karlsruhe at the time, and seemed to have accomplished nothing in his conversion efforts thus far), asking the Karlsruhe church council to force Jews to participate in a disputation with him, "publicly or at the synagogue."[65] The council allowed Bernard to approach Jews but forbade him from entering the synagogue without its permission or forcing anyone to engage in a disputation with him. Though he was obviously eager to participate in actual conversions, Bernard's success in this—just as in his schnapps business—seems to have been very limited. This is perhaps the source of a nasty comment made by Georg Konrad Rieger about Bernard. Shortly after Oppenheimer's trial, Rieger wrote that Bernard "could accomplish little with the Jew [that is, Oppenheimer] because he cannot hold his ground when it comes to matters of religion."[66]

The sources also tell us a few things about Bernard's friends and benefactors. Some of Bernard's admirers were his students and colleagues, people who had heard him lecture, read his books, or met him in person and appreciated his sincerity or the breadth of his knowledge. This, for instance, was the case of the University of Tübingen chancellor, Christoph Matthäus Pfaff, an important theologian with a dominant personality, who was also a strong supporter of the study of Semitic languages as basis for biblical exegesis.[67] In introducing Bernard's first book, Pfaff wrote warmly about Bernard in a sentence that is as indicative of the venom of Bernard's opponents as it is of Pfaff's warm support. Bernard, Pfaff wrote, was "a sincere friend of Jesus Christ, without any falsity, who withstood enough tests of his Christian faith and continues to do so now."[68] "Sincere," "without falsity," "withstood many tests," "continues to do so now"—in a single sentence, Pfaff echoed four times the voices of Bernard's enemies. Pfaff was not alone in his warm feelings toward Bernard, though. The important scholar Johann Gottfried Tympe, who heard Bernard lecture in Jena, had only good things to say about him, as did the important Pietist theologian Friedrich Christoph Oetinger, who studied the Psalms and later also rabbinical literature (including Albo's book) with Bernard in the late 1720s.[69] Finally, August Friedrich Bök, who taught philosophy at Tübingen later in the eighteenth century and perhaps had even known Bernard in person, could still claim, twenty-five years after Bernard's death, that the lecturer had "left behind a number of students who honor his memory to this day and are still praising his teaching."[70]

And then there was also family life. In 1723, Bernard married the widow Maria Margaretha Krieger (née Wagenknecht) from

Tübingen.[71] Maria Margaretha and her first husband had three children, two sons and a daughter, and they lived in a townhouse at the corner of Holzmarkt and the Neue Strasse, which Maria Margaretha invited Bernard to share after they got married.[72] (It was in the "little kitchen" of this house that Bernard tried to install a stove for the distillation of schnapps in 1726.) Nothing is known about the exact nature of Bernard's first marriage, except for two potentially revealing incidents that occurred after Maria Margaretha's death on January 2, 1728. The first was that almost immediately after his spouse's passing, Bernard got into a legal dispute with his wife's daughter that brought both of them before a local magistrate on several occasions.[73] The second was that Bernard remarried less than seven months after Maria Margaretha's death.

Bernard's second wedding took place on July 20, 1728, in the small village of Wannweil, a few miles east of Tübingen.[74] The bride's name was Margaretha Agnesa Goebel. Bernard kept his first wife's house in Tübingen, and he and Margaretha Agnesa occupied it together until his death in 1751. While living there, the couple practically adopted Margaretha Agnesa's niece, Anna Catharina Goebel, the eldest daughter of Margaretha's late brother Johann Philipp. In the joint last will and testament Bernard and his second wife drew up in February 1743, they wrote about Anna Catharina that she "lived with them for many years" and that "they practically raised her." Though she was already married at the time to a baker, Bernard and Margaretha Agnesa still treated Anna with "parental love" (as they put it) and declared her their universal heiress in case they both died.[75] Bernard does not seem to have left any biological children behind at his death.

These details might seem excessive, but they should, I think, give us pause. We know close to nothing about Bernard's father, Baruch: his exact identity; his possessions or occupation (a schnapps distiller and tavern keeper, perhaps?); whether he was still alive when Moses (Bernard) left home; or if he had ever come to know about his son's conversion. What we do know is that Bernard never had children of his own and that even a quarter century after coming to Württemberg he still thought about the obligations of Jewish children toward their parents. In his account of his meetings with Oppenheimer, Bernard tells us that they discussed exactly this topic. The time was the anniversary of Oppenheimer's father's death, his *yahrzeit*, and Bernard reminded Oppenheimer about Jewish customs in this respect.[76] This was at least a quarter of a century after Bernard had seen his own father for the last time.

Bernard's marriages and personal relationships are important for a second reason as well. The inheritance law of Württemberg demanded that in the case of the death of a family member, household property be distributed among the surviving spouse and children. This is why the law demanded that a detailed inventory of one's property be drawn at crucial junctions in life: marriage, death, and divorce, but also after certain types of criminal arrest. This legal background explains why Bernard and his first wife's daughter got into a prolonged dispute in 1728 and why Bernard and his second wife decided to draw a very detailed joint last will and testament in 1743 to prevent any legal disputes after their deaths.

The legal documents produced as a result of Württemberg's inheritance laws are quite revealing in Bernard's case. Three inventories and one joint last will and testament testify to many aspects of the material environment in which Bernard lived. Among many other things, they list the number of rooms, closets, beds, and other pieces of furniture in his house; the quality, color, and value of linens and clothes he and his wives possessed; and the titles and monetary value of the books they kept at home. The latter group of items is especially revealing because it sums up nicely several crucial aspects of Bernard's professional life. Bernard possessed a whole range of Bibles in different languages, a testimony to his activities as a lecturer on all aspects of the Old Testament; he had a series of Jewish and Christian commentaries on aspects of the Pentateuch, the Psalms, and the Prophets, all pointing to his engagement in polemics against Judaism; and he had a series of devotional Christian books attesting to his adopted Christian faith.[77] Finally—and this is apparent especially later in his life—the inventories paint a picture of Bernard's professional decline. In the inventories of the 1720s (during his first and second marriages), one doesn't find any of Bernard's own books. But in 1743, Andreas Christoph Zeller, the university's historian, reports that Bernard had not been able to find a publisher for several completed manuscripts, and upon Bernard's death in 1751, no less than 300 copies of his last book (published originally seven years earlier, in 1744) were listed in an inventory.[78] This material testimony to the lecturer's declining popularity later in life is corroborated by the cool reception of his latest book by the most important Württemberg theologian of the day, Johann Albrecht Bengel, in 1746.[79] Reading the documents today, one has the feeling that by the mid-1730s, Bernard was quickly reaching the limit of what he could achieve academically with the cards he'd been dealt in life.

It was around this time that Oppenheimer appeared in Stuttgart and rose quickly to prominence as the duke's personal banker and advisor. What Bernard thought about him while he was in power is uncertain. What we have is only what Bernard claimed retrospectively to have felt about the rise of the court Jew. "I never met Süss at the height of his power," Bernard insisted in 1738, "nor have I ever had the wish to do so. . . . Once he grew in riches and importance he became disgusting to me, so I avoided him, indeed I prophesied his downfall long before it happened."[80] A fulfillment of Bernard's prophecy or not, in March 1737 Duke Carl Alexander died unexpectedly. That same night Joseph Süss Oppenheimer was arrested; soon afterward he was put on trial.

Two Trips to Stuttgart

Nine months before he stepped into Oppenheimer's cell in the Herrenhaus, Bernard had already been summoned to Stuttgart to assume a modest role in the fallen court Jew's trial. This had to do with Bernard's academic expertise. Among the many items the court officers found in Oppenheimer's and his treasurer Isaac Samuel Levi's possession after their arrests were hundreds of letters, receipts, and short notes written in Yiddish. The members of the judicial committee could not decipher these documents themselves, let alone evaluate their content. They needed a "Jewish expert." They called Bernard.

First, they requested an official decree in the matter. On May 7, 1737, the four members of the inquisition committee—von Pflug, Faber, Dann, and Jäger—asked for permission to have Bernard translate the documents into German. "It is altogether possible," they wrote in their request, "that [these documents] contain nothing of interest." Still, they might hold some interesting details and they had already been confiscated and entered into the court's records. The inquisition committee was well aware that sending the documents to Bernard might compromise the investigation if word got out about any sensitive content. Consequently, "without compromising them, the letters need to be sent to Lecturer Bernard in Tübingen with the request that he translate them as quickly as possible . . . reveal their content to no one, and send a faithful translation back to the committee."[81] A day after the committee made its request, on May 8, 1737, Carl Rudolph approved it.[82]

Many months later, Bernard too would recall these events. In his account, the "Jewish letters" were not sent to him; he had to travel to Stuttgart twice to read and translate them. He described these trips as arduous and extremely unpleasant. "Because there were so many of them [the letters], I had to devote over a month to making excerpts from some for the benefit of the princely committee. . . . It was certainly a burdensome and bitter work [*beschwerlich und saure Arbeit*], more so than any I had ever done in my life. Still, I wanted to show my respect and submission to the princely committee and so I spared no effort and worked assiduously and avidly until I read through all of the letters and translated the important ones into German."[83]

The original notes and letters Bernard translated in the late spring or early summer of 1737 were later destroyed by the court (why is unclear), but two other groups of sources did survive: originals of similar letters from Oppenheimer's personal archive in Frankfurt and Bernard's own reports to the judicial committee in Stuttgart. The first group of documents, about fifty letters in all, was seized from Oppenheimer's apartment in Frankfurt after his arrest but for unknown reasons did not find its way to Stuttgart.[84] It survived intact in Frankfurt, was later transferred to Koblenz—the details of this voyage should not concern us here—and reached the state archives in Stuttgart only in 1928. Reading these notes and letters today, one gets a distinct sense of the kind of materials Bernard read, excerpted, and translated in the much more numerous collections the committee asked him to investigate in Stuttgart. Some of the Frankfurt documents are full-length letters asking Oppenheimer for financial assistance, others are receipts for various transactions, and yet more are single-line notes addressed to Oppenheimer by various (sometimes unidentified) people. Though all these sources are written in Yiddish, they come in different sizes and shapes and some are hardly legible. No wonder that Bernard found the task of reading and translating such notes so incredibly arduous.

The second group of sources is even more revealing. Here, in Bernard's own handwriting, are lists, excerpts, and a few full translations of hundreds of letters, receipts, and notes the Tübingen lecturer read during his two trips to Stuttgart, a unique window not only into Oppenheimer's life and business transactions but also into what Bernard was now learning about the past activities of the famous court Jew. Bernard's lists are divided into two groups. The larger of the two, containing 331 items, includes parts of the personal archive of Oppenheimer's private treasurer Isaac Samuel Levi in Stuttgart, while the smaller one, containing 177 documents, holds various notes addressed primarily to Oppenheimer himself.[85]

The documents Bernard read and translated in the spring of 1737 allowed him a glimpse into Oppenheimer's inner sanctum, past the double façade of the rumors and prejudices against the court Jew on the one hand and Oppenheimer's self-projected image on the other hand. There were a handful of very interesting notes here from Oppenheimer's mother, and a few more from his half brother Daniel Oppenheimer.[86] A couple of additional personal notes came from unnamed "affectionate" women (a later hand added here in red in the margins: *Huren*, "whores").[87] But far more important in Bernard's lists is the very concrete evidence for the geographical extent, quality, and monetary value of Oppenheimer's business transactions. Oppenheimer had contacts in every direction: in Neckarsulm, Mannheim, Landau, Heidelberg,

Frankfurt, and Bingen in southwest Germany, but also in Metz, Munich, Braunschweig, Halle, Berlin, Prague, and Vienna. The geographical extent of this business network was impressive enough, but so too was its quality. With one notable exception, the following family names might mean little to the modern general reader. But to Bernard, who at one point in his life wandered as a poor Jew in central Europe, they must have meant a lot: they represented some of the wealthiest and most influential German-Jewish families of the eighteenth century. Here are letters from members of the Margalith family (also known as Margolis, Margaliot), the extended Oppenheimer clan, the Ulmanns, and (though this family's meteoric rise still lay in the future) even the Rothschilds.[88]

As Bernard was translating the letters in May or June of 1737, he also saw concrete evidence of the immense sums of money Oppenheimer had been handling before his arrest. Many of the receipts or notes he examined mentioned sums of money so insignificant that Bernard didn't think they were worth mentioning,[89] and others were for sums of money ranging from a few dozen to a few hundred gulden.[90] Other receipts and letters, however, must have caused Bernard's eyes to pop out of his head. In October 1736, one Benjamin David from Prague offered Oppenheimer a single precious stone for 50,000 reichsthaler (100,000 gulden); another receipt for several precious stones purchased by Oppenheimer (exact date unknown, but early 1730s) adds up to a total of 70,500 gulden; and yet another adds up to the truly astonishing sum of 244,100 gulden.[91] These were not secondhand, half-mythical accounts of the fallen court Jew's erstwhile wealth and power; these were actual receipts, sent to Oppenheimer's treasurer Isaac Samuel Levi and sometimes to Oppenheimer himself, which Bernard touched with his own hands and read with his own eyes—he, a man whose entire middle-class house was worth only 300 gulden and who at one point in his life tried to make ends meet by distilling schnapps in his "little kitchen" despite his neighbors' complaints.

Considering everything we now know about Bernard's life, his claim that translating the "Jewish letters" during his two trips to Stuttgart was more difficult than any work he had ever done must be deemed hyperbolic. Surely, Bernard had worked harder and faced greater difficulties beforehand, facing (in Chancellor Pfaff's memorable words) "enough tests of his Christian faith."[92] Perhaps what Bernard meant by this remark was consequently more than immediately meets the eye. Reading the notes about Oppenheimer's business transactions was a deeply bitter work for Bernard not only because it was extremely arduous or because of what it told him (Bernard) about Oppenheimer. What was so difficult about this experience for Bernard was that it highlighted the huge difference between how Oppenheimer had lived all those years and how he himself had.

The Four Confiscated Letters

In the published account of his meeting with Oppenheimer, Bernard mentioned the first two trips to Stuttgart he undertook on behalf of the inquisition committee. What he decided not to mention was the fact that he got involved in Oppenheimer's trial for a third time before his rendezvous with Oppenheimer in the Herrenhaus. The omission of this third involvement is significant, because it reveals important clues about Bernard's selection criteria in shaping his narrative: the way he crafted his story as much by excluding certain details as by including others.

The time was mid-September 1737. Bernard was in Tübingen and Oppenheimer and some of his alleged accomplices were in the prison fortress of Hohen Asperg. In Stuttgart, dozens of Jews had been held captive ever since Oppenheimer's arrest in March, including Oppenheimer's private treasurer, Isaac Samuel Levi, the man whose business correspondence Bernard diligently deciphered for the inquisition committee in the late spring. That the situation of the imprisoned Levi and his coreligionists caused much anxiety to their relatives, friends, and business associates in Württemberg and abroad needs little explanation.

On September 19, 1737, the Württemberg authorities confiscated four more Yiddish letters concerning Oppenheimer's case.[93] They had been smuggled into the duchy from Mannheim. The exact circumstances of the confiscation are somewhat unclear, but it seems fairly certain that it was the wife of one of Mannheim's Jews, Isaac Abraham Canz, who was caught carrying the letters into the duchy. The first letter was addressed to the treasurer Isaac Samuel Levi by his father Samuel Isaac, also a resident of Mannheim, while the other three were sent by Isaac Abraham Canz himself to the Ludwigsburg Jew Maram Kahn. As in the case of Oppenheimer's personal archive in Stuttgart, the inquisition committee needed an expert to decipher and translate the four letters' content. On September 25, 1737, they sent them to Bernard's attention in Tübingen.

Unlike Bernard's previous work on behalf of the inquisition committee, the translation work of the four confiscated letters was not very time-consuming. "I have done my best to translate the letters into German word by word," Bernard wrote back to the committee already on September 29, "to do so in the most accurate way, and to send [the translations] back to the committee together with the original letters." Before he gave the inquisition committee the entire package, however, Bernard used the opportunity to remind Regent Carl Rudolph of the committee's obligations toward himself. "His Princely Highness knows personally," Bernard wrote the same day he sent the committee his translations, "that I have been already called on two separate occasions to assist the inquisition committee in Süss's case. In reading through Süss's Yiddish correspondence I spent seven days in a first trip and twenty-five days in a second. This caused me to cancel my [university] colloquium and thus to lose 25 gulden, not considering the uncovered expenses during my stay in Stuttgart." Surely, he wrote, he should now be compensated for this "demonstrated diligence"? In order to further highlight his value to the inquiry into Oppenheimer's affairs, Bernard added a prologue to his four translations in which he tried to explain why the letters revealed "Jewish machinations" against the Württemberg authorities in general and Süss's inquisition committee in particular. "In these matters," Bernard wrote, "I had been entertaining my suspicions for a long time."[94]

Bernard's assertions notwithstanding, the four translations he sent back to the committee did little to prove the long-held suspicions he harbored against certain Jews. On a purely descriptive level, they were remarkable testimonies to the deep anxiety felt by many Jews during Oppenheimer's trial and an important reminder that even as it was unfolding, the case of Jew Süss was much more than the story of Joseph Süss Oppenheimer alone. As the trial of the famous court Jew progressed, it touched the lives of many dozens of Jews and their families, and these people, while they did not share Oppenheimer's fate, were nonetheless deeply implicated in his ordeal in various ways.

Consider the case of the first of the four letters, addressed to the treasurer Isaac Samuel Levi by his father in Mannheim. It is true, as Bernard claimed, that the father was deeply concerned about the ongoing inquisition into different financial affairs by the son. The letter says nothing about "Jewish machinations" against the government, though. Rather, it shows the natural concern of a father for his son and the great anxiety the latter felt in light of the ongoing events in Württemberg. "I urge you my dear child to send me a letter with the next post, because I tremble with worries," Samuel Isaac wrote in his letter. "Write to me if I should come down [to Württemberg] and if by doing so I won't cause more damage than good. People have warned me against it, because if I came down [to Württemberg] and something bad happened to me, who would help me?" Samuel Isaac concluded his letter by saying that "God shall be your helper again and lead you out of the duchy in peace. I plead with you my dear child to have patience and place your trust in God Almighty. . . . I do not know what else to write, my head is spinning."[95]

The three letters Canz sent to Maram Kahn had a different tone, but they too showed their author's deep concern about his personal safety and the ripple effect of Oppenheimer's trial for Jews both near and far. Bernard was right in one respect: in one of his letters, Canz was clearly trying to make sure that he, Maram Kahn, and Kahn's erstwhile competitor Elias Hayum would all represent the same version of events to the inquisition committee if asked about a certain financial transaction. "Do me a personal favor," Canz wrote, "go to Elias Hayum and share with him all that I write to you now, so that we will all speak with one voice, as it were."[96]

In contrast to Bernard's assertion, however, Canz's letters demonstrate better the frictions between Jews than their common conspiracy to commit perjury. What in Samuel Isaac's case caused a father to "tremble with worry" about the fate of his son, made Canz plead with, then directly threaten, his coreligionists rather than conspire with them. "Several people have told me," Canz wrote to Maram Kahn in his first letter, "that I will have to go to Stuttgart and present myself to the inquisition committee. I urge you to give me good advice what to do." When Maram Kahn and Elias Hayum did not respond to this plea, Canz began to use ever more threatening language. "Tell Elias Hayum that he shouldn't even think about leaving me in the lurch. . . . Tell him [that if he does not answer me] I shall come to Stuttgart and what I shall say to the inquisition committee will certainly not please him." And again: "I wait for a rapid answer [from you] with the next post. . . . Otherwise, if I must come down to Stuttgart, it will not be good for Hayum, so he should make sure I am not summoned there. . . . I am as good a Jew as he and will wait another eight days, but then I have to come down to Stuttgart." And one last time: "My dear Maram. Do me this one favor and tell Hayum and his wife what I say. They will not believe [my threats are real] until they see me there [in Stuttgart]."[97]

Bernard's translations of the four confiscated letters are important as windows into the lives of at least some Jews during Oppenheimer's trial. On at least two different levels, they are also quite helpful in drawing attention to Bernard's own actions in the same period. The translations show us how Bernard, while he indeed translated the letters most literally (the originals are in the file and can be compared with the translations), nonetheless chose to interpret them to the inquisition committee in the worst possible light. Of all the different things he could have said about Samuel Isaac's and Canz's letters, Bernard chose to emphasize only one: Canz's failed attempt to align his story with Maram Kahn's and Elias Hayum's. As a storyteller crafting a narrative, Bernard's move here was a double one: he first reduced the text of the four confiscated letters to only one issue about one person (Canz's supposed perjury), then turned this one dimension into a general statement about all Jews (their "machinations"). Here is Bernard at his most simplistic anti-Jewish moment.

What is true in the case of Bernard's treatment of the confiscated letters in his correspondence with the inquisition committee is also the case, mutatis mutandis, in his decision to omit the incident altogether from his later published account about his meeting with Oppenheimer. Any form of history telling entails a simplification: we make sense of the past not only by narrating certain things about it but also by leaving out certain facts. Excluding the stories of other contemporary Jews from his account of Oppenheimer's case should be viewed not as a mere lapse on Bernard's part, then, but as part of the very way the Tübingen lecturer was trying to give meaning to his account. It shows us how Bernard concentrated on the life of a single individual (Oppenheimer) at the expense of many others, thus reducing the story of Oppenheimer's trial to the story of the accused alone. Including Maram Kahn, Elias Hayum, and Canz in the published account would have only distracted the reader from Bernard's main point in his story.

In any event, after the translation of the four confiscated letters in late September, Bernard was not personally involved in Oppenheimer's case for a few months, although some members of the inquisition committee raised the idea (which was then rejected) to have him participate in the interrogation of Isaac Samuel Levi in November.[98] We hear about Bernard again on January 9, 1738, when the Württemberg Administrative Council, in its approval of Oppenheimer's death sentence, also decides to allow two Jews to visit Oppenheimer in the Herrenhaus. This should be done, the Council notes in its resolution, *cum Bernhard ad audi-*

endum, "with Bernard present and listening."[99] Then, on January 29, 1738, six days before Oppenheimer's public hanging, Bernard was finally called to fulfill this role. A couple of months later, Bernard published a long account of what happened next in the form of a dialogue between himself and an imaginary friend. In the following pages, this account is reproduced in an abridged version due to the length of the original text. Particular passages whose meaning might not be immediately clear to the modern reader are marked and explained in the footnotes.

Bernard begins with a description of a meeting in Tübingen, on Wednesday, January 29, 1738. It is one day before Oppenheimer's transfer to Stuttgart from Hohen Asperg.

BERNARD: On January 29, I received a message from Professor Harpprecht,* in his role as a member of the princely committee, that Süss's case not only became very serious but that it was also about to conclude. I was called to meet with the committee's president, Privy Councilor von Gaisberg.†

FRIEND: This was nothing unusual, because I hear that you were involved with Jew Süss more after his fall than earlier, in his good happy days.

BERNARD: I had never seen Süss at the height of his power nor had I ever had the wish to do so. I often wondered why he did

---

* Georg Friedrich Harpprecht Sr. (1676–1754) was a professor of Roman law at Tübingen and therefore Bernard's senior colleague at that university. He is discussed at some length in the first chapter of this book.

† Ernst Conrad von Gaisberg (1681–1738) was the president of Oppenheimer's inquisition committee. He was also vice president of Württemberg's high court of appeals (*Hofgericht*) and the Oberhofmeister of the Collegium Illustre in Tübingen. In this last capacity, von Gaisberg had an apartment in the Collegium, very close to the theological seminary, where Bernard once studied. It is probably there that the two met on January 29, 1738.

not follow the old Jewish proverb: Jews and poverty go together like a horse and carriage. Once he grew in riches and
importance, he became disgusting to me, so I avoided him;
indeed I prophesied his downfall long before it happened.[*]
But I want to tell you about my meeting with His Excellency
Privy Council von Gaisberg. As soon as I came to visit His
Excellency, he ordered me to go to Stuttgart without delay and
to wait for further instructions there, at the city hall, on Friday,
January 31, at two o'clock in the afternoon.[†]

FRIEND: If I'm not mistaken, this was the third time you went to
Stuttgart in this affair?

BERNARD: Yes, but the first two times were devoted to the Yiddish letters, and because there were so many of them I had to
devote over a month to making excerpts from some of them
for the princely committee.[‡] It was certainly a burdensome
and bitter work, more so than any I had ever done in my life.
Still, I wanted to show my respect and submission to the committee so I spared no effort and worked assiduously and avidly
until I read through all of the letters and translated the important ones into German.

FRIEND: My dear lecturer! Was this last trip to Stuttgart as burdensome as the first two? And for what business exactly was
your presence needed in Stuttgart this time around?

BERNARD: This you can judge for yourself when I tell you about
the tasks I was given.[§] The first thing the committee laid be-

---

[*] The significance of this passage will become clear later in Bernard's account.

[†] Stuttgart's town hall was where the inquisition committee had met in November and
December during its verdict deliberations.

[‡] That is, the inquisition committee assigned to Oppenheimer's case.

[§] Bernard now turns to the description of his meeting with the committee in Stuttgart
on Friday, January 31, 1738.

fore me was a simple prayer book, known as *seder tefilot* by the Jews. The members of the committee told me that Nathan the Jew* had sent this book to Süss following the latter's request, marking in it a prayer that Süss could use in his situation. I opened the book at the appropriate page, and couldn't stop myself from laughing: Nathan the Jew marked a prayer in the book in which a sick person asks for the restoration of his health. What idiocy! It seemed almost like a practical joke!†

FRIEND: Still, I assume that the committee wanted to hear about the content of this prayer?

BERNARD: Yes. I read the prayer to the committee.

FRIEND: As far as I know, and as I have heard and learned, Süss did not understand Hebrew at all. What purpose could there be for his praying and confessing in Hebrew?

BERNARD: My friend, it is true that Süss did not understand Hebrew more than a common Jew. He couldn't read Hebrew books. But you have to understand that the Jews believe that when they pray in Hebrew—even if they don't understand a word of it—it is far more pleasing to God than prayers in any other language.‡ In addition, the Jews use a German-Jewish [bilingual] edition in order to understand the contents of the prayers.

FRIEND: My dear lecturer, so far you have told me about Süss's prayer and confession to my great benefit and astonishment.

---

* Also known as Marx Nathan, also known as Mordechai Schloss.

† Bernard highlights here his knowledge of Judaism, which he will continue to do throughout his account. Significantly, he claims to know Jewish customs not only better than his Christian audience but also better than actual Jews like Marx Nathan and (as we shall see) Joseph Süss Oppenheimer.

‡ The question whether a Jew is allowed to pray in a language other than Hebrew is a complicated one, addressed, among many others, by the Mishnah (Tractate Sotah 32:1), the Talmud, and the Shulchan Aruch (Orach Chayim, 101:4).

But you still haven't explained to whom Süss was supposed to confess and what was your role in all of this.

BERNARD: The Jews confess to no one except for God and themselves, and because Süss asked to see Nathan the Jew, I was ordered to go with the latter, to listen to their conversation, and to find out what Süss wanted from Nathan.

FRIEND: Did the committee not order you to do some work toward Süss's conversion?

BERNARD: I myself suspected they would. So I asked the committee: "Am I allowed to discuss religious matters with him?" But they responded: "It is not the right time for this."

FRIEND: One would have had to wait for a special time indeed with someone like Süss! But God holds the key to our hearts, and when he opens a door, we must enter, without delay and with full speed.*

BERNARD: After considering the issue, the committee decided to postpone the matter for the time being.

FRIEND: So nothing came out of this first order of the princely committee?

BERNARD: On the contrary, my friend. Accompanied by Secretary Pregizer, Nathan and I went to visit Süss.

Next, Bernard turns to his first meeting with Oppenheimer. It took place in Stuttgart's Herrenhaus on Saturday, February 1, 1738.

FRIEND: I have no doubt that the Süss you met was in a bewildered state.

---

* Bernard is unusually impatient with the committee here. Eager to proselytize, he claims that if a good opportunity presents itself, one should always try to convert Jews. Compare Bernard's similar frustrations in Karlsruhe described earlier in this chapter.

BERNARD: My friend, it is almost beyond belief how dreadful was the first sight of this suffering man. The person I saw before me seemed to have little in common with the eminent and splendid man of the past. He was little more than a walking corpse, so brittle he threatened to crumble if you touched him. Pain and fear ate away at his flesh like worms at a real dead corpse and his face, already unpleasant before,* became outright disgusting now that it was covered with a thick black beard resembling moss on a gravestone. His formerly alert eyes were like two expunged candles, the little movement still in them so extraordinary that one could hardly tell their affects. His clothes contributed further to his unusual appearance. He covered his lusterless hair with a green cap and tied a silk handkerchief around his neck. The rest of his body was covered only by a white undergarment which, during his long arrest, fell apart almost completely, just like its wearer.

FRIEND: Oh, what miserable, unhappy remains of a formerly so eminent, gallant man, whom God had decided to display as a horrible warning sign to us! It is true, as it is said about the evil man in the Book of Job, chapter 15: "He believeth not that he shall return out of darkness; He shall not be rich, neither shall his substance continue; The flame shall dry up his branches; and fire shall consume the tabernacles of bribery," and so on, and so on.

BERNARD: My thoughts were wandering in almost the same direction, but the desire to meet Süss did not allow me to indulge in them much longer.† Süss, as soon as he saw us, pulled

---

* Bernard seems to contradict himself a bit. Just a few pages earlier, he claimed he had never seen Oppenheimer before they met in the Herrenhaus.

† Significantly, perhaps, Bernard writes that his thoughts were running *almost* in the same direction as the description of the evil man in Job 15. ("*Fast* eben dahin giengen

himself together, and hurried toward us. I was the only one he did not recognize, so he asked the secretary who I was. The secretary answered that I had been sent by the princely committee. Then Süss responded at once: "ha, ha, I already know who he is. The gentleman knows Hebrew as much as I do, or even better. He is welcome here."

FRIEND: A nicer reaction than one would have assumed. I see that your reputation by him wasn't bad.[*]

BERNARD: Yes! But because he knew I was a Christian who came to visit him for a specific purpose,[†] he said immediately: "The gentleman should know that I have resolved to die as a Jew." And then he cried with a shrieking voice: "Shema Yisroel, Odonoi Elohenu, Odonoi Echod, Odonoi Hu Elohim, Odonoi Hu Elohim."[‡] These last words he repeated seven times with such a loud voice that I feared he would faint. I praised his confession of faith but also said to him that in this case the Jews have no advantage over us Christians, because we too confess unequivocally that the Lord our God is One. At the same time, I added, it is not enough to just mumble or prattle the words. One must also make the effort to recognize and understand correctly the one and only God.[§] As for Süss, he

---

meine Gedancken." My italics.) To which direction might Bernard be alluding here he does not say. At this point in the story, one can only speculate that Bernard may have had a specific biblical figure in mind (a king, perhaps?—compare Job 15:24–26) that fell from power after transgressing against God's commands.

[*] Although they had never met face to face before, Bernard claims that Oppenheimer knew who he was. He does not explain why.

[†] That is, to convert him to Christianity.

[‡] The famous Jewish confession of faith: Hear, Oh Israel, the Lord is our God, the Lord is One.

[§] Bernard is trying to draw Oppenheimer into a theological conversation here. His is a double move: he both implies that Oppenheimer is ignorant (thus challenging him intellectually) and also argues that Christians, just like Jews, believe in only one God. The latter excused himself by saying that he was in no state to have a scholarly disputation with me. "I am absolutely determined to die as a Jew," he said. "I beg the princely committee to please not send me any Christian priests. I have the utmost respect for you and would, if you wish, kiss your feet thirty times, but in religious matters I shall not listen to anything you say because I am absolutely resolved to die as a Jew."

FRIEND: I'm a bit surprised that he would have so much respect for Christian priests whom the Jews usually call by the most degrading names. Still, what did you think about Süss's strong resolution?

BERNARD: I had my own thoughts on the matter, to be sure, but I had to follow the instructions of the princely committee and postpone such a conversation until the right moment. In the meantime, Secretary Pregizer asked him: "Why doesn't he eat from the dishes sent to him?" Süss responded: "If I wanted to eat, I would have to do it in the Jewish manner* and therefore get a Jewish cook. But if I took a man to do this job and were to die in prison, people would say that my cook handed me the poison. And if I took a woman to prepare my food for me, the Christians would say that even in prison I needed a whore."

FRIEND: These were wise words one wouldn't expect from such a disturbed man. But didn't he also want to justify himself in your eyes and diminish or even excuse completely his past crimes?

---

is a claim Jews strongly reject, contending that Christians believe in three Gods, not one: the Father, the Son, and the Holy Spirit. For the relationship between the Shema and Christian-Jewish polemics, see Jacob Katz, *Exclusiveness and Tolerance: Studies in Jewish-Gentile Relations in Medieval and Modern Times* (Oxford: Oxford University Press, 1961), 18–19.

* That is, eat kosher.

BERNARD: No. Hardly had the secretary finished talking with Süss about his fasting before the importunate began a rant against the princely committee. He yelled that they had sentenced and condemned him to death but were incapable of giving any reason for it. Then he turned to Secretary Pregizer and told him: "You wrote down the entire protocol, give me then one single reason why I should die! The members of the princely committee cannot list a single one! I am not aware of such a reason myself, yes sir, I am almost forty years old now, and I cannot come up with a single case in which I sinned either against God or man that couldn't be made good by paying fifty—no, twenty—gulden." And upon saying this he grabbed the secretary's face with both hands and said: "My dear secretary, you would greatly recommend yourself to me if you managed to arrange that an appellation committee would be called, composed of three members from Württemberg and from other lands [in the Holy Roman Empire] three Catholics, three Lutherans, and three Calvinists. I have no doubt that it would bring my innocence to light." But when the secretary told him about the impossibility of granting him this request, Süss said: "If the problem is with the large number of members in the committee, give me only three foreign members. For that I won't only give all my property, I promise also to distribute 100,000 reichsthaler [200,000 gulden] among the poor."*

FRIEND: Oh, innocent Süss! It seems from his behavior that his case was one of great obstinacy.

---

* Apparently, Oppenheimer did not know that Harpprecht and especially Schöpff were staunch opponents of the idea that any verdict of a Württemberg court could be appealed outside the duchy. Ferdinand Graner, "Zur Geschichte des Hofgerichts in Tübingen," *Württemberigische Vierteljahrshefte für Landesgeschichte, Neue Folge* 32 (1925/1926): 85–89.

BERNARD: So it was, my friend. In him I could feel nothing but an unrepentant heart. He ranted and raved for a while longer to our great annoyance, rejecting out of hand any counterarguments. Nothing we did could put him in a good disposition,* so I tried to come up with ways and means to bring him some relief, to help a breath of fresh air, so to speak, enter into his poor soul. Alas, for human eyes it all seemed to be in vain. There was not the least sign of recognition or common sense in him, his ill humor and reluctance to listen were extraordinarily strong. At last I spoke to him in a serious tone: "My Süss! He wishes, according to his own repeated requests, to die as a Jew. He would therefore believe what the Jewish books say. Now you acknowledge in your prayers that at the beginning of every Jewish New Year, God writes down a list which he then seals on Yom Kippur, the Day of Atonement. In this list, God determines not only who will live and who will die in the following year, but also the type of death of each individual, whether usual or extraordinary, by fire, water, sword, and so forth.† Five months have passed since the Jewish New Year began, which means that God had already determined his death and its type five months ago. What cause does he have, then, to rant and rave so against the princely committee!"‡

* In an effort to establish Oppenheimer's obstinacy (a classic Christian criticism of the Jews), Bernard pretends not to understand why Oppenheimer couldn't be put "in a good disposition" on the eve of his execution. Later in his account, the Tübingen lecturer would be much more sympathetic toward Oppenheimer's predicament.

† The allusion here is to the famous piyyut (liturgical song) *Unetanneh Tokef*, which is part of the Rosh Hashana and Yom Kippur liturgies. Bernard does not mention a crucial part of the piyyut, however. According to *Unetanneh Tokef*, even if God determines every man's fate between Rosh Hashana and Yom Kippur, "Repentance, prayer, and charity can still avert a severe decree."

‡ This is the only time in their conversation that Bernard gets close to asking Oppenheimer a direct question. Following the rules of an academic disputation, he nevertheless changes course at the very last minute, turning his question into a statement.

FRIEND: It was very fitting to try to convince him by using the principles of his own religion and to entangle him in his own web, as it were.

BERNARD: That was exactly my intention. But he replied to me thus: "Every New Year, God also determines each man's food for the next twelve months. But this is no reason to be lazy and lie down in bed; one must also do one's duty. I too have to take care of my own life."

FRIEND: How did you respond to this objection, and how did you carry on the conversation?

BERNARD: I saw that I could accomplish nothing with him in this respect, so I left the matter at that. Then Nathan handed him the abovementioned prayer book. Süss grabbed the book quite willingly and as his eyes fell on the marked prayer he said, "Yes, this is right." But when I told him about the contents of the prayer and exposed his ignorance in these things by explaining that this prayer had nothing to do with his present predicament, he listened to me patiently, accepted my words, and said: "What should I confess, then?"

Another book was lying on his table. I took it up, looked up a regular confession in it where the sins were specifically named, and urged him to read through the list earnestly and to pray to God for forgiveness especially concerning those sins he had committed against other people. Alas, Satan would not allow any good thoughts into his heart anymore. Although he took the book willingly, he almost immediately threw it away and started all over again with his usual diatribes against the judges, declaring his innocence.

FRIEND: I am convinced that Süss belonged to that type of obstinate Jews whose hearts are rendered completely numb by Satan.

BERNARD: Indeed, one could witness most violently how Satan played with him. When the conversation dealt with worldly things, Satan let him speak and act in whatever way he wished, but as soon as one spoke with him about matters of the heart, Satan locked and bolted it so that no good could enter into it.

Finally, his intense anger and indignation subsided a little and he stopped his extraordinary rants and ravings against the princely committee. For a moment, it seemed he would take hold of himself and finally calm down. Alas, it was not to be. According to custom, he demanded to see two rabbis,* from either Frankfurt or Heidelberg, so he could practice before them a *mesirat moda'ah*, that is, a confession of faith. He was told that this was impossible, but I also told him that this could take place in front of two common Jews, so he chose Nathan and yet another Jew for that purpose.

FRIEND: For my benefit, I beg you to give me a good and complete explanation and description of this *mesirat moda'ah*.

BERNARD: It is basically this: A Jew makes a special confession so that all that he shall say, do, or think from that point on, if it contradicts his confession, will be considered null and void.† At any rate, he continued to complain about, and fulminate against, the princely committee. I finally interrupted him by saying: "My Süss, you complain about the death sentence so indignantly, but also want to pass for a humble and reasonable Jew. No gentile has ever let himself be seen behaving in such a wild manner. Doesn't he know what Agag did,

---

* According to the criminal legal code in the Holy Roman Empire, a condemned man had the right to see two priests before his execution.

† Bernard had dealt with the *mesirat moda'ah* and similar issues in his *Unpartayische Beurtheilung des Eyd-Schwurs Eines Juden gegen einem Christen . . .* (Tübingen: Cotta, 1728).

and with what self-composure he chased away the bitterness of death?"*

FRIEND: Nicely done, Herr Lector! You cornered Süss into a trap there.

BERNARD: No! He said: "Agag was a gentile, who did not have a part in *'olam haba*—the world to come—but my case is different, because I have a part in it. This is why I have to fight for my life."

FRIEND: What? You want to say that Agag confronted death with such happy countenance because he had no part in the world to come? And Süss wanted to continue living because a better life was awaiting him on the other side of death? What nonsense from a man already struggling under the heavy hand of death! It seems to me that Süss was already feeling the presence of his horrible eternal fate even days before the death that would deliver him thence. I think that what he really meant to say was this: Agag, a gentile, was able to face death so well because—this was Süss's opinion—he was like stupid cattle about to be slaughtered. But with him, Süss, it was different, and he knew very well what awaited him on the other side as an eternal reward for his deeds on earth.†

---

* Agag was the king of the Amalekites, a people whom God ordered the Israelites to annihilate down to the last man (Deuteronomy 25:17–19; 1 Samuel 15:2–3). Nevertheless, King Saul spared Agag after a battle (1 Samuel 15:7–9). The sparing of the Amalekite king's life enraged the prophet Samuel, who confronted Saul and prophesied his downfall. Finally, Samuel had Agag brought in front of him and hacked him to pieces (1 Samuel 15:33). According to one common interpretation of this episode, Agag faced Samuel "without the bitterness of death," which can mean either that Agag did not expect to be slain by Samuel or that he did expect it, but kept his composure nonetheless.

† The entire exchange about Agag has a distinct feeling of scholarly disputation about it. Earlier in his account, Bernard claimed that Oppenheimer was an "ignorant Jew," who could not read Hebrew and proved unwilling to engage in exactly such a "scholarly disputation." Bernard's inclusion of the exchange about Agag's story might consequently be less an accurate description of Oppenheimer's speech and more a suggestion by Bernard of a

BERNARD: Would you have really expected any better from a man who was condemned by God's judgment so violently? Imagine such a blasphemous man to yourself: a man who led such a glamorous, happy life, who possessed so much prestige and enjoyed every conceivable honor and privilege, a man, finally, whose every wish had always been fulfilled and every order followed. Imagine and judge for yourself what it must have felt like to have all your privileges taken away from you, to be put in the most miserable condition, with handcuffs and heavy chains, the death sentence read to you.*

FRIEND: After all you have told me, I can easily imagine how upset and restless he must have been. I can easily imagine how such a quick, unexpected, and extraordinary change would cause him extreme pain, how his long and hard captivity and the reading of the death sentence would multiply his worries and sorrows, how, finally, his fast-approaching hideous end would awaken in him the greatest fear and dread. He must have realized that he would not die a blessed man even according to the rules of his own religion and that he must go to hell after his death, where he would suffer and be tortured for all eternity.

BERNARD: So it is, my friend! But you are mistaken if you think that the Jews who end up in hell have to stay there forever and without interruption. Because according to Jewish belief, Jews condemned to hell are let out every Sabbath and new moon only to be locked inside again afterward, and when a Jew leaves

---

parallel between Oppenheimer and another biblical figure, related to (but perhaps not identical with) Agag.

*Bernard's attempt to step into Oppenheimer's shoes here is quite extraordinary and stands in stark contrast to the lecturer's previous attempt to describe Oppenheimer as utterly unreasonable.

behind a son who prays for his deceased father, that son can free him completely from hell by praying.

FRIEND: It is really unbelievable that the Jews, who are after all reasonable human beings, believe in such nonsense!

BERNARD: This is undoubtedly a great superstition among the Jews that they believe in such things as much as they believe in the Ten Commandments. Still, this is why they believe it is very good when a son says kaddish* or a similar prayer in the synagogue over his dead father, as it is said in the story about Rabbi Akiva.†

FRIEND: Oh inconsolable Süss! Who would wonder now that he was so scared. After all, he left no son by a Jewish mother‡ who could pray for him after his death.

BERNARD: I am happy to see that you are now convinced by this man's mixture of madness, rage, and suffering. Now you can perhaps understand why it was useless to try to have any kind of serious, reasonable conversation with him. So I decided to conclude our conversation. I only asked him if he would give me permission to come see him again: I wanted to bring two Jews with me in front of whom he could per-

---

* A central prayer in the Jewish liturgy, one version of which (the mourner's kaddish) is recited by a close relative of a deceased person in his or her memory and for the sanctification of the name of God. If a deceased person's son is alive, it is his obligation to recite the kaddish.

† The reference is to the Rabbi Akiva's story about the "Restless Dead." The story is reproduced in Micah Joseph Berdichevsky, *Mimekor Yisrael: Classical Jewish Folktales*, ed. Emanuel bin Gorion, trans. I. M. Lask (Bloomington: Indiana University Press, 1976), 2: 685–686.

‡ A reference to the possibility that Oppenheimer may have had sons by non-Jewish women. Indeed, Oppenheimer's (Christian) girlfriend Luciana Fischerin bore him a child during the trial (Oppenheimer was unaware of this). The child died even before Oppenheimer's execution. Relevant documents are reproduced in Hellmut G. Haasis, *Joseph Süß Oppenheimers Rache: Erzählung, biographischer Essay, Dokumente aus der Haft und dem Prozess* (Blieskastel: Gollenstein, 1994), 243–249.

form his *mesirat moda'ah*. He thanked me for my effort and asked me to return.

FRIEND: My dear lecturer! You must have communicated the entire progression of this conversation to the princely committee?

BERNARD: Yes! I mentioned the entire conversation I had led with Süss to the committee and received permission to go see him again, accompanied by Herr Secretary Pregizer, Nathan the Jew, and Seligmann Schechter* [another Jew], at two o'clock in the afternoon on the following Monday. This way, if he still wished it, he would be able to make his *mesirat moda'ah* in front of the two Jews while I would supervise the whole thing, making sure the Jews do not talk with Süss about the princely committee or reveal to Süss the exact method of his execution.

Bernard concludes his account with a description of his meeting with Oppenheimer two days later, in the Herrenhaus, at 2 o'clock in the afternoon on Monday, February 3, 1738, one day before Oppenheimer's execution.

FRIEND: And how did you find him this time?

BERNARD: He was wearing a coat but also his *tefillin* (phylacteries) and was reading the confession in the same book which, in our previous meeting, I had recommended to him. But as soon as he caught a glimpse of us, he stood up and rushed forward, making a very unpleasant grimace. He had just fasted in memory of his father, who had passed away a few years ago.†

---

* This man was known by different names. His exact identity is discussed at length in chapter 3 of this book.

† Again, Bernard claims that Oppenheimer's father had died not long before the trial and not in 1707, as documents from Heidelberg make abundantly clear. StdA Heidelberg H55, n.p.

FRIEND: I still have to wonder why, toward the end, Süss had become so infatuated with the Jewish religion, confessing it openly and without any embarrassment. After all, in his former, affluent life he dismissed the notion of God, and—when asked which religion he felt closest to—used to answer: "All religions are equal in my eyes."

BERNARD: The rabbis have a nice saying about such a case, which you can find in the second chapter of Tractate Sanhedrin in the Talmud: When a thief cannot steal any longer he turns devout.* Süss was a doomed man facing complete ruin. His entire devotion was made of nothing but a few external ceremonies with which he tried to fool himself and the people around him. He continued in his stubbornness, uttering words full of bitterness over his death sentence, crying for revenge. Finally, he asked what type of death awaited him. Nathan told him: "This we cannot reveal to you just yet." These words irritated him further, so he ranted and raved almost a full hour in the room. Finally he said: "I must die, innocent, like a martyr. God will look after me and punish the judges." I responded: "I am surprised that he reacts so restlessly and apprehensively about his own death sentence. If he is indeed to die a martyr, he must rejoice in his own approaching death, of turning into a *kadosh* or a saint.† Dying in such a way is worth more than the whole world and should therefore give him a great sense of consolation." But even these words failed to pacify him because his bad conscience told him something else. This is the reason he said to me: "Oh, what a bad consolation!"

---

* חסריה לגנבא נפשיה לשלמא נקיט. מסכת סנהדרין, פרק שני, דף כב.

† As we shall see later, Bernard's own words here would come back to haunt him.

FRIEND: I see that you have practiced much patience with him.

BERNARD: Yes, I had to consider his precious soul. That was the reason I started talking to him once again, even more forcefully and convincingly than before. I told him: "In the past, you have relied so much on your intelligence and common sense, I know that you think very highly of your own acumen and wisdom and that you understand how to live reasonably. But I have to tell you that in the two days I have met you I did not see or hear much proof of that." He asked me in a soft, quiet voice: "Why?" I told him: "Your wish and desire that the princely commission would allow you to perform a Jewish *mesirat moda'ah* in front of two Jews was received and accepted. We see him now sitting over his tefillin and his prayer book, acknowledging his sins and humbly begging God for forgiveness and an eternal life. But despite all of this, he persists in his obstinacy, ill humor, and restlessness. How can he turn to God in prayer in such a state of mind and confess his sins to Him honestly? How could even a single good thought arise from his heart to God in heaven? Behaving in this way is useless and unreasonable." He asked me: "What shall I do?" I spoke to him: "Why don't you take up that prayer book and make your confession of faith before these Jews?"

FRIEND: I find it surprising that he did not mistreat you. After all, he always had an arrogant spirit. In other cases, he let no one convince him of anything.

BERNARD: Time can and does change many things. At that moment, he was really very peaceful and humble. He took up the prayer book and began to read the confession of faith from the book. I walked over and placed myself next to him, helping him start reciting the confession. The first line went just fine, but already by the second line he stumbled upon a series of Aramaic words and Hebrew abbreviations which, as is common among the Jews, he was used to only mumbling to himself without worrying about their actual meanings. So I helped him by reading aloud such words and expressions, and he repeated after me. But whenever I stopped helping him, he began once again to mumble the lines quickly to himself as if time were pressing, prattling the last words quickly to himself without any attempt to understand them. Süss understood very little about God. Still, he followed me and wanted to know if he should say anything else. So I showed him the rest of the text he had to read.

FRIEND: All this time, what did the other two rabbis do?

BERNARD: The entire time they both just stood there like statues without uttering a word, until I told them: "Now it is your time to speak, Süss is done with his confession of faith." Upon this, they began to jabber and mumble the indulgence formula with the same hastiness as Süss.

FRIEND: My dear lecturer! What could have caused Süss to make this confession of faith?

BERNARD: You must have heard what a sly and devious person he had been when he was still flourishing and enjoying the highest reputation. Even when he was approaching the end, he still wanted to continue to practice his dark arts, to lead Christians astray and to cheat them. This is why he demanded to have his *mesirat moda'ah* before two rabbis: so that if he would have to act against it with thoughts, words, or deeds, perhaps prompted by fear or intimidation, it would all be null and void. As a cunning man, he must have thought to himself: "The princely committee would expect me to convert if I recognized that it would save my life, or at least that it would postpone my execution. But in this way, I could convert to Christianity, behave externally as a Christian, and deny my true religion, and yet all of it would mean nothing at all, I shall remain a Jew at heart."

FRIEND: How could he have known all of this? One could not find anything to this effect in the Talmud or in any other rabbinical text.

BERNARD: This is a common trick by the Jews, and they use the *mesirat moda'ah* often in their business handlings, because they believe that this would be the easiest way to avoid falling into sin. It was probably in this way that Süss had known about it. Be that as it may, after the *mesirat moda'ah* his mood did not get better at all, he still remained the old Süss. After the prayer was over, he tossed the book away disdainfully and began again a tirade against the members of the princely committee.

FRIEND: Aren't the Jews supposed to forgive their enemies after making their confession even if they still think these have wronged them?

BERNARD: Yes, according to their faith, they are not allowed to harbor any hatred or even grudges against their enemies. Alas, Süss stubbornly rejected all good advice and refused to desist from his curses and insults, continuing to insist that he was innocent and that he would die an innocent man.

FRIEND: Did he also refuse to forgive those Jews who testified against him during the trial?

BERNARD: He said: "I shall forgive my fellow human beings and my coreligionists who gave a false testimony against me. J. U. claimed I owed him 65,000 gulden, although I do not owe him a single farthing. M. C., who raised six different claims against me of which even one would have been enough to send me to the gallows, presented a promissory note for 6,000 gulden against me although he always owed me money, not the other way around. I'd like to know whose hand wrote that note."*

FRIEND: Why couldn't Süss relax his hateful and hostile attitude toward Christians? Don't the Jews follow their own religion and forgive their neighbors, both Jewish and gentile, their sins?

BERNARD: My friend! You shouldn't look for any logic or coherence in the Jewish religion, even if they speak highly of it themselves and believe that, as Abraham's descendants, they alone possess wisdom and we Christians are nothing but fools compared to them. You must judge the Jews only according to the Talmud. What that book says, they believe with all their hearts, be it as stupid, illogical, and unreasonable as one could only imagine. This is why they don't care to listen to one's thorough, clear, and convincing arguments, and they wouldn't take the time at all to pay attention to any contradiction in their teachings and to judge them logically and fairly, whether they correspond to the truth or not. Their teachings are full of superstitions, absurdities, and nonsense. The rabbis explain the Holy Scripture as they see fit, and even if it results in complete nonsense, the Jews have to believe in this and treat the rabbis' explanations as if they were the truth itself.

FRIEND: This, then, was the reason that Süss couldn't forgive the Christians. Just like other Jews, he believed in the false expla-

---

*J. U., as Bernard himself would later claim, was Jakob Ullmann of Mannheim (UA Tübingen 38/10, 1–Nr. 7.2). M. C. must be Maram Cahn (Kahn, Kam, and so on) from Ludwigsburg, an old business rival of Oppenheimer's.

nations of the rabbis. Undoubtedly, you tried to change his false beliefs?

BERNARD: No! I desisted from talking to him at all, I recognized his evil obstinacy. So I kept quiet. But he began once again to bemoan his approaching wretched death, scheduled for the following day, and regretted that his eminent family would be cursed through it. He said to me: "Herr Professor must have heard about my grandfather Rabbi Selmele Chasan, that is, Rabbi Salomon, he was a cantor in Frankfurt, the like of his voice had not been heard in many centuries among the Jews."

FRIEND: Because Süss asked you whether you knew his grandfather, he must have known you had been born a Jew.* Had he ever used bad or harsh words against you, or treated you badly in any other way?

BERNARD: On the contrary, he always behaved toward me in a friendly and pleasant way. Think about it: he made a last will and testament, included me as one of his inheritors in it, and left me 30 gulden.† I could see that he was well disposed toward me but could also conclude from the circumstances that one could not speak with him seriously about matters of religion. One had to leave him to God's mercy. He abhorred the thought of eternal life, the bliss of the hereafter, and the enjoyment of Paradise; he ridiculed the prayer book, he tossed it away from him, he gave a *mesirat moda'ah*; he was bound and determined to die as a Jew and wouldn't let himself be drawn into any conversation about religion. Indeed, he would talk about nothing but his own innocence and insist on it most

---

* Significantly, Bernard talks about his Jewish past only toward the very end of the account about his meeting with Oppenheimer. This corresponds, as we have seen, to his usual practice to play it down.

† The last will and testament will be discussed in the next chapter of this book.

passionately. I decided to say nothing about conversion and simply leave him be. So I turned toward the door, about to leave him, and said to him: "Now it is time to go back, I wish that he would find a merciful God in heaven; if you look for Him, surely He will let you find Him." He thanked me for all my troubles, took my hand in his, pressed it, and cried loudly several times: "Is this my consolation?" I continued toward the door, but right before I reached it he tugged at my coat. I turned around and asked him what he wanted from me. He said: "Be so kind, and ask the princely committee to allow my body, when I am dead, to be buried in a Jewish cemetery." I told him: "This shall be done." But he cried one again: "Is this my consolation?" Upon this, I addressed him seriously and said: "Now I can see that he never read the Bible seriously, otherwise he would have recalled the history of King Saul, who had to hear from the Prophet Samuel that he would die the following day in the battle against the Philistines.* King Saul was surely as smart as you, and if you were in his shoes, you would probably say: I am not so stupid as to go to battle on the morrow; I'd rather stay here and save my life. But Saul thought: Because this is God's will, I shall go and fight tomorrow; I'd rather die following God's will than live against it. Now all of us must follow God's will in the same way." He told

---

* There are two references here to the story of Saul and Samuel. The first is to 1 Samuel 15:27–28, which describes how after a confrontation between the two men, Saul held and tore Samuel's mantle. Upon this, Samuel said to Saul: "The Lord hath rent the kingdom of Israel from thee this day, and hath given it to a neighbour of thine, that is better than thou." The second reference is to 1 Samuel 28. On the eve of Saul's final battle with the Philistines, the king's prayers to God remained unanswered. Terrified, Saul called on the witch of Endor to raise Samuel from the dead (the prophet had died in the meantime) only to be reminded by the dead prophet of the divine decision to tear the kingdom of Israel from him. The terrified Saul then refused to eat or drink but eventually went back to camp. The following morning, Saul died in battle.

me: "I know this history very well, but as opposed to Saul, I do not know if it is indeed God's will that I should die, I know myself to be innocent." I answered him: "He should be assured that not a single hair can fall from our heads without God's will." And with these words I ended my speech, and left him. But as I reached the guard, I saw him running after me, and so I said: "Go back, you are not allowed beyond this point." But he followed me farther and cried four times one after the other: "Oh, wretched me! Had I met the dear man four weeks ago I would have become a different person!" I let him cry, left him, and told the princely committee everything I had heard and seen.

FRIEND: Did you communicate Süss's last wish to the princely committee?

BERNARD: I thought about it, but did not really care what would happen to his body after his death.* I knew the details of the death sentence that would be announced to him the following day,† and I had already seen with my own eyes the red-painted cage that was prepared for him. I further respected and praised humbly the mighty hand of God, which took him so quickly and suddenly, striking this evil dastard, who brought about so many Christian sighs and tears, with a just, well-deserved punishment.‡

---

* In the original biblical story, the Philistines fastened King Saul's and his sons' bodies to the walls of their city, Bethshan. The following day, the men of Jabesh Gilad (members of Saul's own tribe), rescued the bodies, burned them, and buried the remains in their territory (1 Samuel 31:11–13).

† Bernard is slightly unclear here. The death sentence had already been read to Oppenheimer the previous day. What would be announced the following day, before the actual execution, was just the method of execution.

‡ Compare Samuel's famous words to Agag: "And Samuel said, As thy sword hath made women childless, so shall thy mother be childless among women. And Samuel hewed Agag in pieces before the Lord in Gilgal" (1 Samuel 15:33).

Epilogue

There were certain things about his encounter with Süss that Bernard never fully explained. Shortly after Oppenheimer's arrest, for instance, two court officials broke into his apartment in Frankfurt am Main. Assisted by a local clerk and a Württemberg councilor, they later took a detailed inventory of Oppenheimer's belongings and sent it to Stuttgart. Among many other items on their lists were jewels, bed linens, pieces of furniture, utensils, pictures, prints, and various documents. And then a truly revealing discovery. Among the approximately eighty books whose titles the court officers meticulously recorded are three books by one Christoph David Bernard, lecturer at the University of Tübingen: a Hebrew grammar, a treatise about the validity of Jews' legal oaths, and a commentary on Isaiah 7.[100]

In describing their meeting in the Herrenhaus, Bernard claimed he had never seen Oppenheimer before, so he had no explanation for why the prisoner recognized him immediately after hearing his name. Here, on Oppenheimer's bookshelf in Frankfurt, is the explanation. Even if Oppenheimer had never met Bernard in person before January 31, 1738, he still recognized him as the author of three books he had in his possession (perhaps even sent to him by Bernard himself, at some point), books from which he also gathered at least the basic facts about Bernard's life, including his line of work—a university lecturer of Hebrew—and the conversion from Judaism. This is why Oppenheimer reacted in the way he did, moving from puzzlement before hearing Bernard's name to recognition immediately thereafter to crying the Shema Israel seven times after recalling the conversion. We see here clear evidence that important parts of Bernard's account must have been truthful not only because of the lecturer's precarious social position as a convert, but also because he reports things that are clearly supported by independent evidence.

This does not mean, of course, that Bernard's story is unadorned or completely (or even mostly) truthful. Bernard's account is highly stylized, it contains obvious falsities (about Oppenheimer's father, for instance), and it does not tell us all that Bernard knew about Oppenheimer's case (the four confiscated letters). But the question about the objectivity and truthfulness of Bernard's account is perhaps not the principal one we should consider in his case. The importance of Bernard's story derives less from what it tells us about Oppenheimer than from what it says about Bernard himself. On one level, this is perhaps obvious. Throughout his account, Bernard constantly displayed his abilities and skills, trying to remind contemporary Württemberg of his worth. At times he is a Hebrew teacher, at others an exegete of the Bible and an expert on Jewish oaths, and at others still he is a religious disputant and proselytizer of Jews. Bernard does not merely describe Oppenheimer; he constantly uses his meetings with the famous court Jew to demonstrate his knowledge and expertise. His story is not just a description; it is above all a performance.

The performance-like element in Bernard's story is also evident on another level, which is perhaps less immediately evident to the modern reader but is important and indeed crucial nonetheless. Throughout his story, Bernard alludes to the biblical story of King Saul's downfall: his wrongful sparing of Agag the Amalekite's life and the just punishment meted out to Saul for it. Early on in the account, Bernard's allusions are implicit. First he compares himself to a prophet ("I prophesied his fall long before it happened," he writes about Oppenheimer), and later he quotes some very suggestive verses from the Book of Job. Soon enough the allusions become explicit: Bernard mentions Agag's story directly in the description of the first meeting with Oppenheimer, and he chooses to end his entire account not with a description of Oppenheimer's execution (as most contemporaries did) but by evoking two famous scenes from chapter 15 of 1 Samuel. Here, first, is Agag's execution by Samuel, and here, too, the tearing of the Kingdom of Israel from Saul's hands and its transfer to David, "thy neighbor, that is better than thou."[101]

King Saul's downfall is a good, if imperfect, allegory of Oppenheimer's story. At least to Bernard, the parallels seem to have been clear: just like Saul, Oppenheimer died after falling from a powerful political position, his kingdom (read: power) taken away from him, his dead body put on display on a town's walls; just like Saul, Oppenheimer stubbornly disobeyed God, reaching for a prophet's hem before hearing his awful sentence, and was finally left without a son to recite a kaddish over him.[102] Of course, one should not stretch the parallels too far. Oppenheimer was not a real king, he obviously did not die in battle, and on several occasions he clearly failed to play the role of the ancient Israelite king Bernard assigned to him. What was Bernard's purpose in constantly reminding the reader about the parallels with King Saul, then? What, if anything, did Bernard try to do or perform by evoking this story repeatedly, indeed by ending with a direct reference to it?

Many educated readers of Bernard's account knew St. Augustine's book *The City of God*. St. Augustine was the most important Church Father in Western Christianity, and his fifth-century masterpiece was the most fundamental book about the relationship between Christianity and other religions, including Judaism. In his book, Augustine interprets in detail King Saul's fall from power.[103] In his account, Saul represents the carnal, earth-bound Jews while David stands for the higher, spiritual kingdom of Christ. In Samuel's tearing the kingdom of Israel from Saul's hands and giving it to David, Augustine saw a prophecy about the Jews' fall and the passing of God's favor to Christ and his followers, an interpretation that was also often derived from Matthew 21:43.[104] Bernard's description of his last exchange with Oppenheimer is consequently almost too good to be true; its allegorical, Christian-theological meaning was certainly impossible to miss. "David is better than thou, King Saul," the convert Christoph *David* Bernard seems to tell the terrified Oppenheimer and by extension all other Jews. "David shall prosper while thou shalt not be rich, neither shall thy substance continue; The flame shall dry up thy branches" (Job 15).

Alluding to St. Augustine's interpretation of King Saul's story might have served another and even deeper purpose in Bernard's account. Throughout all his years in Württemberg, Bernard had to withstand "enough tests of his Christian faith" (Chancellor Pfaff): discrimination, prejudice, and even outright ridicule and hate, all because of his Jewish past. At times, he must have felt that a convert from Judaism could never be considered a true Christian no matter what he did or for how long. This is where the allusion to King Saul's story, if understood in the spirit of St. Augustine, could have been especially powerful as the implicit message of Bernard's entire account. Following the Jews' rejection of Christ, Augustine believed God had taken the kingdom from them and given it to their neighbor "that is better than thou." But unlike many eighteenth-century Württembergers, Augustine did not believe that Jews, if converted to Christianity, somehow still remained inherently Jewish and did not join the true community of Christ. After all, though not a former Jew himself, Augustine too was a convert. In his exegesis of Saul's story in *The City of God*, Augustine elaborated this point in a way that must have echoed powerfully Bernard's own sentiments on the matter. Jews were not all of one kind, Augustine insisted; there was a "grain, as it were, in that chaff. For certainly thence came the apostles, thence so many martyrs, of whom Stephen is the first, thence so many churches, which the Apostle Paul names, magnifying God in their conversion."[105] Augustine's and Bernard's point was consequently not only that "Jesus Christ was born a Jew" (as Martin Luther famously preached to his readers in 1523), but also that the early Christian community, almost down to a man, was composed of former Jews. The apostles were former Jews, as were the early martyrs. Jewish converts, from the Church's earliest history, had always magnified God's name in their conversion. Was not St. Paul (Saul of Tarsus) a convert? Was not St. Stephen a former Jew? If conversion was impossible and proselytes remained constantly under suspicion, what then would be left of Christianity?

The story of Bernard's involvement in Oppenheimer's case might have ended with this powerful message if only everyone else had taken the time to read St. Augustine as carefully as he had. Alas, they did not. Thus, about two months after the execution, Bernard simply had to react. The reason was a small Jewish pamphlet, printed in Fürth near Nuremberg, which Johann Helwig Engerer, a chaplain in Schwabach, mailed to Bernard.[106] There, in tiny Hebrew letters and in a mixture of Hebrew and Yiddish, Bernard read that Marx Nathan, Jew Seligmann, and several other Jews had elevated Oppenheimer to the status of *kadosh*, a holy man. They asked their coreligionists to call Oppenheimer "righteous and holy," to add the line "may the memory of this righteous man be a blessing" to his name, and to remember that he had died a martyr, for *kiddush ha-shem*. The pamphlet even included a short description of the second meeting in the Herrenhaus (which Bernard attended with Nathan, Seligmann, and Pregizer), though it did not mention Bernard's name even once. Bernard, who in his own account had almost completely sidelined the other participants in his meetings with Oppenheimer, was given a taste of his own medicine.

Upon reading the pamphlet, Bernard became furious. According to his own account of the conversations in the Herrenhaus, Bernard had used what he thought was the utterly absurd idea of Oppenheimer turning into a martyr after his death to humiliate the prisoner. ("You must rejoice in your own approaching death," he told the inconsolable Oppenheimer with what seems like schadenfreude; dying as a *kadosh* "is worth more than the whole world." To which Oppenheimer reportedly replied: "Oh, what a bad consolation!"). Now, however, the absurd had become reality. It was all Marx Nathan's fault, and Bernard, who previously had either ignored or gently ridiculed the man, now wrote about him using extremely negative language. It is doubtful whether "he can even understand his daily prayers," he wrote about Nathan; he and the other Jews involved in publishing the pamphlet were "dogs" and "scavengers."[107] That these common, ignorant Jews would bestow the title *kadosh* on Oppenheimer was "really unbearable."[108] Bernard then wrote a fiery refutation of the "canonization manifesto" (as he called it) to which he also added his own German translation of the pamphlet. In footnotes throughout the text, he stressed that Oppenheimer's past behavior had condemned him in the eyes of "both God and man" and that "throughout his life [he] showed not the least sign of piety or holiness." He went much further now in his negative portrayal of Oppenheimer than ever before, calling him damned, cursed, infamous, outright disgusting, and devilish. "This a holy man to celebrate or be proud of?" he asked rhetorically.[109] Bernard was fit to be tied.

A distance of three centuries and all the common uncertainties that accompany attempts to penetrate the minds of other human beings make it difficult to be sure about what Bernard really meant by his vituperative language here. Was he angry only at Oppenheimer, Marx Nathan, or even the entire Jewish community in Württemberg? Was he perhaps blowing off steam because other, unnamed individuals kept misunderstanding or ignoring him? The extensive documentation of Bernard's life in Württemberg presented in this chapter and the repeated allusions to King Saul's story in Bernard's published account seem to point in this direction. Bernard might not have engaged Oppenheimer in a conversation quite in the same way he and some modern historians claimed he had. No matter: the Tübingen lecturer's intention in crafting his account was less to describe a conversation that had already taken place than to instigate a new one that he felt was badly needed. The notion of disputation is central here, but it has to be qualified. All along, Bernard was engaged in a disputation with his adoptive Christian community as much as—if not even more than—with the Jew Joseph Süss Oppenheimer of Heidelberg. This is not to doubt that many of the details in Bernard's description of his meetings with Oppenheimer were true. Rather, it is to suggest that beyond or alongside its descriptive level, there was also a fundamentally important performative aspect to Bernard's account. Only by including this second level of reality in our analysis can we hope to grasp the full meaning of this convert's tale.

Third Conversation

READER: What an interesting man, this Bernard!

AUTHOR: A very interesting man indeed, regardless of whether he told the truth about Oppenheimer or not.

READER: I tend to agree, and the way you mapped out his life and place in the world worked quite well, I think, perhaps better than in Jäger's case. Now, I remember from the introduction that you're about to turn to the story of Mordechai Schloss (also known as Marx Nathan), the same "ignorant Jew" who accompanied Bernard into the Herrenhaus and later commissioned the so-called canonization manifesto. Before we get to that story, however, I would like you to clarify two—no, three—points.

AUTHOR: I suggest we start with the first point, move on to the second, and conclude with the third.

READER *[laughing]*: Thank you for this very wise advice! But seriously, you argue that the way St. Augustine interpreted King Saul's story in *The City of God* is key to understanding Bernard's tale. I'll grant that your argument is suggestive, but where is the definitive proof for it? Bernard never once mentions St. Augustine in his account.

AUTHOR: I asked myself: Why would a man like Bernard, whose entire social position was dependent on being considered truthful, introduce several blatantly fictional elements to his story? Consider his portrayal of Oppenheimer as a completely ignorant Jew but also the long scholarly exchange between Oppenheimer and Bernard about the fate of King Agag the Amalekite. Was Oppenheimer actually ignorant or not? Or think about the final scene in the story, where Oppenheimer tugs at the lecturer's coat, just like Saul in 1 Kings 15. This is completely implausible. It's too good to be true.

READER: Your point?

AUTHOR: That Bernard introduced these fictional elements for a reason. He was willing to take the risk of telling blatant lies in order to reach a deeper theological truth. In this respect, we should think about his tale as a true story that never happened. It was true, though it contained many fictional elements.

READER: But what is the place of St. Augustine in all of this? How could Bernard expect his readers to know they should go to *The City of God* to look for St. Augustine's interpretation of King Saul's story?

AUTHOR: One can support this hypothesis with both specific evidence and general arguments. For instance, it is clear that Bernard's patron at the University of Tübingen, the theologian and former university chancellor Christoph Matthäus Pfaff, read Augustine's works closely and deployed his ideas specifically in thinking about the possibility of authentic conversion. The same is also true for some of Pfaff's students.[110] Even more generally, Bernard could reasonably expect his more educated readers—especially, but not exclusively, at the university—to turn to the most important book ever written about the connections between the Old and New Testament and find out for themselves what the Christian message of King Saul's story was. This was one of the first steps I myself took after noticing the constant allusions to the Israelite king in Bernard's account. And lo and behold: St. Augustine's interpretation of King Saul's story mentions Jewish converts in a way that echoes Bernard's own thinking about the matter, only more elegantly, powerfully, and authoritatively than he himself ever could. Ralph

Waldo Emerson writes somewhere that in the great works of the past "we recognize our own rejected thoughts. They come back to us with a certain alienated majesty." I think this is exactly what happened here.

READER: But why couldn't Bernard just tell his readers directly to look up that passage in *The City of God*?

AUTHOR: The whole point of Bernard's account—the "oriental trickery" of it, if you will—was to make people think this was about Oppenheimer when in fact it was about Bernard's experience as a convert. Bernard knew that if he wrote only about his personal situation, no one would be interested, no one would care. He had to do it subtly. He did it through Oppenheimer and perhaps through St. Augustine, too.

READER: This is a good segue into my second question. Having read about Jäger and Bernard so far, I feel that I know quite a bit about the two men but that I'm no closer to understanding Oppenheimer. The notorious court Jew is like a pictorial negative space in your narrative—you paint a wide tableau only to leave his own figure blank.

AUTHOR: It's like waiting for Godot, no?

READER: Exactly, it's like waiting for Godot.

AUTHOR: I suspect that some of my other readers can already guess the answer to your question. My intention in writing this book was never to compose yet another supposedly definitive biography of Jew Süss. Rather, it was to write a new history of his trial. (The two topics are by no means identical.) And because, during his trial, Oppenheimer was incarcerated, he was far from the public eye, with his point of view suppressed and his voice always controlled by others. I disagree with historians who claim that we can at any point observe Oppenheimer directly or hear his actual voice. To my mind, such claims are at best wishful thinking, at worst a patronizing fantasy about granting Oppenheimer an agency that in practice he never really exercised. Oppenheimer's absence from my narrative in the previous two chapters is consequently not a problem I failed to solve, but an aspect of his story around which I structured my narrative. You are right: Oppenheimer is the book's absent center; he is its pictorial negative space, its structuring absence.

READER: Do answer this one final, and rather personal, question, then. While reading Bernard's account, it dawned on me that my own existence in the pages of this book could be related to it. Both you and Bernard decided to include imaginary interlocutors in your accounts. Was his work perhaps the inspiration behind my own creation?

AUTHOR: Great question, but No. Bernard's interlocutor is a stooge, a yes-man who never once challenges his creator seriously. Your case could not be more different. As you may remember from this book's introduction, your figure, though fictional, is based on some very real people who over the years heard me talk about this book and challenged my arguments, sometimes quite harshly. One of the main considerations behind your creation was my wish to both acknowledge these critics' concerns and address them directly. I also use the fictive nature of a dialogue with an imaginary reader to acknowledge and indeed draw attention to the literary elements in my own account. As a writer, I do not stand outside literary traditions and practices. I try not to be their servant, however, but to use them to my own advantage. This is evident in the gospel-like structure of this entire book, in the many literary allusions in it, in the mixture of genres I use, and not least in the way I choose to end a chapter and begin a new one. Now turn the page. You'll see immediately what I mean.

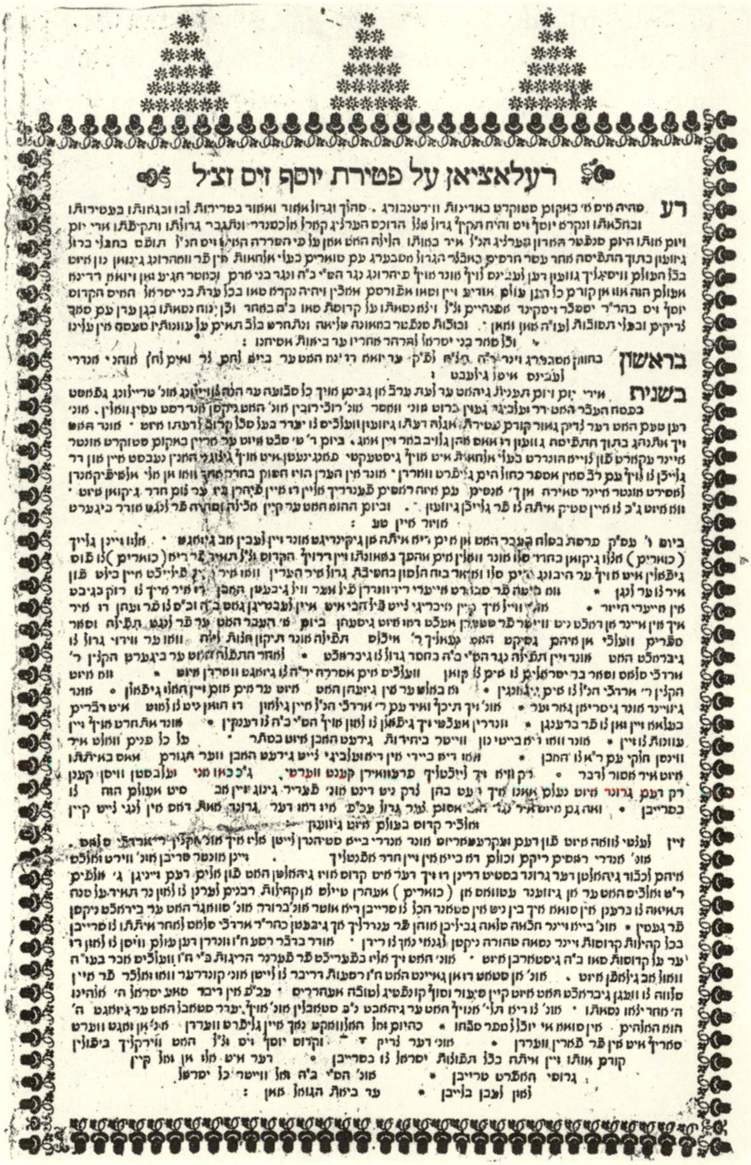

רעלאציאן על פטירת יוסף זיס זצ"ל

FIGURE 7. Mordechai Schloss and Callman Seligmann. *The Story of the Passing of Joseph Süss, May the Memory of the Righteous Be a Blessing* (Fürth, 1738). *Source*: Private collection.

CHAPTER 3

Joseph and His Brothers

And as soon as he saw him, Joseph Süss
fell upon the man's neck, and cried
and shouted a great deal.
—The Story of the Passing of Joseph Süss,
ZT"L, 1738

In the beginning was the ghetto. Joseph Oppenheimer's relationship with other Jews is incomprehensible without it as both a
physical place and a symbolic reference point. If this is true in
general, it is particularly true in the case of the only eyewitness
account of Oppenheimer's trial to have been written by a Jew (figure 7).

The commissioner of the eyewitness account was Mordechai
Schloss. Schloss was a native of the Frankfurt ghetto—the famous
Judengasse, or "Jewish Lane"—and he remained connected to his
birthplace by strong family, commercial, and cultural ties
throughout his life. Schloss's Frankfurt background shaped his
uneasy relationship with Oppenheimer on many levels, and it
shows through in the account he eventually commissioned about

the fate of his fellow Jew. Schloss's account is crucial in deciphering the Jewish side of Oppenheimer's story. In order to make
sense of it, one needs to understand Schloss's relationship with
Oppenheimer, and in order to do that, one must begin with the
ghetto.

Schloss lived the first thirty-three years of his life on the Jewish
Lane.[1] He was born there in 1674,[2] two centuries after Frankfurt's
Jews were ordered to leave their homes in the city and move to an
enclosed alley just outside the old city walls. Originally intended
for about fifteen families, by the 1670s the long and narrow Lane
had become home to a community of 2,500 Jews. Prohibited from
leaving their neighborhood after dark or on Sundays and Christian holidays, some of Frankfurt's Jews referred to the Lane as
their "New Egypt." They felt exiled in it, like their ancient forefathers in the Land of Goshen.

Modern historians like to paint a more complex picture of the
Lane than the one invoked by the epithet "New Egypt." Consider,
for instance, the case of the dress code that applied to Jews like
Schloss. Jewish men in Schloss's time were required by municipal
law to wear wide-brimmed black hats and black robes with white
ruffs, while the women wore white bonnets and long, dark dresses.
Until 1728, Frankfurt's Jews were also ordered to wear a special
yellow circle on their clothes, further marking them off from the
rest of the population. Tempting though it may be, we should not
think of such practices as the consequences of discrimination or
Judeophobia alone. In Frankfurt's hierarchical society, sartorial
distinctions were used for many purposes, not only to distinguish
Jews from Christians, and at least some in the Jewish community
continued to embrace the Frankfurt dress code even when they
had left the city. Thus, one print from the time of Oppenheimer's
trial suggests that Mordechai Schloss still dressed in the typical
Frankfurt fashion even decades after leaving the city of his birth.[3]

He was clearly not obligated to do so: Joseph Süss Oppenheimer and even some Jews in Schloss's own social circle wore very fashionable clothes at the time.[4]

In 1700, more than a century before the introduction of street names and house numbers in Frankfurt, each of the two hundred houses on the Jewish Lane was known by a special name. These timber-framed constructions were owned by the city council, which rented them out only to Jews it deemed worthy of residence permits. Records of the council's frequent inspections of its properties on the Lane, together with various documents from the Jewish community, provide valuable information about the inhabitants of specific houses, including the Schlosses.[5] They tell us that Schloss's forefathers came to Frankfurt in the mid-sixteenth century from the Rhine Valley and that they first settled in a house called "Schloss," a fact that consequently gave the family its name. In 1614, during a general upheaval in the city led by the grocer Vincenz Fettmilch, a local mob attacked the Lane, and the Schlosses, together with the rest of Frankfurt's Jews, were expelled from the city and prevented from coming back for two years. Rather than an unambiguous indication of endemic Jew hatred, this episode too reveals the complex situation of Frankfurt's Jewish community. There is no question that Frankfurt's Jews were hated by some of their neighbors. At the same time, the attack of 1614 was part of a larger conflict (other people were attacked too), and the expulsion of the Jews was eventually followed by their return and a promise by the city council to punish severely anyone who harmed them again. Without underestimating the animosity toward Jews such as Mordechai Schloss and his family, it is important to keep in mind that they also had some very powerful allies.[6]

After the Schlosses' return to the Lane in 1616, one branch of the family moved across the alley to a house called Wilder Mann, a tall and extremely narrow building located a few doors down from the ghetto's central synagogue. During Mordechai Schloss's childhood, his entire family lived in this house, including his father, Nateh (short for Nathan); his mother, Yidle (Yehudit); and his siblings, Moshe, Yaakef, Faysh, Gelbe, and Bluma. Though the father's occupation is not documented, an entry in the community's records indicates that he was in all likelihood a prominent man among the Lane's Jews.[7]

Schloss moved to Württemberg in late 1706 and died there almost four decades later, but throughout his life he remained closely associated with the Frankfurt Lane. The authorities in Württemberg usually referred to him as Marx Nathan of Frankfurt (Marx being the Latinized version of Mordechai and Nathan the name of his father), while to his Jewish coreligionists he remained Mordechai, son of Nateh Schloss of Wilder Mann, or, in short, Mordechai Schloss. (In order to avoid confusion, we will refer to him in this chapter as Mordechai Schloss, regardless of what the various sources call him.) Surviving documents show that Schloss often came back to the Lane and that he retained his Frankfurt residence permit throughout his life.[8] When he died in Stuttgart in 1744, his wife entered his name in the Frankfurt community's commemorative book (*Memorbuch*), an act typically reserved for the more distinguished members of the Jewish community. The book describes Schloss as an especially charitable man, "trustworthy in his [commercial] dealings . . . who went to synagogue daily in the morning and evening and prayed to the great God with devotion [*be-khavanah*]."[9]

Surrounding Schloss as he grew up on the Lane was a heterogeneous group of neighbors. When Frankfurt's city council inspected the ghetto's houses in 1694 and again in 1703, Schloss still lived in the Wilder Mann. In addition to his family, the council's agents found in the house "a baker, who also trades in old iron, his wife, and their two sons, twenty and sixteen years old, who help their father in different ways."[10] Also under the same roof was a couple from the city of Worms and their small child. Adjacent buildings housed, among many other people, a couple of shop assistants and their son "who does nothing," an "idle widow" with her son and daughter-in-law (the latter both money changers), a leatherworker, a rabbi, a man who "trades in whatever he can lay his hands on," and a butcher.[11] This diverse group of people led a rich cultural life. The Lane had four synagogues, a ritual bath, a so-called wedding house (a small banquet hall used for weddings and other celebrations), a hospital, a cemetery, and several educational institutions, mostly geared toward the young. As home to a large community, the Lane was furthermore the site of countless rituals—from the communal daily prayers and the biweekly readings of Torah portions in the synagogues, to annual celebrations of Jewish holidays such as Rosh Hashana and Passover, to rites of passage such as the bris and the bar mitzvah. In addition, over the course of its existence, the Lane was home to many important mystics and rabbis, including several Schlosses.

As a scion of a distinguished Lane family, Mordechai Schloss would have had an education that included at the very least attending the *cheder*, the elementary school for Jewish boys. In the early modern period, the study of the Pentateuch stood at the heart of the cheder curriculum. The Yiddish-speaking *melamed* (teacher) read the weekly portion of the Torah with the children, translated and explained the Hebrew verses line by line, clarified terms, and interpreted difficult passages. This pedagogical method, combined with the need to move to a different Torah portion every week, meant that the pupils studied the early verses of every portion much more closely than later ones. After they spent several years with the Pentateuch, the pupils were made familiar with the elementary collection of oral Jewish law and its commentary and related legends (Talmud). Thus, the melamed taught his students both some basic knowledge and elementary learning skills, including at least a modest command of Hebrew and Aramaic and a familiarity with some basic interpretative methods.[12]

Like practically any social group, the Lane's Jews had their own collective memory: their way of constructing, keeping, and passing along their heritage and identity to future generations. They did so through communal institutions, public rituals, textual records, and even physical objects. The weekly readings of the Torah were of course crucial in this respect, as was the annual reading of the Haggadah at Passover. More local in nature but also important were the already mentioned Memorbuch, which was kept in the central synagogue; the records of the gravediggers (*pinkas ha-kavranim*); and the inscriptions on the gravestones in the Lane's cemetery. In the century following Mordechai Schloss's birth, the Lane also became famous for its annual Purimspiel—an enactment of biblical stories in the style of the commedia dell'arte—and as a center for the trade in Hebrew and Yiddish books. (Before emancipation, Frankfurt Jews were not allowed to actually print books in the Lane, but non-Jewish printers, outside the ghetto, certainly did so.[13]) Among the works read and traded on the Lane were biblical commentaries as well as broadsides of Yiddish historical songs and vernacular pamphlets about recent events. It is the common assumption of the scholarly literature on the topic that these bilingual and Yiddish materials catered to all sectors of Jewish society. Yiddish, after all, was the daily language of all Jews, from the most revered scholars to the least educated.[14]

As the exile of 1614 and the return to the city two years later made clear, Jews in early modern Frankfurt had both enemies—those who forced them to leave—and also some very powerful patrons, who saw to it that they were permitted to return. The Jews' allure to their allies lay in large part in their financial activities, and these, in turn, were closely related to Frankfurt's famous annual trade fairs. Twice a year—once in the fall and once in the spring—Frankfurt opened its gates to merchants from across Europe who for two weeks traded in the city's central marketplace. Some Jews helped effect exchanges among the many different currencies used by the foreign merchants, others were peddlers or small-scale traders, and still others specialized in the wholesale of specific commodities such as linens, wax, old and new clothes, Hebrew and Yiddish books, jewelry, gold, silver, and other metals. Many Jews also worked as moneylenders or pawnbrokers, especially during the fair. Indeed, almost all the houses on the Jewish Lane served as storage spaces for general wares or hocked items. This must have been the case of the Wilder Mann, too.

Whether at the fair or during the rest of the year, Frankfurt's Jews maintained many contacts with their Christian neighbors as well as with merchants and other visitors to the city, including princes on the lookout for loans and supplies they couldn't get elsewhere.[15] This is how Mordechai Schloss got to know Duke Eberhard Ludwig of Württemberg. By the first decade of the eighteenth century, Schloss was involved in enough commercial and financial activities to have attracted the attention of the duke and his mistress, Christina Wilhelmina von Grävenitz. Contemporary documents from Frankfurt and a legal deposition Schloss gave later in life in Württemberg shed some light on Schloss's relationship with the couple and the sequence of events that led him to move to Württemberg. In 1704, Schloss married Rachel (nick-named Rehle), daughter of the Jew Löw (Leyb) Schwartz, also from the Lane. A year later, his mother, Yidle, passed away in the Wilder Mann. Then, "[i]n the year 1706, Mademoiselle Grävenitz came to Frankfurt, accompanying His Highness the Duke [of Württemberg]." The couple were on their way to Schlangenbad, a spa town near Mainz. "It was then that the duke decided to take me [Mordechai Schloss] with him, appointed me as his court Jew, and granted me privileges to trade freely in Württemberg."[16] Because Grävenitz met Eberhard Ludwig for the first time only in November 1706[17] and because Schloss claims he met the couple together sometime that year, we can be fairly certain that it was toward the very end of 1706 that Mordechai Schloss left the Jewish Lane in Frankfurt to become Eberhard Ludwig's court Jew in Württemberg.

Württemberg

Judging from surviving historical sources from his time in Württemberg, Mordechai Schloss's life in the duchy was not without its tensions. He enjoyed much success, but he also experienced failure and even the occasional brush with the law; he was surrounded by a variety of people, some proving more trustworthy than others; and he seems to have been a prominent member of the local Jewish community although some of his competitors and even outright enemies were Jews themselves. Last but not least of the tensions in Schloss's story is the fact that he had clearly known Christoph David Bernard and some members of Oppenheimer's inquisition committee long before they all got involved in Oppenheimer's case. The Württemberg court that Schloss joined in 1706, despite its aspirations to grandeur, was in fact a rather small place.

Several decades before Oppenheimer's appearance on the scene, court Jews were already a prominent feature of Württemberg's economic and political landscape.[18] Jews were legally prohibited from living in the duchy, but the regent during Eberhard Ludwig's childhood, Duke Friedrich Carl, had hired the Jew Model Löw as a horse trader in 1686,[19] and Eberhard Ludwig himself employed two Frankfurt Jews as his personal agents by 1698. About a decade later, Eberhard Ludwig invited more Jews to assist him in the supply of building materials, luxury items, and credit for the construction of his new palace in Ludwigsburg.[20] Mordechai Schloss belonged to this group of merchants, alongside men like Gabriel Fränkel, Fränckel Levin, and others. Most of the duchy's court Jews came to Württemberg about a decade and a half after Schloss, starting in around 1721. Not all of them stayed for long, but all their names are on record: Hirsch Levi, Hayum Strassburger, David Ulmann, Abraham Hechinger, Elias Hayum, Abraham Joseph Mändel, Callman Seligmann, and about two dozen more.[21]

By the late 1730s, Schloss had a house in Stuttgart. Where exactly this house was located and whether Schloss had also lived in Stuttgart earlier in his life (rather than in Ludwigsburg, for instance) remain open questions. Either way, there was no little irony in the fact that Schloss's children did not grow up in a ghetto like their father before them: there was no need for "Jewish Lanes" in a duchy that for so long completely prohibited Jews from settling within its borders. The Schlosses had three sons—Moshe, Leyb, and Nateh—and two daughters—Yule (Yoela) and Yudle (Yehudit). They employed several servants and even a special Jewish cook from Frankfurt. His name was Hertz Hammel.[22]

One gets a glimpse into the nature and extent of Mordechai and Rehle Schloss's social circle by looking at whom the couple selected as spouses for their children. Moshe worked closely with his father for several years before marrying a Frankfurt girl and moving back to the Wilder Mann around 1730, and Leyb also moved back to Frankfurt, where he was married twice, the second time to Zipora (Feygle), the widowed daughter-in-law of the famous Jewish businesswoman and diarist Glikl of Hammeln. As for the two girls, they were both married to Württemberg court Jews. In her early teens, Yudle was married to Elias Hayum, a young man with a very bright future ahead of him, and six months after Oppenheimer's execution, Yule married Callman Seligmann, her father's longtime commercial associate.[23] During the dramatic events of 1737–1738, Schloss's two sons-in-law played revealing and indeed important roles.

Relying on his connections in the Württemberg court on the one hand and his extensive family and commercial ties in Frankfurt on the other hand, Schloss became a very successful businessman. In 1706 and then again in 1714, 1715, and 1719, he received extensive trade privileges from Eberhard Ludwig. "Together with his associates and servants," the duke wrote in 1714, for instance, Schloss had permission "to trade, negotiate, exchange, buy, sell, or otherwise contract all wares and jewels, of whatever kind, with [any] members of the court, always free of the excise, customs, tolls, daily fees, and other impositions, of whatever name."[24] The court's accounting books record how Schloss used these privileges to provide the duke with various items, including candle wax, napkins, and parts of military uniforms, but also porcelain tableware, damask tablecloths, expensive furniture, and jewelry.[25] The amount of money exchanged ranged from a few hundred gulden for one item in 1717 to over 5,000 gulden for furniture in 1732. One should bear in mind that this trade represented only one part of Schloss's commercial activities. The other part consisted of private transactions that would leave no trace in the ducal accounting books.

In the mid-1720s, during a legal dispute with some of his competitors, Schloss explained the way he ran his business. Accusations against him notwithstanding, he never sought out his customers—they always came to him. "He refused to admit that he ever engaged in hawking or peddling," one document paraphrased Schloss's position. "When a prominent person of the court, a gentleman, or anyone else asked to buy or trade in something, [Schloss] and his people would serve them as best they could."[26] Schloss further insisted he never cheated anyone in his whole life. "*Au contraire*, [Schloss] treated everyone so generously that people often told him they wished the local [Christian] merchants treated them in the same way."[27]

Several documents from the 1710s and 1720s reveal further details about Schloss's modus operandi.[28] He often traveled in person to the trade fairs in Frankfurt, to Mannheim (where he had many business connections),[29] and even to distant Leipzig, where he negotiated and bought different wares and objects for his Württemberg customers. Absenting himself from the duchy for several weeks at a time, Schloss was proud to report that "his products were fresher, more beautiful, and more exquisite" than those of his competitors.[30] He was nevertheless often quite concerned about maintaining his good credit in Frankfurt. This was crucial, because most transactions in the fair were done through bills of exchange rather than in cash. Maintaining one's credit was consequently of the utmost importance.

In 1722, the duke further expanded Schloss's legal rights by allowing him to form a commercial syndicate with several other court Jews, including Fränckel Levin and David Ulmann.[31] The syndicate lasted barely five years, partly because Schloss felt short-changed by his partners. For us, the syndicate's importance lies less in what it achieved financially than in what it tells us about Schloss's social position. Commercial consortiums between Jews were unknown in Württemberg before Schloss's time, and they were in fact explicitly forbidden in Frankfurt because they strengthened the negotiating position of the Jews and put their trade competitors at a disadvantage.[32] That Schloss managed to get an official letter sanctioning the consortium must consequently be interpreted as a sign of great ducal favor. Moreover, the syndicate's original charter identified Schloss as the senior partner in the company. Not only at court, then, but also among his fellow Württemberg Jews, Mordechai Schloss was a leading figure, a successful and respected court Jew, with strong family and commercial ties both in Württemberg and in Frankfurt.

Conflicts and Challenges

A prominent court Jew like Mordechai Schloss was bound to make some enemies. His religion was one source of resentment against him, but it was far from being the only one. Some in Württemberg disliked Schloss as a person, others objected to his special relationship with the duke, and yet others—including several Jews—envied Schloss's commercial success and tried to outbid him for lucrative contracts at court.

The earliest documented conflict involving Schloss dates from the summer of 1716. In August of that year, Schloss ran into a Jewish convert to Christianity in Ludwigsburg and the two men had some kind of verbal altercation. The convert, one Christian Ludwig,[33] claimed later that Schloss had used abusive language against him and even threatened him with physical violence. To support his accusations, Ludwig asked three witnesses to testify in his favor: two local proselytes by the names of Frösch and Weil, and Christoph David Bernard, the protagonist of the previous chapter in this book. By the time of the scheduled depositions, all three witnesses happened to be out of the duchy (Bernard was in Jena). The ducal commissioner had no choice but to dismiss the charges, although he did suspect that Schloss "was not necessarily innocent in the whole affair."[34]

Another conflict connected with Schloss—this time indirectly—took place a few years later, in 1723. It involved Schloss's partner Levin Fränkel, Fränkel's cook Maram Kahn, and Schloss's cook Hertz Hammel.[35] The two cooks had a list of personal grievances against Fränkel to which they also added the accusation that he had imposed himself on his female servants and even impregnated a Christian maid. Just as in the case of Christian Ludwig's complaint against Schloss, Hammel's and Kahn's accusations against Fränkel were eventually dismissed by the court. Their historical significance lies not in whether the alleged events took place (which one cannot determine today one way or another), but in the background the accusations provide for Oppenheimer's later trial. Schloss's conflict with a convert adds to several pieces of evidence that characterize him as especially devout.[36] The incident involving Schloss's cook and his commercial partner Fränkel is even more telling. It demonstrates that accusations about sexual misconduct by Württemberg court Jews preceded Oppenheimer's arrest by at least fourteen years. Significantly, in 1723, unlike in 1737–1738, they had no consequences whatsoever.

In December 1718, several Württemberg merchants lodged their own complaint against Schloss. They claimed that "the Jew [Schloss] and his many associates trade in many different wares and jewels, all for the annual payment of 50 gulden to the local estates but otherwise free of all impositions, customs, tolls, and daily fees." Such a state of affairs was intolerable to the "[Christian] burghers and subjects who, though obedient, are burdened by taxes to the point of losing their livelihoods." The merchants singled out Schloss as a particular problem. His many trade privileges "benefit tremendously the Jew and his many associates but at the same time prevent others from earning their daily bread and cause much harm to the duke's financial interests by freeing [Schloss] from tolls."[37]

Eberhard Ludwig remained unpersuaded by these arguments, and shortly after receiving the merchants' complaint, he reconfirmed Schloss's trade privileges. Then, in 1723, the merchants tried their luck again. "The free commerce of the Jews brings [Christian merchants] to the brink of complete ruination," they wrote. Ever since their last correspondence with the duke, "the damaging commerce of the Jews, instead of subsiding, had only intensified" because many foreign Jews had managed to infiltrate into the country and "all year round move from house to house, offering their wares."[38] Having received no response from the duke, the merchants began adding a more urgent tone to their correspondence. "The commerce of the Jews causes us immense suffering so that in the future, without [ducal] interference, we shall not be able to either earn our basic sustenance or stem the tide of the ever increasing protestations of the general population [against the Jews]."[39] Schloss, who was asked early on to respond to the complaints, replied sardonically. He wrote to the duke that despite the merchants' protestations over their inability to feed their families, "several of these merchants had been somehow able to make a profit of several hundred thousand gulden" in the preceding several years.[40]

A more serious challenge to Schloss's business came from within the ranks of the Jewish community. In November 1720, Model Löw, one of the earliest court Jews to settle in Württemberg, wrote to the duke that for over thirty years, he "had always been a true servant of the dukes of Württemberg, performing my duties honorably so that no one had ever lodged a single complaint against me." This idyllic situation had been disrupted by Mordechai Schloss. "I have been—alas!—prosecuted by this Jew whose actions are furthermore damaging well beyond the case of a single man." Löw claimed that Schloss "seeks to prosecute honorable people, he misuses ducal favor, and he causes immense losses to the duke and the local estates by not paying excise and tolls."[41] There was an easy remedy to this situation, Löw continued: to give him (Löw) Schloss's lucrative contracts for supplying the court with candles, torches, tableware, and other commodities. Whereas Schloss received 1,000 gulden a year for his contracts, Löw was willing to take only 500.

Three years later, Löw lodged another complaint. He accused Schloss of disrespect toward a local official and charged Schloss's partner Fränkel with a long series of abuses including, once again, sexual misconduct.[42] The case was eventually dismissed and Löw himself was incarcerated for several years for making false allegations. (The judges determined that Löw's actions were motivated by pure jealousy.[43]) Löw's significance lies in his being one of several Württemberg court Jews who at points felt pushed aside or even outright cheated by their coreligionists. In 1727, Schloss himself felt this way and dissolved the syndicate he had formed with his associates.[44] In 1729, the tables were turned once again, and Schloss and his son Moshe found themselves arrested and held for four weeks because of a complaint from a fellow Jewish merchant citing the inferior quality of the wallpaper they delivered.[45] Contrary to the impression given by some historians of Oppenheimer's case, the court Jews of early eighteenth-century Württemberg did not form a uniform block. Though they often married into each other's families (Yule, Yudle), and though they did form commercial alliances when it suited them (the syndicate), they also competed fiercely against one another and at times had such serious disagreements that they dissolved their partnerships, ended up in front of a magistrate or a judge, and, despite the strong taboo among Jews to testify against each other in premodern Christian courts, caused one another to be put behind bars. What held their community together was not harmonious consensus or common practices, but individual and highly insecure commercial opportunities at a prince's court. Theirs was above all a community of risk.

Oppenheimer and Schloss

Just like Mordechai Schloss, Joseph Süss Oppenheimer too had business contacts in Frankfurt. In his early years as a financier, he relied on Frankfurt's financial market, and while running the mint in Hesse-Darmstadt, he had also participated in the commerce in precious metals in which many of the Lane's inhabitants were involved. After he sold his mint contract in Darmstadt to two other court Jews—a deal that would come to haunt him later—he tried his luck in Karlsruhe. When his business there didn't take off, he decided to move to the famous trade city on the Main.

Thanks to historians Heinrich Völker and Hellmut Haasis, we know a great deal about Oppenheimer's time in Frankfurt.[46] Oppenheimer decided not to live on the crowded Jewish Lane, preferring instead to rent a small apartment at the Golden Swan Inn, right next to the local post station and about two hundred yards outside the Jewish ghetto. Over the next several years, he expanded his lodgings from two chambers into a small complex of rooms and apartments, complete with a personal secretary, various assistants, and a small archive. Frankfurt's city council naturally disapproved of Oppenheimer's unprecedented move, citing the "immemorial custom" of Jews living on the Lane,[47] but Oppenheimer remained literally unmoved. He had met Carl Alexander in 1732 and become his personal agent (*Resident*) in Frankfurt in late 1733. As such, he demanded to be treated as a princely representative rather than as a Jew: what the city council termed "immemorial custom" was simply a "bad custom" to him.[48] Ultimately, the city council had no choice but to cave in to Oppenheimer's demands. It was in no position to dictate to an official agent of the duke of Württemberg where to reside.

Just like Bernard's seat at the back of Tübingen's Collegiate church or Frankfurt's enclosed Jewish Lane, Oppenheimer's physical place in Frankfurt was a reflection of his social and political position. By refusing to give up his lodgings outside the ghetto, he was making a strong political statement vis-à-vis the city council while also maintaining a physical and symbolic distance from the local Jewish community. It seems very unlikely that Mordechai Schloss was unaware of this double statement. Schloss entertained many business contacts in Frankfurt, he attended the fairs there on a regular basis, and he had a great number of relatives in the Judengasse, including four siblings, a son, a daughter-in-law, and, as of 1733, one or possibly two grandchildren.

While Oppenheimer's position in Frankfurt was on the rise, Schloss's own place in Stuttgart seemed precarious. The death of his old ducal patron Eberhard Ludwig in 1733 was one problem, and the appearance of Oppenheimer on the scene yet another. The packed field of Württemberg court Jews was getting ever more crowded, making it increasingly more difficult for Schloss to turn a profit. The best pieces of evidence for this state of affairs are the ducal accounting books. Before 1732, the books mention

Schloss on a regular basis, documenting him selling candle wax, wine, tapestries, jewelry, furniture, and a host of other wares to the Württemberg court. After Carl Alexander's ascension to the throne and Oppenheimer's rise, the books stop mentioning Schloss altogether. "Now there arose up a new king over Egypt, who knew not Joseph," says the Bible about the similar story of the earliest known court Jew, Joseph son of Jacob. Schloss, even if his entire education amounted to just a few years at the cheder, surely knew this famous verse by heart.

Schloss's fortunes reached a new low during the Grävenitz affair. Whereas in Frankfurt Oppenheimer became Carl Alexander's plenipotentiary and brokered a deal with the disgraced mistress, in Stuttgart Schloss was brought in front of the inquisition committee and "asked solemnly to reply truthfully and under oath to a series of questions."[49] The inquisition committee in the Grävenitz case—still without Jäger, who was not appointed Fiskal until later—wanted to know about the exact nature of Schloss's business and about his relationship with Grävenitz-Würben, her brother Count Friedrich Wilhelm von Grävenitz, and the latter's plenipotentiary Joachim Friedrich von Pfeil.

The record of Schloss's deposition in the Grävenitz case is dated February 19, 1734. In it, one hears echoes of Schloss's tense relationships with Levin Fränkel and Model Löw and can detect further proof (if any was still needed) of the intense competition over contracts at court. If the scribe's language is any indication, one can perhaps even detect in the deposition echoes of Schloss's changing demeanor. The confident court Jew of the early 1720s, the man who rejected dismissively the accusations of local Christian merchants, comes off in 1734 as deferential and hesitant.[50] "What kinds of deliveries he, the deponent, has made to the court?" the judges began their questioning.

*R[eply]. He delivered candles, wine, and for a long time parts of
military uniform, one time he also delivered badly made
wallpaper.*

Q[uestion]. Who signed the contracts with him in each case?

*R. The Marshall [high court official] did so, in the presence of
all the deputies.*

Q. Whether no one profited unlawfully from this, whether in
cash or in kind?

*R. At the signing of the agreement he gave no one anything. But
otherwise, he recalls that when the payment wasn't forthcoming,
he gave the count [Grävenitz's brother] a couple of presents, so
for example to his servant he gave cloth for livery two or three
times until the bill ran to about 200 gulden. And to the countess
[Grävenitz] herself, in order to keep her well-disposed toward him,
he sold wares at a lower price than he himself had paid. . . . In the
end, he also had to sign on the receipt for the livery without getting
paid.*

Q. To whom, then, had he given presents at court . . . in order to
profit by it personally?

*R. When Levin [Fränkel] managed to take from him the con-
tract for the candles, he [Schloss] gave a brown shirt with silver
linings to von Pfeil and asked him to speak with the count on his
behalf. But he never regained the contract.*[51]

The general questions soon turned more specific. By his own
admission, Schloss delivered wine to the court.

Q. Who, then, received the wine? Who signed the contract?

*R. The contract was signed at the office of the Marshall and the
wine was delivered to one of his assistants. Before the signing of*

the contract, however, he [Schloss] first delivered the wine to a servant, who stored it in the cellar.

Q. Whether he did not have to give something in return for getting the contract, and in case he did, to whom?

R. Because of the contract, and because the wine was often left in the cellar for three, five, or even six months before the contract was signed, he once gave von Pfeil some Mosel wine in order to expedite the process. Before signing the contract, he also gave von Pfeil permission to take 50 or 100 bottles— he can't remember the exact number anymore—as soon as the contract was signed.

Q. How high was the price for each bottle?

R. Often 4,000 bottles for 450 gulden.

Q. Since the wine was so expensive, were there no other merchants to whom [the contract] was offered?

R. He doesn't know. The office of the Marshall should know this.

Q. He must know, however, that Jew Model had the intention to deliver wine of similar quality for only 250 gulden?

R. He knew absolutely nothing about that.

The committee completed the interrogation by raising doubts about Schloss's credibility. If we can trust the protocols, Schloss himself was aware of this problem and echoed it in his responses.

Q. He is unwilling to admit he had given any more presents. And yet isn't it true that he had to give something in exchange for the contract for delivering tableware?

A. It's been so long, he can't remember anything anymore. . . .

Q. Whether he wasn't entrusted by some people to change money for them outside the country [Württemberg]?

R. *He would have done it gladly, but no one had trusted him.*

Q. If he could remember anything else that was done against the duke's interest, he should say it right away. Otherwise, he should do it as soon as possible, in writing, and without hiding anything.

R. *He cannot say anything more at the moment. He does know many things, however, and will think it over so that he could ground his statements on a solid basis. Then he will report again and testify under oath about anything else he had done against the duke's interest.*[52]

After the deposition was over, Schloss signed his name at the bottom of the protocol. One month later, in Stuttgart, another hand signed a different document. In mid-March 1734, Carl Alexander decided to further expand Oppenheimer's responsibilities. He sent his Frankfurt envoy a letter detailing the latter's various new tasks, signed it in his own hand, and added a wax imprint of his seal at the bottom.[53] There was nothing out of the ordinary in this turn of events. In a field marked by competition over princely favors and scarce resources, a change in government often marked the decline in the fortunes of one court Jew and the rise of another.

The Two Sons-in-Law

Let there be no mistake about it: there is a great deal about Schloss, his household, and his business that we do not know. We do not have any information about how Schloss usually sounded or with what intonation he replied to the questions put to him by the inquisition committee in the Grävenitz case. (These are important issues because they could inform the way we interpret the protocols.) Unlike in Bernard's or Jäger's cases, there is also no direct documentation of Schloss's education, the books he read, or any substantial texts (other than business transactions and a handful of short letters) he himself composed before Oppenheimer's trial. The archival footprint of people in Schloss's immediate social circle is often also quite small. Only one letter from Rehle Schloss has survived,[54] the documentation about the five Schloss children is sparse at best, and, apart from the cook Hertz Hammel, the exact identity of the servants in the Schloss household is, and is likely to always remain, unknown.

Fortunately, the archival information about Yudle's husband, Elias Hayum, is much better. Hayum was born in 1709 in the village of Pfersee near Augsburg. Although he and his father moved to Württemberg in 1721, they maintained their business contacts in Augsburg at least until Oppenheimer's trial, and they continued to maintain a house in Pfersee for many years thereafter.[55] (Hayum's father eventually died there in 1768.[56]) Why the family moved to Württemberg in the first place or when it formed close social ties with Mordechai Schloss is not documented, but by 1725, young Hayum was clearly already betrothed to fourteen-year-old Yudle Schloss.[57]

After Oppenheimer's move to Stuttgart, Elias Hayum worked with him rather closely. According to a document from 1735, Hayum helped Oppenheimer provide supplies to Carl Alexander's army, and according to a bill from November 1736, Oppenheimer entrusted Hayum with the replacement of hundreds of precious stones from the Württemberg crown jewels in Switzerland.[58] (Some of the stones had to be sold in order to raise money for the prince's personal expenses.) During Oppenheimer's trial,

FIGURE 8. Unknown artist. *Portrait of the Württemberg Court Jew Elias Hayyum*, ca. 1735. *Source:* JMNY, Gift of Dr. Harry G. Friedman, F 5439.

Hayum's name came up again and again as a supplier of silver to the Oppenheimer-run mint in Stuttgart.[59] No less revealing about the nature of Oppenheimer's and Hayum's relationship is a unique portrait of Hayum that was painted in Stuttgart around 1735. (See figure 8.) The only known portrait of a Württemberg court Jew predating Oppenheimer's trial, it shows Hayum as a young courtier dressed in a frock coat and wearing a stylish wig. Similar to Oppenheimer in his worldly appearance, Hayum displayed sartorial preferences that stood in stark contrast to the dress of his father-in-law, the sixty-three-year-old Judengasse Jew.[60]

We also know a thing or two about Callman Seligmann, Schloss's close business associate and Yule's eventual husband, though most of what we know about him dates from after Oppenheimer's trial. Seligmann married Yule Schloss in August 1738 and upon her father's death in 1744 seems to have taken over much of the old man's business.[61] By 1747, the couple had four children and also shared their home with the elderly Rehle Schloss, who seems to have moved in with them after her husband's death.[62] Seligmann was not as shrewd a businessman as his father-in-law. The records show that in the late 1740s and 1750s, while he was trading in various commodities, he had an ever-increasing list of creditors, Jewish and Christian alike. In the 1740s, one Jewish and three Christian merchants filed individual lawsuits against Seligmann, and in the following decade, the list of Seligmann's unsatisfied creditors continued to grow, until he went bankrupt and all his commercial contracts were taken away from him.[63] By contrast, the Jews of Frankfurt wrote about Seligmann very favorably. Upon his death in Stuttgart in 1764, they entered his name in their Memorbuch and mentioned how "his house [in Stuttgart] was open to all," how he provided a safe haven to Jews in distress, and how he always helped others "with all his heart and all his soul."[64] Although all eulogies need to be taken with a grain of salt, this one seems to have corresponded to reality. Documents by the authorities in Stuttgart corroborate the story of Seligmann hiding Jews in distress in the late 1740s.[65]

Considering the crucial role Seligmann played in documenting Oppenheimer's final days, it is quite frustrating that we know so little about his earlier life. A passport issued to Seligmann on July 17, 1732, mentions him as Mordechai Schloss's "commercial consort,"[66] and Christoph David Bernard reports that in early 1738, Oppenheimer called Seligmann "really poor" in contrast to Schloss, whom he considered "rich and in need of nothing."[67] The many gaps in our knowledge about Seligmann might be interpreted in the same light: we know so little about him because he wasn't rich or important enough to draw much bureaucratic attention. As for the reason that Seligmann became associated with Schloss in the first place, only one piece of evidence might be relevant. Callman Seligmann was known among his fellow Jews as Callman Bing, because his forefathers hailed from the small Jewish community in Bingen-on-the-Rhine.[68] For generations, one branch of the Bing family lived on the Jewish Lane in Frankfurt and Callman Seligmann grew up there, in a house just across the street from the Schlosses.[69] This proximity might suggest how Seligmann and Schloss got to know each other and perhaps even what formed the basis for their entire relationship. In any event, the Jewish Lane clearly played an important role in Callman Seligmann's life just as it did in Mordechai Schloss's. These two court Jews had both hailed from "New Egypt." That at the beginning of both their stories stands the famous Jewish Lane is worth keeping in mind as we now turn to the dramatic events surrounding Oppenheimer's fall.

Jewish Reactions to Oppenheimer's Arrest

As it unfolded, Oppenheimer's trial involved many Jews beside Oppenheimer himself. They formed a rather diverse group: some were young and others quite old; most were male, but some were female; and among them, one can find Jews who had been close to Oppenheimer in the past, others who had long been his declared enemies, and still others who were neither friend nor foe. Just like their backgrounds, the reactions of these men and women to Oppenheimer's predicament were varied. There was no one, single, unified response by *the* Jews to the drama of Oppenheimer's trial, certainly not at first.

Among the Jews who were directly touched by Oppenheimer's trial, one group consisted of the accused's close family members. By the time of her son's arrest, Michal Oppenheimer lived with her second husband in the principality of Ansbach, not far from Nuremberg and Fürth. At one point during her son's incarceration, Michal Oppenheimer was caught traveling through Württemberg, apprehended, and questioned briefly by a magistrate before being set free. (Her son was apparently completely unaware of any of this.) Also involved in the trial was Daniel Oppenheimer, Joseph Süss's half-brother. Daniel hired a lawyer to argue on Oppenheimer's behalf in front of the Holy Roman Empire's highest court of appeals in Wetzlar. The appeal was turned down.[70]

A second group of Jews affected by Oppenheimer's trial were the Jewish arrestees. Oppenheimer was not apprehended alone on the evening of March 12, 1737. When, following Oppenheimer's arrest, the local magistrates broke into his home in Stuttgart, they immediately put all members of the household under house arrest and later transferred them to several jails. Oppenheimer's girlfriend Luciana Fischerin was among these arrestees, as were several business associates and assistants and a large number of footmen, manservants, cooks, gardeners, and washerwomen, Jews and non-Jews alike. The most important among the Jewish arrestees was Isaac Samuel Levi, Oppenheimer's personal treasurer. In December 1737, Levi managed to escape from jail in a daring action whose details are unclear. The sources only mention an act of "great violence" in this regard.[71]

The Stuttgart magistrates carefully documented the names of all fifty-five household members they arrested in Oppenheimer's home.[72] Alongside several dozen Lutherans and Catholics, this group also included a handful of Jews. Among the latter, we find seventeen-year-old Yaacob from Frankfurt, eighteen-year-old Benjamin from Bingen, and nineteen-year-old Henlin, a cook-maid from Mannheim. Much older than these three were forty-two-year-old Salomon Mayer from Karlsruhe and fifty-year-old Isaac Leser from Mannheim. Most of the arrestees, regardless of their religion, refused to testify against Oppenheimer. For instance, when Isaac Leser was asked if "he had ever seen or heard that Süss engaged in anything suspicious with other people," he allegedly replied that he had "neither saw nor heard anything suspicious" about his employer.[73]

Though some of Oppenheimer's coreligionists proved loyal, others clearly turned against him. In early April 1737, Jacob Ulmann of Mannheim sent a letter to the inquisition committee in Oppenheimer's case indicating his willingness to come to Stuttgart and share with the inquisitors the "many pieces of information" he had about Oppenheimer.[74] Ulmann, one of the two Jews to whom Oppenheimer sold his Darmstadt mint contract in the early 1730s, had a long-standing financial dispute with Oppenheimer. Now that Oppenheimer was behind bars, Ulmann believed he could force the prisoner to pay him a large sum of money.

More extreme than Ulmann's case was the story of Maram Kahn, a court Jew in Ludwigsburg who asked in early June 1737 to appear in person before the inquisition committee in order to give incriminating testimony against Oppenheimer.[75] His request granted, Kahn came to Hohen Asperg in the middle of June. During the several days he spent with the inquisition committee, he reportedly claimed that the duke had good reason not to trust Oppenheimer, because the latter, "although he carried the title of financial councilor, in fact cared only about his own personal interests and . . . instead of filling the [state's] coffers only emptied them."[76] If we choose to believe Christoph David Bernard on this point, Oppenheimer knew about these two testimonies. "J. U. claimed I owed him 65,000 gulden," Bernard reported Oppenheimer as saying, "although I do not owe him a single farthing." As for Maram Kahn, the man had "raised six different claims against me of which even one would have been enough to send me to the gallows."[77]

A final example of a Jew who reportedly testified against Oppenheimer is Isaac Salomon Landau. Landau, a former associate of Oppenheimer's who is reported to have been the man who had introduced the court Jew to Carl Alexander in the first place, was arrested in the wake of Oppenheimer's fall and interrogated on several occasions. According to the protocol of his second interrogation (September 18, 1737), Landau accused Oppenheimer of a long series of brutal acts (*Brutalitäten*) as well as outright blasphemy. "If [Oppenheimer's] case were to be sent to three different rabbis," the scribe reported Landau's speech, "they would unanimously condemn him to be stoned to death."[78]

Not all Jews' reactions to Oppenheimer's fall were extreme or even directly related to Oppenheimer himself. A good example of a balanced view is Elias Hayum. As a close associate of Oppenheimer's, Hayum was apprehended in late March, interrogated, and kept in prison for about ten days. The protocols of his interrogations portray him conceding that Oppenheimer was no angel but still refusing to demonize his fallen patron. Perhaps contributing to Hayum's release from prison was a letter sent to the inquisition committee by his wife (and Schloss's daughter), Yudle.[79] It is the only time she appears in the trial's records.

As for Mordechai Schloss and his soon-to-be son-in-law Callman Seligmann, the picture is a bit complicated. What the two men felt in the immediate aftermath of Oppenheimer's arrest is not documented. With Elias Hayum in prison and Yudle in distress, they probably shared the feelings of other Jews whose relatives had been arrested. (Some such reactions are recorded in the four Yiddish letters Bernard translated in the summer of 1737.[80]) The only surviving text by Schloss from the early part of Oppenheimer's trial is nonetheless very revealing. In a letter Schloss sent to the Stuttgart authorities on May 16, 1737, he thanked them for protecting him in the past. "Now, however, when we [the Jews] walk the streets, local artisans and other young men constantly call us all kinds of nasty names, push and taunt us, yes, even throw stones at us to the point that we fear for our lives. Just a few days ago, someone threw a stone at my future son-in-law [Callman Seligmann] that, had it hit him, could have been his end."[81] In evaluating Jewish reactions to Oppenheimer's arrest, we need to keep Schloss's letter in mind: although Jews could and did react in many different ways to Oppenheimer's fall, not everything was under their control. Very far from it.

The September Deposition

The archives are silent about Schloss's whereabouts over the next four months, although they do document that several other Jews—including Elias Hayum, who had been released from custody in the meantime—bought some of Oppenheimer's confiscated property when it was auctioned off at this time.[82] The inquisition committee's main concern at this point in the trial lay elsewhere, however. After the preliminary phase of the investigation in Stuttgart, the committee members moved in early June to Hohen Asperg, where they interrogated Oppenheimer and several crucial witnesses over the next three months. Only in mid-September, once they were back in Stuttgart, did they find time to summon Schloss to testify. The absence of documents about

Schloss from the period of May to September 1737 is conse-quently interesting in itself: it indicates that the inquisition com-mittee did not think Schloss could be a key witness against his coreligionist.

Finally, on September 16, 1737, Schloss appeared before the committee. Jäger, Faber, and Dann were present in the room, with Pregizer assisting them as scribe and von Pflug absent. The pro-tocol from the meeting has survived and gives an impression of Schloss as a man very eager to please the inquisition committee even if at first he hesitated to incriminate Oppenheimer outright. At the beginning of his deposition, Schloss reportedly insisted that "he does not want to say anything that might hurt Süss, God forbid, because Süss had done him neither harm nor good." A few sentences later, however, Schloss seems to have already changed his mind, claiming that Oppenheimer had always been a person about whom "no one had anything good to say."[83]

Schloss's deposition did not stop at this general remark. Ac-cording to Pregizer's protocol, Schloss reported to the committee that his contacts in Frankfurt assured him that Oppenheimer had had very little credit and property before he moved to Württem-berg and that "no one knows where he had gotten any credit at all." Furthermore, and "as the whole world knows," Oppenheimer had "never let anyone stand in his way," threatened to send disobedient people "to Hohen Asperg and other prisons," and humiliated many honorable people right in front of Duke Carl Alexander. Concluding the deposition's first part was Schloss's general claim that "there are a great many examples that show how Süss was master without parallel when it came to pressuring people to do as he pleased."[84]

The second part of Schloss's deposition gets more specific. In reply to a series of questions about Oppenheimer's business practices, Schloss reportedly said that Oppenheimer had cheated Carl Alexander by falsifying accounts (for example, receiving multiple payments for selling the duke the same precious stones) and that he had lied to the Württemberg territorial estates on more than one occasion. According to the account, Schloss admitted that he hadn't been privy to any such actions on Oppenheimer's part, but he insisted that he nonetheless had credible information that Oppenheimer had done all these things.[85] Thus, next to incriminating statements relating to the accusations of usurpation of power and lèse-majesté, Schloss's deposition supported the claim that Oppenheimer had stolen from the prince's own purse as well as from the state's and the estates' coffers. He was a traitor *and* a thief.

Some of the statements attributed to Schloss in the protocols strike the modern reader as possibly disingenuous. More than six months after the beginning of Oppenheimer's trial, the scribe reports that Schloss claimed he had no idea what the committee might want to ask him about. According to the trial records, when Jäger and his associates asked Schloss whether "the witness [Schloss] had been coached by someone or spoken to one of the other witnesses concerning what he would tell [in his testimony]," Schloss replied that "he doesn't have the slightest idea what questions are to be put to him and could therefore not have discussed them with anyone beforehand."[86] At other times, the statements in the deposition are verifiably false. In the late 1720s, Schloss and his son were placed behind bars for four weeks, and during the Grävenitz trial Schloss was interrogated by a judge. Still, according to the trial records, when the inquisition committee asked Schloss in 1737 whether he had ever been implicated in a criminal investigation before, Schloss replied in the negative, claiming that "[h]is whole life he had never stood before a magistrate."[87]

What can we make of Schloss's deposition, then? What, if anything, does it tell us about Oppenheimer, and what does it teach us about Schloss? We know that Schloss feared for his life during the early months of Oppenheimer's trial, that his words could have been easily distorted by the inquisition committee or the scribe, and that his deposition, as reported, was not completely truthful. As such, the value of Schloss's testimony as evidence against Oppenheimer is questionable at best. Where the deposition does come in handy is as evidence about Schloss. At the bottom of two different copies of his September deposition, Schloss signed his own name. Even if he hadn't said what was attributed to him in the deposition, Schloss's signatures attest to the fact that at the very least he knew what the committee claimed he had said. The historical value of Schloss's September deposition comes down to this, then: when, a few days before the execution, Schloss met the condemned man in the Herrenhaus, Schloss knew he had played a part—however small and unintentional—in impugning the reputation, and ultimately destroying the life, of Joseph Süss Oppenheimer.

The Story of the Passing of Joseph Süss, ZT"L

Six months after his deposition and about two weeks after meeting Oppenheimer in Stuttgart, Mordechai Schloss helped publish a short account of Oppenheimer's life. Its title is *The Story of the Passing of Joseph Süss, ZT"L (May the Memory of the Righteous Be a Blessing)*. Its author is not named in the document, and determining the identity of the scribe is a complicated matter, as we will see. Even aside from the question of its authorship, though, the account is an extraordinary document. In brief, decisive, and at times very moving passages, it tells the story of Oppenheimer's rise to power, his arrest, trial, and execution. Although Oppenheimer's story had been told before, and although it was to be recounted over and over again in the following months and years, *The Story of the Passing* is unique. It is the only document we know of that was composed by Jews in the immediate aftermath of the execution, and it told Oppenheimer's story from an overall very sympathetic perspective.[88]

The text begins in Hebrew, with a hint that Oppenheimer's past actions had not all been altruistic.

> Be it known that there once was a man in Stuttgart in the state of Württemberg, who became ever greater in the stubbornness of his heart and his pride, in his wealth and his wisdom, and he was called Joseph Süss. This Süss became a high counselor to Duke Carl Alexander, and rose in importance with each passing day. One day, his master the duke passed away. That very night, Süss was arrested by dint of royal edict, was chained by bonds of iron, and was placed for a duration of eleven months in Hohen Asperg, the great fortress, where he was surrounded by guards who were men of war.

Echoing or perhaps replying to accusations against Oppenheimer by other Jews, *The Story* claims next that Oppenheimer had committed many transgressions against God and man, but also that once he had repented and especially after he died for the sanctification of God's name, his place among the righteous in paradise was guaranteed. The term "righteous" is worth keeping in mind here: it appears half a dozen times in the short *Story* and will consequently come to play a crucial role in our interpretation of it.

> The life story of Süss is known far and wide, as are his actions against the almighty God and against human beings.

But because the time of his judgment had arrived and the time of his departure from this world, we must first of all publicly announce his name to the whole world, and ask that his name be read out in every Jewish community: The martyr Joseph Süss ben Issachar Süsskind Oppenheim of blessed memory, whose soul departed in sanctification of the Lord's name, may his soul rest in paradise with the other righteous individuals and repentants forever and ever, amen and amen. And because he passed away in possession of a full belief in God, and wholeheartedly regretted the transgressions he had committed, neither we nor any members of the Jewish faith should ponder upon them until the arrival of the Messiah.

After this first section, written in Hebrew, the text switches to Yiddish and starts recounting the story of Oppenheimer's demise. It does so in a seemingly disorganized chronology, beginning with Oppenheimer's incarceration in Hohen Asperg, which it wrongly dates to September (it began in June), and continuing with the events of the previous Passover when, according to the inquisition committee's documents, Oppenheimer was bedridden with fever.

Firstly, while Joseph Süss was imprisoned in the Asperg fortress, from Rosh Hashana 5498 [that is, 1737] until the day of the trial, he subsisted solely on thin bread and water.

Secondly, he fasted each and every day, and only when evening fell did he eat something, and each week he fasted two or three entire days. Last Passover, he subsisted solely on bread,* water, and turnips. The reason for all this was

---

* It is a common practice in Jewish sources to call Matzo bread, which seems to be the case here as well. It seems highly unlikely that *The Story*'s author, who after all recommends Oppenheimer for his devotion and promises to him a place among the righteous in the

revealed by the wholly righteous person prior to his death, and anyone of intelligence can understand his reasoning. And the way in which he acted within the prison is truly incredible.

Finally, on Wednesday the ninth of Shevat 5498 [January 30, 1738], Süss was transferred to Stuttgart under the guard of 200 men of war with drawn sabers and loaded muskets, and a large assembly of people all around, beyond enumeration, as the sand which is upon the seashore. Süss was placed in Stuttgart near the market square, in a single room, where it is customary to imprison the criminals, with a guard of twenty men and several officers. And this transfer alone, until he arrived at this room by way of the city, was tantamount to a first death.* And on that day, he did not ask or demand any food or drink, except for a kettle of tea.

Next comes the story of how Oppenheimer heard about his death sentence and how several priests (*kemarim*[89]) tried to convert him. For the first and only time in *The Story*, a specific portion of the Bible is mentioned.

On Friday, the eve of the holy Sabbath on which the Torah portion Beshalach is read, he was informed of the death sentence against him. Immediately, several priests entered his room, who attempted to effect an upheaval of his faith. And

---

world to come, would also ascribe to him the eating of (leavened) bread during Passover, which carries with it great punishment by God or man (Exodus 12:19).

* Trials and executions in early modern Europe were highly symbolic rituals. They aimed to express in visual and often outright theatrical form the court's interpretation of the execution as the reestablishment of social order after a violent crime had been committed. In this particular passage, *The Story* portrays Oppenheimer's judicial process from the condemned man's point of view. As such, it subverts the court's intention. About the symbolic aspects of early modern executions in the Holy Roman Empire, see, most importantly, Richard J. Evans, *Rituals of Retribution: Capital Punishment in Germany, 1600–1987* (Oxford: Oxford University Press, 1996), esp. 65–108.

the righteous Joseph Süss of blessed memory immediately
fell to his knees and with his arms raised high, said in these
words, and with great import: Gentlemen, what you are perhaps thinking of asking me? I request that you spare me
these words; withdraw, and go back to your homes. Because
I am left without much time to become reconciled with my
Lord, blessed be He and blessed be His Name. Do not dis-
turb my rest any longer. And that is what happened.

Mirroring other known accounts of the same scene, the author of
The Story describes next an emotional encounter between Oppenheimer and Schloss. The mentioning of "last Sunday" in the
passage implies that the text was written in the week following the
execution. That upon seeing each other, Oppenheimer wept on
Schloss's shoulders but not vice versa should also be noted.

Last Sunday, Joseph Süss asked for and received a Jewish
prayer book and other books. These were the prayer book
of Rabbi Michels,* with prayers in great benevolence to the
Blessed Be He, and a midnight *tikkun* [in Jewish liturgy,
prayers of repentance]. Following the prayer, Joseph Süss
asked to see Rabbi Mordechai Schloss and other Israelites
[*beney Yisra'el*]. This request of his was granted to him by
the authorities. And so, the aforementioned Rabbi Mordechai came to him, and as soon as he saw him, Joseph Süss
fell upon the man's neck, and cried and shouted a great deal,
and immediately told this Rabbi Mordechai that the time
was too short to engage in matters of this world. Rather, he
had to think of the Blessed Be He and regret the transgressions he had committed.

* This is, in all likelihood, Yehiel Michel ben Avraham Halevi Epstein, *Seder Tefilah
Derekh Yeshara* (Frankfurt am Main, 1697), which is a bilingual Yiddish-Hebrew prayer
book (siddur).

Afterward, the two men spoke alone and I am forbidden to say what they spoke. Verily, I do not have enough quills and ink to describe his passing from this world. What's more, it is difficult for me owing to my great sorrow. Nevertheless, it is true that the world has not seen such a righteous man as Süss for a very long time.

During that last meeting with Schloss in Stuttgart, Oppenheimer dictated his last will and testament, two other copies of which have survived among the trial documents.[90] *The Story* lists Schloss, the scribe, and other persons as witnesses, while avoiding mentioning by name the convert Bernard, who was also there.

Witnesses to his last will and testament were the secretary and other persons, as well as myself and Rabbi Mordechai Schloss and other lower-ranking officers, and all were present in the room and signed their names, and this will be to the greater honor of Süss. And the reason for this is that of all of the property of this righteous man, only the amount of 6,000 gulden remained, and of that sum he gave something to the priests, but the majority he gave for the benefit of Jewish communities for the sake of study of the Torah and so that they would light an eternal flame for him in his memory for a full year's time. In short, I cannot describe everything, but neither did he forget his mother and his brother and brother-in-law.

Implying that its author was witness to the execution, *The Story* then claims that

Süss remained in his full wits, and asked Rabbi Mordechai Schloss that following his death he write to all of the holy communities, asking them not to recall his pure soul reproachfully or refer to it in an evil connotation, God forbid, but through God's help no such thing occurred. In any event, after this his soul departed, as he was calling "Hear O Israel, the Lord is our God, the Lord is one." And fifty-two steps led to the gallows, and as he climbed each one of them he said, "The Lord is God."

The Story concludes by reflecting on the reason for its own composition.

> In conclusion, who would be able to recount his praises? And prior to his death the saintly righteous man Joseph Süss of blessed memory instructed, in a true and full heart, that [someone] write about how he died and send the report to all of the Jewish diaspora and to warn against arrogance, and that the Blessed Be He will with God's help keep all of Israel alive until the arrival of the redeemer, amen.

That is it. The entire account fits onto a single-page pamphlet.

Joseph the Righteous

What we know about the immediate context and the possible intent behind *The Story* comes from four rather disparate—yet equally problematic—groups of sources: (1) *The Story* itself; (2) the published writings of Christoph David Bernard as well as his legal deposition; (3) the documents created by the inquisition committee; and (4) four annotated translations of *The Story*, which appeared almost immediately after the publication of the original, as well as a few other related pamphlets. None of these sources are unbiased, and all of them contain interesting contradictions. Taken together, however, they help paint a potentially very revealing picture of Schloss and his immediate social circle in the aftermath of Oppenheimer's execution.

The author of *The Story* identifies himself in the text only as Schloss's companion during the visit to the Herrenhaus. ("Witnesses to his last will and testament were the secretary and other persons, as well as myself and Rabbi Mordechai Schloss.") Who was this author, then? In his detailed account of the same meeting, Bernard usually called this man Jew Seligmann—which could mean several different Jews who went by this name in late-1730s Stuttgart[91]—and the inquisition committee, in referring to the same individual, used two other names, Seligmann Schlachter and Salomon Schächter. Finally, Schloss's future son-in-law—the man who was attacked in May by an errant stone—was known among Christians by the surname Seligmann, but his given name was Callman, not Schlachter or Salomon, and among Jews he went by the only glancingly related name of Callman Bing. Luckily, Bernard clarifies this confusion for us. As a convert who straddled multiple social worlds, Bernard knew that although different groups used different names for *The Story*'s author, they all meant the same person. According to several different passages in Bernard's writings, Jew Seligmann, also known as Seligmann Schlachter and Salomon Schächter, was Schloss's soon-to-be second son-in-law and consequently the same man the Württemberg authorities usually called Callman Seligmann and the Jews Callman Bing.[92]

The second important clue about the creation of *The Story* is its very language. Despite its first paragraph, which is written in Hebrew, *The Story* is predominantly a Yiddish text, a fact that places it quite firmly within a large group of seventeenth- and eighteenth-century Yiddish sources that reported contemporary events to Jewish communities across Europe. We know from the work of historian Chava Turniansky that such texts depicted a wide variety of events, including fires, natural disasters, wars and sieges,

persecutions of Jews, trials and executions, and the deaths of rabbis and other famous men.[93] We also know that they were addressed to laypeople and educated readers alike. While *The Story*
does not check all the boxes when it comes to this genre (most
important, it does not contain rhymed verses and is therefore not
a Yiddish *lid* or poem), it shares with it the language of composition, the type of event it describes, and some common literary
devices, such as strategic omissions, hidden messages, and Juda-
ization (giving Jewish meaning to an otherwise nonreligious
event). Indeed, a comparison of *The Story* with a Yiddish poem
from late seventeenth-century Prague about the execution of a
Jew reveals many concrete parallels, including similar descriptions of the fasting of the condemned man, the refusal to convert,
the meeting with other Jews, the term "holy martyr" (*ha-kadosh*),
and much more.[94]

Seligmann's authorship notwithstanding, our sources agree
that Schloss was the moving spirit behind *The Story*, and two of
them also mention Fürth as the place of publication.[95] Where the
sources sharply diverge is on the question of the exact motivation
behind the publication of the account.

As the cause of its own creation, *The Story* mentions a request
made by Oppenheimer himself, who "asked Rabbi Mordechai
Schloss that [someone] write about how he died and send the report to all of the Jewish diaspora."[96] According to this narrative,
Oppenheimer stood behind the composition of *The Story*. Because
he couldn't write it himself, he asked Schloss to find someone to
do so and Schloss, in turn, passed the job onto his junior business
associate and soon-to-be son-in-law, Callman Seligmann.

The convert Bernard naturally disagreed with this claim very
strongly. He thought that the motivation behind *The Story* was the
arrogance of a few ignorant Jews, "who wholeheartedly rejoiced

at the opportunity to declare a new saint" for their religion.[97] It was their own perfidy, rather than Oppenheimer's supposed righteousness, that made Seligmann and Schloss publish their account. Bernard furthermore refused to accept the idea that anything could have happened during the meeting between Schloss and Oppenheimer (which he also attended) without his knowledge. As "Jew Seligmann knows all too well," Bernard wrote, "I was sent to Süss [together with Schloss and Seligmann] with this one and only intention, to pay close attention to the exchange he would have with Schloss."[98]

One doesn't need to share Bernard's cynical view of Seligmann and Schloss to suspect that there might have been more behind the publication of *The Story* than immediately meets the eye. The stark contrast between Schloss's September deposition and the post-execution account might point to a sense of guilt on Schloss's part—a change of heart not by the condemned man but by his one-time competitor. Schloss might have been motivated by more than rote obedience in granting Oppenheimer's dying request. He had his own compunctions to work out in the process.

A similar combination of factors can be seen in the case of Callman Seligmann. Unlike Schloss, Seligmann was a poor man. The account he authored after Oppenheimer's death appears so heartfelt that it is difficult to doubt its sincerity: he wrote that he didn't "have enough quills and ink to describe [Oppenheimer's] passing from this world" and that "[w]hat's more, it is difficult for me due to my great sorrow." And yet the same Seligmann also approached the inquisition committee immediately after the execution in the hope of getting some financial remuneration for his trouble in visiting Oppenheimer in prison.[99] This is not to suggest that Seligmann authored the account simply in order to make a quick buck. Rather, it is to stress that under the extreme circumstances of

Oppenheimer's execution, Württemberg's Jews had to take many things into consideration beside the question of what happened to Joseph Oppenheimer. There were bills to pay, people to support, mouths to feed. Writing about Oppenheimer had to take the past, but also the present and the future, into consideration.

And then there is one last and extremely intriguing possibility. As in Bernard's account, Jäger's *species facti,* and many other texts—premodern and modern, Jewish and non-Jewish alike—the true motivation behind the publication of *The Story of the Passing of Joseph Süss* might be contained in the text itself, albeit in a hidden way, as a semisecret code or message. (Embedding secret codes—*remazim*—in their texts was a common practice among Jews in the early modern period as a way of evading censors, keeping the less educated in the dark, and so on.) Seligmann seems to suggest the use of *remazim* when he states that when it comes to the meaning of a certain episode in Oppenheimer's life, "anyone of intelligence can understand it," even if he himself is not allowed to openly state what it is.[100] Seligmann's claim that Schloss and Oppenheimer also "spoke alone and I am forbidden to say what they spoke" strengthens this suspicion further. If he was truly forbidden to say anything at all about this conversation, he should perhaps not have mentioned it in the first place. But if there is a secret message in *The Story,* what could it be?

One of the four German translators of *The Story,* echoing a widespread contemporary leitmotif,[101] raised one possibility. "Joseph the Righteous" (*Yosef ha-Tsadik*) was the common Jewish appellation for the biblical Joseph, the famous interpreter of dreams who was sold into slavery by his jealous brothers. Was it a mere coincidence that *The Story* kept referring to Oppenheimer with a similar phrase? The anonymous translator also found it interesting that *The Story* mentioned the Torah portion Beshalach in the text. Other than the reference to Passover 1737, this is the only time *The Story* makes a reference to a story other than itself. The translator knew, of course, about the Israelites' Exodus, commemorated in the Jewish feast of Passover, and in a footnote to his translation he wrote that when he looked up the Torah portion Beshalach, he immediately noticed that it contained a reference, right in the first few verses, to the fulfillment of the Israelites' promise to bring the bones of Joseph the Righteous with them when they eventually left Egypt for the Promised Land. In his account, the convert Bernard claimed that Oppenheimer had pleaded with him to bury his bones according to Jewish ritual, and we know from the work of Hellmut Haasis that the inquisition committee feared the Jews might try to do just that and consequently placed a guard next to the gibbet containing Oppenheimer's corpse.[102] The unnamed translator of *The Story* thought along similar lines. The mentioning of Beshalach and the repeated references to Joseph Oppenheimer as righteous had a special meaning.[103] *The Story*, the translator concluded, contained a clear message that the Jews planned to rebury the bones of this, "their modern-day Joseph the Righteous," just as they had done with those of the biblical Joseph before him.

* * *

It is of course impossible to know for certain what lay behind Schloss's and Seligmann's publication of *The Story*. Unlike the one who can "probe the heart and discern hidden motives" (Jeremiah 17:10), we do not enjoy direct access to Schloss's and Seligmann's inner thoughts. In the particular case of these two Jews, the problem is further compounded by their account's many ambiguous passages. What was the true intention behind the inclusion of the reference to Beshalach, for instance? Should we read anything into the term "Joseph the Righteous"? Is there anything unusual about Schloss and Seligmann referring to their coreligionists as

Israelites (*beney yisra'el*) rather than, simply, Jews? And most intriguingly: Why does *The Story* mention the emotional conversation between Oppenheimer and Schloss only to add that it cannot say anything about its contents?

It is possible and indeed likely that there is nothing unusual about *The Story*, that it is just another Yiddish pamphlet about a Jewish criminal turned martyr, one among several dozens we know about.[104] And yet the detailed documentation about Schloss's life presented in the preceding pages, together with *The Story*'s repeated allusions to Joseph the Righteous, the Israelites, and even the scene in which Oppenheimer falls on Schloss's neck and "cries and shouts a great deal" raise another possibility, highly speculative though it may be. Schloss and Seligmann may have consciously modeled *The Story* on the life of the biblical Joseph, and they may have done so with a very specific purpose in mind.

It is important to stress, first of all, that any contemporary reader with a modicum of biblical literacy would have been familiar with some version of the account of Joseph's life. He or she would have known about the conspiracy against Joseph by his brothers, his being sold into servitude, and the time he spent in prison after being falsely accused of trying to rape his master Potiphar's wife. The reader would have also been familiar with the story of how Joseph eventually emerged as Pharaoh's powerful advisor and how, many years after he had left home, he met his brothers in Egypt, revealed his true identity to them, and forgave them for all they had done to him.

Schloss's and Seligmann's Yiddish-reading audience didn't need to have a good command of Hebrew or Aramaic in order to know the basic outlines of Joseph's story. Beside the men's cheder lessons, and beside, too, the weekly readings of the Torah in the synagogue, Jews of both sexes discussed the Exodus during Passover, and all of them had plenty of access to the story in Yiddish. The fourteenth-century Cambridge Yiddish Codex, the earliest known literary document in Yiddish, already contains a vernacular version of the story of the false attempted rape allegation against Joseph the Righteous, and the many popular early modern Yiddish renderings of biblical stories such as the important compilations *Ma'assebuch* and *Tseno Ureno* (*Ts'ena u-R'ena*) include valuable comments about the same biblical episode as well. Indeed, in the first decade of the eighteenth century, the story of Joseph the Righteous was the topic of a Purimspiel right at Schloss's and Seligmann's doorstep in the Judengasse in Frankfurt.[105] On at least one occasion, it had already even served as an allegory for the story of another famous court Jew, Berend Lehmann of Halberstadt.[106]

Some of the Yiddish accounts of Joseph's story portray him as a victim of false allegations.[107] They emphasize that it was Potiphar's wife who tried to seduce Joseph, not the other way around. If Schloss and Seligmann tried to invoke this particular interpretation in *The Story*, they engaged in what we may roughly call the inversion of the inquisition committee's account: rather than Oppenheimer being a rapist (as Jäger, for instance, tried to suggest), Schloss and Seligmann represent him as an innocent victim of rape allegations. This interpretation would fit in nicely with other creative interpretations in *The Story*, such as the claim that Oppenheimer fasted for religious reasons (rather than having his food rations reduced drastically by the inquisition committee, as the trial records show), or that during Passover of 1737 he decided to subsist only on bread, water, and turnips. According to the inquisition committee's reports, Oppenheimer was sick at that time and unable to eat even had he wanted to.[108]

Perhaps even more intriguing as possible candidates for *The Story*'s hidden message are several important interpretations of the opening lines of the very Torah portion *The Story* mentions, including the interpretation in *Tseno Ureno* and its own source, the ancient collection of legends *Genesis Rabbah*. According to these accounts, as the Israelites were about to leave Egypt, they were preoccupied with their silver and gold, caring for their own property above all else. Moses was the only exception. He remembered the Israelites' old promise to Joseph to take his bones with them to the Promised Land. If Schloss and Seligmann intended to use this story as a parable about Joseph Oppenheimer's case, they seem to have cast themselves in the role of Moses, and other Jews—think here of Jacob Ulmann, Maram Kahn, Isaac Salomon Landau, and perhaps even Elias Hayum—as those greedy Israelites who cared about property and money instead of their obligation to their (dead) brother. Such a reading would emphasize the negative role of many Jews in Oppenheimer's story. After all, didn't many of them envy him? Didn't some of them even betray him?

This brings us to the final, most extreme, and most poignant speculation about Schloss's and Seligmann's possible hidden message. In *The Story*, Schloss and Seligmann do not enumerate Oppenheimer's "transgressions against the almighty God and against human beings," and they insist that "neither we nor any members of the Jewish faith should ponder upon them until the arrival of the Messiah." *The Story* is about a final forgiveness. It is about leaving the factual accuracy of Oppenheimer's past aside. What he did or did not do is now irrelevant.

In the Jewish tradition, the story of the biblical Joseph has often been interpreted through a similar lens.[109] In the Bible, much happens after Joseph recognizes his brothers in Egypt, but eventually he forgives them for having betrayed him. When he finally decides to reveal his identity to them, he first goes to a room in his house and weeps bitterly. Then he goes outside, reveals his identity to his brothers, and falls and weeps on the neck of his younger brother Benjamin, who was still very young when Joseph was sold into slavery. Finally, he kisses all the other brothers and weeps over their necks, too. Significantly, they do not reciprocate the gesture.

We are now finally in a position to clearly state what is surely the most speculative version of what passed between Schloss and Oppenheimer after the latter, in the words of *The Story*, "fell upon his [Schloss's] neck, and cried and shouted a great deal." When Joseph Süss saw Schloss, he didn't only tell him to bury his bones according to the Jewish tradition. Like his ancient namesake, he also wept three times: once over his own fate, once over his closest family, and once over his Jewish brethren, including Schloss, whom he forgave despite all they had done to him. Interpreted in this way, *The Story* truly does become an account about Joseph and his brothers, complete with a land of Egypt, a prince and his Israelite advisor, brotherly competition and betrayal, imprisonment, and eventual forgiveness and reconciliation. Most important, for a brief and fleeting moment we might finally be hearing parts of Schloss's conversation with Oppenheimer in the Herrenhaus. The Bible tells this story in a way that takes one's breath away. When Joseph finally confronted his brothers, after all those years and all that had passed between them, he fell on their necks, kissed them, and cried. "I am Joseph your brother, whom you sold into the land of Egypt. Now therefore be not grieved, nor angry with yourselves, that you sold me hither . . . for it was not you who sent me hither, but God" (Genesis 45:5–8).[110]

Fourth Conversation

AUTHOR: So, what do you think?

READER: I think it's a very powerful way of ending the story. The chapter is also very well structured and the documentation supporting it is detailed to a fault. Halfway through the reading, I asked myself why you were discussing such minute details as who Schloss's two sons-in-law were. By the time I finished the last paragraph, I could see your point.

AUTHOR: I hear a "but" coming.

READER: I don't have a "but" so much as a series of interrelated observations. The first one is this: One doesn't have to be persuaded by your argument about the ultimate intention behind the publication of *The Story* to appreciate your placing the stories of the two Josephs side by side. If nothing else, it helps us stretch the power of our historical imagination. For instance, while reading the chapter I couldn't help thinking that both stories contain not only scenes of brotherly competition and betrayal, but also a father figure over whose favor the brothers compete: Jacob in the biblical story of Joseph and his brothers, the duke in the case of Oppenheimer and other Württemberg court Jews. Juxtaposing the two stories sharpens our sensibilities as readers in both directions. In fact, I just reread the relevant chapters in Genesis, and your story about Schloss, Seligmann, and Oppenheimer made me see the biblical Joseph in a new light. A proto court Jew is not a bad description for what he was.

AUTHOR: I am very pleased to hear you say this.

READER: At the same time, I do not regard the chapter as completely convincing, either. Indeed, I share the chapter's own

assessment that its reading of what passed between Oppenheimer, Schloss, and Seligmann in the Herrenhaus is extremely
speculative. As far as we know, Schloss and Seligmann never
published anything other than *The Story*, and nowhere are we
presented with evidence that either one of these Jews was so-
phisticated enough to come up with the nuanced message the
chapter ultimately ascribes to them.

AUTHOR: So you think I have overintellectualized the whole
thing?

READER: Perhaps. And even if you haven't, you must know that
the biblical story of Joseph and his brothers is so rich and
open-ended that comparing it with *The Story* opens many interpretative avenues, not only the one you yourself follow in
the case of Schloss and Seligmann.

AUTHOR: There is no disagreement between us about this point.
Recall that the chapter explicitly mentions how one of the four
German translators held his own views about the intention behind *The Story's* publication, views he too based on the text's
allusions to the biblical Joseph.

READER: I would like to offer a third interpretation as well, if I
may. In my reading, *The Story* is less about the relationships
between different members within the Jewish community in
Württemberg than about the personal transformation of Joseph Oppenheimer on the eve of his death. *The Story* tells us
that although Oppenheimer had committed many transgressions against "the almighty God and against human beings,"
he was in fact a changed person after his arrest and "wholeheartedly regretted the transgressions he had committed." Especially illuminating in this regard is *The Story's* claim that
Oppenheimer's transfer from Hohen Asperg to Stuttgart "was

tantamount to a first death." According to many religious traditions, a major spiritual event in one's life can so transform a human being that afterward he or she cannot be considered again as the same person at all. I think this is what Schloss and Seligmann meant when they wrote that "neither we nor any members of the Jewish faith can ponder upon [Oppenheimer's transgressions] until the arrival of the Messiah." Upon realizing his imminent death, Oppenheimer deeply repented for the transgressions he had committed and was thus transformed into someone else. His old ego had died already several days before his physical body was strangled on the gallows.

AUTHOR: I like your interpretation so much that I'd like to develop it even further. The foremost Jewish exegete of the entire Pentateuch, Rabbi Shlomo Yitzchaki (commonly known as Rashi), mentions the possibility that a man may die more than once. Indeed, Rashi makes this point in his interpretation of the very story of Joseph and his brothers. According to the Bible, after Joseph's brothers had sold him into slavery, they misled their father Jacob to believe his beloved son had been devoured by a wild beast. Jacob's pain was so acute, Rashi explains in his commentary, that it was tantamount to a first death; Jacob felt completely abandoned by God, as only the death of a child can do. Many years later, when Jacob received the news that Joseph was alive after all, his spirit revived and he said, "I shall die this time [that is, having died once already] having seen your face and knowing you are still alive" (Genesis 37:35; 45:27; 46:30, with Rashi commentary).

READER: This brings me to my final observation. That you so readily accept an interpretation that is diametrically opposed to yours is quite curious. Why aren't you trying to hold your ground a little longer? Moreover, throughout the chapter you have made many allusions to the biblical story of Joseph and his brothers even when Schloss and Seligmann did not do so themselves. Consider the very title of the chapter and the invocation of famous verses from the books of Genesis and Exodus (for example, "In the beginning was the ghetto"; "And then arose a new king in Egypt"). I take all of this to mean that you want your readers to think about your account in the same way you thought about Bernard's. You have been trying to accomplish something through these repeated references to, and interpretations of, the biblical story. What matters to you is less that your readers be convinced by your particular interpretation than that they view Oppenheimer's story through a biblical prism.

AUTHOR: I like where you're heading with this. Please continue.

READER: And then it finally hit me. You do many things in this chapter: you describe the events of Schloss's life, you analyze communal and state documents, you quote from legal depositions, and you try to speculate about the true intentions behind the publication of *The Story*. But you also do something else, above and beyond all these activities: you try to fulfill a request.

AUTHOR: If your suspicion is justified—and I don't say it is—let me at least state that it was certainly not done intentionally. I did not set out to write this chapter with the task of fulfilling a long-forgotten request in mind.

READER: This only makes it all the more interesting. But let me first of all spell out to our readers what request we're referring to. If, as Schloss and Seligmann claim in *The Story*, Oppenheimer had indeed instructed them to spread his side of the story, your chapter helps to achieve that goal. And if, as Schloss and Seligmann also claim, Oppenheimer wished that people would not discuss his guilt and instead study the Torah in his honor, the chapter helps him achieve those goals, too. On a deep structural level, this entire chapter seems like an attempt to fulfill what Schloss and Seligmann say was Oppenheimer's last will and testament. Haven't we just read what seems like Oppenheimer's version of his own story? Have we not also bracketed the question of his guilt? And have we not, through the repeated allusions to the story of Joseph the Righteous and through at least three different interpretations of it, have we not, I say, also studied the Torah, at least for a little while?

AUTHOR: What you say of this chapter may very well apply to the book as a whole.

READER: Indeed. It is a strange but moving thought. And its logical conclusion is this: intentionally or not, this book implies that it too is part of Oppenheimer's story and perhaps that I, as a reader, play a part in the story as well. By reading this chapter and this book as a whole, I fulfill what Schloss and Seligmann claimed had been Oppenheimer's final request.

AUTHOR: I like this line of thought very much. You know, a text can be a claim about reality, and it can also be used polemically to intervene in an ongoing extratextual conversation. Jäger's *species facti* is an example of the former case, Bernard's account of the latter. But I think we often forget that composing or reading a text can also be a simple act of kindness, above and beyond all descriptions and interpretations, praises and condemnations. In *The Story*, Schloss and Seligmann are doing that kind of textual work themselves. They do not list Oppenheimer's transgressions; they insist no one should think about his guilt until the arrival of the Messiah; and they even include enough mystery in their account ("anyone of intelligence can understand it," "I am not allowed to openly state what it is") to entice us to open the Bible and study it. *The Story* thus helps us do what it prescribes.

READER: Surely, then, a book that holds these aspirations cannot be considered a work of professional history?

AUTHOR: Your question is based on the assumption that the past is dead and buried and that the role of the historian is to keep it that way. Thomas Mann, in his own rendering of the story of Joseph and his brothers, knew better. The dead are among us, Mann claimed; they direct their gaze at us, and we gaze back at them in return. The clear separation between the living and the dead is consequently both real and fictional. The dead are present in the land of the living, which is another way of saying that we, the living, always and everywhere, inevitably also inhabit the land of the dead.

FIGURE 9. Unknown artist. Frontispiece to volume 16 of David Fassman, *Gespräche in dem Reiche derer Todten* (Leipzig: Wolfgang Deer, 1737). *Source*: BSB München, Res/h.misc. 83–226.

CHAPTER 4

In the Land of the Dead

"Confess the whole truth about your
life, Jew! No concealment can help
you now, in this place."
—David Fassmann, *Conversations in
the Realm of the Dead*, 1738

In a fictional account published about three months after Oppenheimer's execution, the notorious court Jew, now a resident of the
netherworld, tells the story of his own death. The account begins
with a description of Oppenheimer's spirit leaving its dead body
near Stuttgart and traveling toward Acheron, the river that sepa-
rates the land of the living from the realm of the dead. Then,
crossing the river on Charon's mythical boat, Oppenheimer meets
the spirits of other dead courtiers and gives them what he claims
is a full and honest account of his earthly existence. Oppenheimer's tale covers all aspects of his life, from his birth in Heidelberg, through his many criminal actions in Württemberg, to the
events of his arrest, trial, and execution. It is, both literally and
figuratively, an incredible story.

Though obviously fictitious and at times outright bizarre, Oppenheimer's purported story from beyond the grave is also extraordinarily telling: it teaches us a great deal about David Fassmann, the author of the account; it reveals an equal amount about early eighteenth-century political culture, of which Oppenheimer's case was an expression; and it even provides some essential clues about Oppenheimer himself and our own uneasy relationship to his story. As such, it is a fitting concluding chapter to the present, polyphonic history.

Leipzig

Halfway through his life's journey, at age thirty-two, David Fassmann settled in the city of Leipzig. He had grown up in Oberwiesenthal, a small village in Germany's remote Harz Mountains.[1] Having lost his father at a young age, Fassmann was raised by his maternal grandfather, Oberwiesenthal's Lutheran pastor.[2] The old cleric taught the boy several languages and made sure his handwriting was especially handsome. In 1697, Fassmann began attending school in the town of Ansbach, and four years later he left for the University of Altdorf near Nuremberg. What Fassmann intended to study there is unknown.[3] The grandfather died shortly after Fassmann started attending lectures, and the young man—apparently completely penniless—had to forgo his secondary education and look for employment.[4]

Many years later, just before he published Oppenheimer's fictitious confession from beyond the grave, Fassmann jotted down a few more (questionable) comments about his own youth and upbringing. According to these autobiographical notes, Fassmann led an exceptionally adventurous life after leaving Altdorf. He worked in the cities of Nuremberg, Regensburg, Dresden, and Warsaw; he traveled across eastern Europe, through present-day

Germany, France, England, and Italy; he was a scribe, a travel companion, and a soldier; he took part in one great war and many smaller campaigns; and he met some of the great rulers of the age, including the pope, the Russian czar, Louis XIV, and even Carl Alexander of Württemberg. According to Fassmann's autobiographical notes, the foreign languages and perfect cursive handwriting his grandfather had taught him never failed to gain him employment in different courts and cities. Through his many odd jobs, he acquired an insider's view of European politics. Through his extensive travels, he developed what he described as a "cat-like ability to always land on one's feet no matter how violent the fall."[5]

Extensive research in Oberwiesenthal, Ansbach, Nuremberg, Dresden, Halle, and several British archives could corroborate very few of Fassmann's claims about his pre-Leipzig existence. Fassmann reports, for instance, that he worked as a clerk in Nuremberg in the 1710s and that he was part of the Saxon delegation to Frankfurt am Main in 1711. And yet the extremely thorough records of Nuremberg's employees in the 1710s never mention a David Fassmann, and an extraordinary detailed list of the Saxon delegation's participants in 1711, down to the cooks and the cooks' assistants, does not mention Fassmann by name. Similarly suspicious are Fassmann's claims that he was associated at one point with the British Lord Chancellor, that he traveled to Italy in the late 1710s, and that he spent time studying with the famous theologian Hermann August Francke in the city of Halle. No independent documentation corroborates any of these claims, and some evidence even seems to refute them.[6] The only semi-reliable information we possess about Fassmann's life before his move to Leipzig is that he was a very heavy drinker, an aspect of his life on which both Fassmann and his enemies agreed. In his autobiographical account of 1737, Fassmann admits that he developed a drinking problem early in life; his only known portrait, drawn by one of his bitterest critics, depicts him with a beer glass in one of his hands and a wine decanter tied to a rope around his neck (figure 10).[7]

Whatever he had done earlier in life, Fassmann's presence in Leipzig is documented from late 1717 on. The Saxon city he entered that year was still a walled settlement, surrounded by lines of fortifications, bastions, towers, and a water-filled moat. Its closed appearance notwithstanding, in many respects Leipzig was a remarkably open place. In the first two decades of the eighteenth century, an influx of migrants doubled the city's population, from 15,000 inhabitants to slightly over 30,000. Outside influence came in other ways, too. The city had a newly constructed stock exchange, which had been built according to the latest fashion in Italian architecture, as well as older structures such as the city hall and several other civic buildings all of which one visitor described as "beautiful and absolutely magnificent."[8] Leipzig also possessed a famous boys' music conservatory, the St. Thomas School, soon to be headed by one Johann Sebastian Bach. Because Bach's activities in Leipzig included directing the music in all of the city's churches, at many civic events, and occasionally even in one of the city's famous coffeehouses, Fassmann may very well have heard many of Bach's pieces live just as the great German musician performed or conducted them for the first time.

Where Fassmann first settled in Leipzig is not documented, but after a while, he found a permanent abode in the so-called Stepfen House, about three hundred yards west of Leipzig's main marketplace and about the same distance north of the St. Thomas Church.[9] In 1723, he is documented living there, giving private language lessons. A second major location of Fassmann's activities

FIGURE 10. Unknown artist. "The Court Fool" (caricature of
David Fassmann), ca. 1736. Frontispiece to Friedrich August Hackmann,
*Der, im Wein-Faß begrabene Paul Gundling, Geheimer Staats- Kriegs- und
Domainen-Rath, raisonniret mit David Faßmann . . .* (Freybourg, 1736?).
Source: UB Halle.

was the printing house of Wolfgang Deer in the Grimmaische Lane, in the eastern part of Leipzig. This part of the city was adjacent to Leipzig's world-famous university, with its "innumerable scholars whom it does not take much to engage in conversation."[10] Just three years before Fassmann's arrival in Leipzig, the university's theologians had caused a sensation. Though anti-Jewish sentiments were definitely common in early eighteenth-century Leipzig—Jews were not allowed to settle permanently in the city before the mid-nineteenth century—in 1714 the theologians published an expert report condemning blood libels against Jews as utterly absurd.[11] In Leipzig, as in many other places in early modern Germany, attitudes toward Jews were by no means uniform or simplistic.

That so many people moved to Leipzig in the early eighteenth century was a consequence of the city's prosperity, and that, in turn, owed much to Leipzig's trade fairs. Over the centuries, Leipzig had managed to acquire a special Imperial privilege to hold three two-week-long fairs every year: after the first Sunday following Michaelmas (September 29), on New Year's Day, and three weeks after Easter. The special privilege gave Leipzig a veritable monopoly over large-scale trade, considering that no other town within a seventy-mile radius was allowed to hold a fair at the same time as the Saxon city. The success of the fairs was also due to Leipzig's advantageous geopolitical location. Unlike its rival trade city Frankfurt, Leipzig was situated firmly within the commercially dynamic Protestant north, and it remained unaffected by the ongoing military struggles between Louis XIV's France and the small southwestern German states, including Württemberg.[12] Most important, Leipzig was located at the intersection of several crucial trade routes. As such, it was an ideal meeting place for international merchants, a hub or central node in the European—

and even Eurasian—trade network. "All the world's curious objects, all conceivable precious things pass through this trade city,"
proclaimed one eighteenth-century author.[13] The city was full of
foreigners, reported another: "Hungarians, Transylvanians, Turks,
Greeks, Arabs, Chinese, Persians, Czechs, Russians, Dutch, and
Englishmen are present here, all wearing their special costumes."[14]
The writer Gotthold Ephraim Lessing put it best in 1749 when he
wrote to his mother, "I am traveling now to Leipzig, where one
can see the whole world writ small, as it were."[15]

Many eighteenth-century writers, including Fassmann, were
deeply interested in international politics. Moving to Leipzig
made sense to them. From there, they did not have to travel far to
collect information for their stories; they stayed in Leipzig, where
the world and its stories came to them. It is no coincidence that
the world's first daily newspaper appeared in Leipzig in 1650 or
that the most important German political journal of the early
eighteenth century, *Die europäische Fama*, was printed there as
well. In fact, before 1750, the vast majority of German journals—174 out of 240—were published in Leipzig.[16] The Saxon city
was the veritable epicenter of the German news network.

Above all, perhaps, early eighteenth-century Leipzig was famous as a center for the book trade. Unlike France or England,
the Holy Roman Empire of the German Nation was not a centralized polity; it did not have a clear political or cultural center like
Paris or London. The commerce in books during the Leipzig fairs
developed as a distinct response to this situation. Instead of cor-
responding with, or sending their wares to, hundreds of small-
and medium-size towns across Germany, writers, printers, publishers, and booksellers met during the Leipzig fairs, examined
new titles, exchanged existing ones, signed contracts, and had
their wares examined by the university scholars who also served

as Saxony's book censors.[17] Though the annual fairs in Frankfurt served much the same purpose, it was clear by the early eighteenth century that Leipzig was becoming the center of the book trade in central Europe, eclipsing its rival city on the river Main especially with regard to German (rather than Latin) books and Protestant publications.[18]

Most of the book trade in Leipzig took place at two of the main city markets and in a handful of streets around the university, including the Grimmaische Lane, where Deer's publishing house was located. It was in this part of town that book traders unloaded their wares after arriving for the fair and exchanged them for other books or (more rarely, because of possible tax implications) paid for new ones in cash or bills of exchange. More than any other German city, Leipzig was flooded by books of various origins, quality, and type. In the late 1730s, while Fassmann was collecting materials for his account of Oppenheimer's life, Leipzig had twenty permanent bookstores, fifteen printing houses, twenty-two bookbinding stores, eleven copperplate engraving ateliers, and three type foundries. During the Michaelmas and Easter fairs, these numbers swelled dramatically. In 1740, 187 major book firms from no fewer than sixty-nine different locations across Europe set up booths at the fair, while many other traders who could not afford the high travel costs were represented in Leipzig by local agents.[19] Even if they originated or eventually ended up elsewhere, a vast number of books, tracts, journals, newspapers, broadsides, and leaflets passed through Leipzig at one point or another. This was also true for much of the literature about Oppenheimer's trial and execution, including Bernard's account of the Herrenhaus meeting, a German translation of Schloss's and Seligmann's pamphlet, and printed copies of the verdict Jäger and his associates reached, all of which, as we shall see, were read by Fassmann, personally, in Leipzig.

From the fall of 1717 until his death a quarter of a century later, Fassmann was a fixture of the Leipzig book fairs. His "book fair works,"[20] as he once called them, included writing pieces for his publisher Deer early enough so that the latter could show them to the censor, then print, sell, or exchange them at Michaelmas or Easter. Deer paid Fassmann shortly after the fair. This overall arrangement never changed. After his move to Leipzig, Fassmann continued to give private language lessons at least until 1723, and between 1726 and 1731 he spent five eventful years in Prussia.[21] Even then, however, he did not stop sending his materials to Deer in Leipzig. From 1717 on, publishing in the Leipzig fairs remained a constant feature of his life.

Indeed, once he had settled in Leipzig, Fassmann started publishing almost immediately. His first book came out late that same year. It showed few signs of the brilliance and success that were to come, though it did demonstrate how Fassmann had already started concentrating on the topic that would occupy his entire career: contemporary courtly politics. The book was a rather tedious examination of the ongoing political struggles in England between the Whig and Tory parties, which Fassmann claimed (perhaps falsely) he had experienced firsthand a few years earlier while serving as the travel companion of a relative of the Lord High Chancellor of Great Britain.[22] Over the following twenty-five years, Fassmann published many other works, including three princely biographies, a long book about various political and amorous affairs in European courts, a manual on writing good poetry, and a whole journal he devoted, in the spirit of a beloved eighteenth-century genre, to the adventures and observations of a fictional Chinese visitor to Europe.[23] "So long as God wills it," Fassmann wrote in the year of Oppenheimer's trial, "I shall continue to enjoy reading books and writing them."[24] Leipzig was the perfect place for both activities.

All of his other literary projects notwithstanding, Fassmann devoted the lion's share of his energy after 1717 to one particular literary project. Very soon after his move to Leipzig, he hit on a simple idea that, in just a few years, made him a household name across Germany, placed his finances on a sound basis, and even earned him a royal invitation from the Prussian king in Berlin. Fassmann's idea also brought him countless imitators, much envy and bitterness, and even outright enemies who hoped to see him hanging from the gallows, and the sooner the better. Like many successful writers before and after him, Fassmann did not create something out of nothing but instead adapted an old literary device to a new context. The new context was the proliferation of Baroque political culture in central Europe in the decades after about 1650; the old literary device was the ancient genre of the dialogues of the dead.

Katabasis

The history of dialogues with the dead extends back thousands of years. Such dialogues appear in fictional descriptions of a descent into the realm of the dead—*katabasis* in Greek—in the Akkadian *Epic of Gilgamesh* in the third millennium B.C.E., in Homer's *Odyssey*, in Virgil's *Aeneid*, and in Dante Alighieri's *Divine Comedy*, not to mention many lesser works before or since. For Fassmann, most important among such models was a group of dialogues of the dead composed by the second-century Roman satirist Lucian.[25] If we want to understand Fassmann, we consequently have to understand Lucian first.

In his dialogues, Lucian transports his readers to Hades, the Greek realm of the dead, and introduces them to the afterlife's inhabitants. Here they find Pluto, the ruler of Hades; Charon, the boatman who transfers the newly deceased across the river

Acheron; and Cerberus, the terrifying multiheaded dog who guards the entrance to the afterlife. Here, too, are famous historical and mythological figures such as Alexander the Great, Achilles, Agamemnon, and Hannibal, as well as some famous Greek writers and thinkers, like Socrates and (a favorite of Lucian's) the satirist Mennipus.

Before climbing onto Charon's boat, Lucian's dead leave behind all of their possessions. These have no meaning in the afterlife. Then, while the ancient ferryman carries them across the river and past Cerberus, Hades's veteran inhabitants watch them, bemused by the new arrivals' reluctance to accept their fate. Once they safely disembark on the shores of Hades, the dead often change their minds. "Now I realize that glory is useless, however much men above hymn its praises," says the dead Achilles in one of Lucian's dialogues, then continues: "Among the dead all have but equal honor, and neither the beauty nor the strength we had remain with us, but we lie buried in the same darkness, all of us quite alike, no one better than the other." Another of Lucian's characters repeats the same point. "No one is handsome here. In Hades all are equal, and all alike."[26]

Death as the Great Equalizer is one of several elements that characterize Lucian's dialogues and, though they are by no means completely identical, Fassmann's dialogues as well. The realm of the dead recognizes no distinctions of time, place, or status between its inhabitants; it brings together what life kept apart. Thus, the dead King Philip of Macedon can join his son Alexander in conversation about the latter's passing (which took place a decade after King Philip's own death), while Alexander, in his turn, can speak with the famous Carthaginian general Hannibal, who died a century and a half after him. In death, the elevated can speak with the poor, gods with mortals, philosophers with one another, and Charon with all. Inhabitants of the netherworld can approach one another without fear and strike up a conversation. When, in one of Lucian's dialogues, Heracles threatens the philosopher Diogenes with a thrashing for his purported insolence, the latter's reply leaves him speechless. "Why should I fear you now?" asks Diogenes, "I have died once and for all."[27]

The brilliance of Lucian's dialogues and the great influence they exerted over the centuries can be attributed to other factors beside their ability to cross boundaries of time, space, and personal status. Three in particular seem to have influenced Fassmann. The first was the use of the dialogue form itself, which allows Lucian's characters to compare and verbally engage with one another in a way other forms of discourse—Fassmann especially detested the rigid form of the scholarly dispute—could never achieve.[28] Lucian did not pick out his characters randomly. He chose them so that their conversations would shed light on a given topic. Thus, in one dialogue Lucian includes Alexander, Hannibal, and Scipio Africanus (the Roman general who defeated Hannibal in 202 B.C.E.), in order to discuss the meaning of military success, and in another he engages the Greek heroes Ajax and Agamemnon in a conversation in order to make a point about the Homeric sagas.

Another important aspect of Lucian's dialogues is their unmistakable slapstick humor. The ferryman Charon, for instance, repeatedly curses his passengers, only to be repaid in the same coin. "I'll throttle you, you blackguard, if you don't pay for your journey," he says to the newly deceased Mennipus in one dialogue, to which Mennipus replies, "And I'll smash your head with a blow from my stick."[29] Laughter is crucial in Lucian's realm of the dead. Thus, when Charon issues orders to his ghostly passengers before they climb aboard his boat, he tells them to strip themselves of all earthly possessions: money, beauty, and flattery have no place in the netherworld. Laughter, on the other hand, is allowed.[30]

One final element of Lucian's dialogues was especially crucial for Fassmann's adaptation of the genre after 1718. Lucian's land of the dead is a place of certitude. Now that the interlocutors have all died, they could finally look with direct eyes at their actions in the world of the living. This is one reason for the dead's incessant laughter. "On earth laughter is fraught with uncertainty, and people often wonder whether anyone at all is quite sure about what follows death, but here one is able to laugh endlessly without any doubt."[31] Though Lucian's characters do lie occasionally, their prevarications are always exposed as useless. What could the dead possibly hope to gain by not telling the truth? King Philip, Alexander the Great's father, makes this point clear in one of Lucian's dialogues. When the king senses his dead son is trying to evade the truth even after death, he asks him, "Aren't you ashamed? Won't you learn to forget your pride, and know yourself, and realize that you are now dead?"[32]

The Truthfulness of Dead Courtiers

Imitations of Lucian's dialogues were not unheard of in the early eighteenth century. A few decades before Fassmann moved to Leipzig, the celebrated French writer Fontenelle had composed a brilliant adaptation of the genre, and only six years before Fassmann began to publish his own dialogues, Fontenelle's compatriot, François Fénelon, had published his. The clear influence of such writers on his own work notwithstanding, Fassmann differed from his predecessors in important respects. He drilled down with the same literary equipment, as it were, but in a new field. Sometime in early 1718, he decided to imitate Lucian's dialogues in order to explore political, rather than moral, issues. Almost as soon as he broke ground, he realized he had hit a subterranean reservoir of immense dimensions. The result was a remarkable commercial success.

Fassmann's concentration on contemporary politics manifested itself above all in the typical interlocutors of his dialogues. Earlier imitations of Lucian tended to include gods, heroes, and philosophers. Fassmann's interlocutors, on the other hand, were almost always members of the contemporary courtly world. They included monarchs, ministers, royal confessors and preachers, ladies-in-waiting, and royal mistresses. In his choice of characters, Fassmann turned the genre itself into a political message. Following a common Baroque understanding of politics that emphasized its secretive aspects, Fassmann defined courtly politics simply as "the art of simulation and dissimulation."[33] Decisions in court society were made by the prince himself and a handful of his close advisors. They alone knew the truth about what was afoot, but only once they were all dead would they ever dare tell it publicly. The message of Fassmann's dialogues is consequently contained already in his choice of genre and characters. Members of Baroque court society live in an almost phantasmagorical world, a place full of secrets and lies. Their stories are worth listening to only when they come from beyond the grave.

The political critique that stood behind Fassmann's choice of characters was also decisive in determining the topics and even length of his dialogues. Previous dialogues of the dead focused primarily on moral questions. They discussed the vanity of man, the uselessness of riches, or the respective values of ancient and modern philosophy. Fassmann's dialogues tend to concentrate on more mundane matters, usually of historical nature, though they, too, occasionally discuss lofty questions. This explains in part the extraordinary length of Fassmann's dialogues. While previous works in the genre tended to be very short, an average Fassmann dialogue runs for about seventy octavo pages. It takes much more time to discuss the intricacies of the Baroque court than the uselessness of money after death.

Quantity is also important in understanding Fassmann's oeuvre. While Lucian wrote thirty dialogues of the dead, Fénelon sixty-six, and Fontenelle thirty-one, Fassmann published close to two hundred and fifty such pieces, including four dialogues that touch on Oppenheimer's case more or less directly. In total page numbers, this means an overall production of over 18,000 octavo pages over barely two decades, without including Fassmann's many other publications during the same time. All of this certainly tells us something about Fassmann's remarkable energy. But princely courts were not unique to Baroque-era Germany, nor is lying a uniquely German trait. Why did Fassmann's dialogues sell by the thousands, then? Why was there no equivalent corpus in French or in English?

We have already seen how the book trade in Leipzig and Frankfurt developed as a response to a particularly German situation: the lack of a clear cultural center in the Holy Roman Empire. The extent and popularity of Fassmann's works seems to have owed much to the same factor. France's court society was the most celebrated of its day, and one could quite easily have written a dialogue of some of its dead members. Indeed, both Fontenelle and Fénelon wrote several conversations in that vein. But such dialogues were limited because France's court society was concentrated in Versailles and the number of influential French courtiers, let alone monarchs, was limited. How many times can a dead Louis XIV retell his life story before he becomes repetitive? The same was true in other centralized countries such as England and Spain. The centralization processes in those countries had long ago reduced the number of courts to essentially only one. There was little room there for a large number of dialogues of the dead that concentrated on politics.

The situation in the Holy Roman Empire could not have been more different. Because early eighteenth-century Germany had hundreds of different courts, a political version of Lucian's dialogues could find an almost unlimited number of possible topics and interlocutors there. This was the reservoir Fassmann discovered when he began writing his dialogues in 1718. Moreover, in the century and a half following the disastrous Thirty Years' War (1618–1648), German states were notoriously vulnerable to foreign intervention, so events in foreign courts became especially interesting to German readers. It couldn't have taken Fassmann long to realize all of this. Almost immediately after they hit the streets of Leipzig, copies of Fassmann's political adaptations of Lucian's dialogues started selling by the thousands. He called his dialogues *Conversations in the Realm of the Dead*. He promised they would not bore his readers.[34] He kept his word.

Conversations in the Realm of the Dead

Fassmann's first *Conversation* went to press late in the summer of 1718 and was on sale at the Leipzig fair in September.[35] Its two interlocutors were King Louis XIV of France (who had died in 1715) and the Holy Roman emperor Leopold I (who had died in 1705). Fassmann could hardly have chosen more predictable characters with which to start discussing court culture. Before they passed on to the world of the dead, Louis and Leopold had been the heads of the two most prominent European courts, in Versailles and Vienna, respectively.

With only minor modifications, the structure Fassmann developed for his first *Conversation* would remain the same throughout the next twenty years. After a short introduction to set the scene, the two (or, more rarely, three) interlocutors speak at length about their respective lives before a messenger arrives from the land of the living, reading a handful of newspaper and journal articles about contemporary events and listening to the interlocutors' reactions. Known simply as the Secretarius ("secretary"), this messenger might very well be a personification of Fassmann himself, since according to his own biographical notes, Fassmann had been a secretary before moving to Leipzig and he became one again in 1726 for five eventful years, as we shall soon see. Fassmann never changed the tripartite structure of his *Conversations*. It was as if the first prototype of his literary device had proven so effective that there was no need for any further modifications. His extraordinary productivity in the next two decades also owed much to the fact that he lived near his sources—Leipzig's many newspapers and human sources—and that his publisher Deer, for financial reasons, often pressed him to compose the *Conversations* very quickly. Professional scholars might have time to "devote several months to the composition of only a couple of pages," Fassmann commented once with a tinge of bitterness. As for himself, "in six months I need to produce as many *Conversations*."[36]

The fact that the *Conversations* have a uniform structure and were written in rapid succession should not be taken to imply that they contain identical content. On the contrary, once his device was ready, Fassmann could use it to explore a whole variety of life stories. Between 1718 and Oppenheimer's trial, Fassmann told the life stories of almost three hundred dead individuals, including eighty-two monarchs, nine popes, forty-nine generals, twenty-five ministers, five court ladies, and seven mistresses. The life stories he depicted side by side always shared something in common with one another. This is why he chose them in the first place. But Fassmann's characters are also always unique in some way, thus making the *Conversations* effective on at least two levels. They can be read as independent biographies or as a comparison between two or more lives.

Although Fassmann's *Conversations* enjoyed immediate commercial success, his readers also found many faults in them. Some critics were quick to point out that Fassmann's imitation of the old genre of the dialogues of the dead, written in haste, was not always of the highest literary quality. Imitating ancient authors was of fundamentally positive value in early modern Europe, but it had to be done in good taste, with elegance, and usually (though not always) in Latin. Fassmann clearly did not check these boxes. Some reviewers consequently found his *Conversations* simply quite tasteless.[37] With good reason: the *Conversations* do include a disproportionate number of assassinations, instances of excessive drinking, amorous adventures, and—especially important for understanding Oppenheimer's case—many executions, including botched ones.[38] There is a bit of the tabloid in Fassmann's *Conversations* and a whole lot of low-brow, morbid humor. In that respect, they were indeed a rather vulgar imitation of a classical genre.

But Fassmann's work also had its admirers.[39] Perhaps because of the *Conversations'* often sensationalist flavor, they proved extraordinarily popular and led to many imitations. Fassmann complained about this sincerest form of flattery with a bitterness that by the late 1730s verged on exasperation. His own dialogues, he insisted, aspired to be much more than the sensationalist rubbish of his imitators. His copycats were nothing but "apes, telling foolish, idiotic, unfounded, and nonsensical tales . . . that contribute nothing to the education of the public."[40] His own work was strikingly different. Taken together, the *Conversations* formed a general reference work for the politics of the early eighteenth century, a way one could acquaint oneself with individual figures, common themes, and general developments across Europe even if one lacked formal education. Fassmann advertised this aspect of his work explicitly as early as 1719, in the first collection of *Conversa-tions* he translated into English. The collection included, he wrote, "several great personages, deceased, that rehearse to each other the history of their life and time, and the springs [origins] of their politics and conduct, so that the whole performance is a good history of all of Europe for many years backward."[41] The point of Fassmann's *Conversations* was consequently not only to entertain, but also to educate. "The primary plan of these *Conversations*," he once wrote, "is to combine entertainment with serious reflection and history with moral judgment."[42]

Mimesis and Imitation

Fassmann always walked a fine line between truth and fiction. The dialogues themselves are of course a figment of their author's imagination, but the life stories they depict are supposedly real. This welter of the actual and fictional was fundamental to Fass-mann's literary career, not least because it allowed him to talk about court society while at the same time protecting himself from censorship. "By choosing to write the histories of persons who are long dead," Fassmann wrote on one occasion, "one is free to depict both their virtues and vices; writing about a living figure is a different matter. Here one must deal with the truth much more cautiously."[43] For similar reasons, Fassmann was also forth-right about his sources. He kept a record of—and indeed often openly cites—the very real books and journals he used in crafting his accounts.[44] This was important as a means of avoiding trouble with the censors. If a story had already been published elsewhere, its contents were not Fassmann's responsibility.

In general, Fassmann's system worked quite well. For over twenty years, thick volumes of his *Conversations* came out one after the other, almost without interruption. On three occasions, however, the system broke down, with revealing consequences. The first instance occurred in the early spring of 1725, when Russian Empress Catherine I, still very much alive, filed a complaint against Fassmann with the Saxon authorities.[45] The empress complained that Fassmann's description of her and her late husband was rude, impertinent, and false. On May 1, 1725, court officials in Leipzig acted on this complaint by interrogating the publisher Deer and then asking him to summon Fassmann to his store. Fassmann indeed appeared later that day, admitted he was the author of the relevant *Conversation*, and tried to persuade the officials he wasn't at fault. Two days later, he composed a letter in his own defense, explaining that he had based all his descriptions on already published materials and attaching copies of the exact sources he had used, complete with the relevant paragraphs underlined in dark blue pencil. The Leipzig magistrates remained unimpressed. Deer's remaining copies of the relevant *Conversation* were confiscated, an interrogation was launched into the particular censor responsible for the examination of Deer's publishing house, and Fassmann was sent to jail for four weeks.[46]

David Fassmann knew perfectly well that a prince's court was by its very structure a dangerous environment, full of cabals and intrigues, mutual suspicions and open competition. In one of his early *Conversations*, Fassmann claims that "there is no better metaphor for the court of a great prince than that of a wild, turbulent sea, full of submerged rocks one might hit at any moment and drown."[47] The court, he adds, "is a place where no friend is ever close enough not to become an enemy later. The court's soul is its secrets. For a courtier to share his inner thoughts with another amounts to giving the latter a knife with which to stab him in the back."[48] Fassmann repeats this message in a great many *Conversations*. That despite all of this he decided to move to Prussia in 1726 and become a courtier himself comes consequently as a surprise. Why he did so is unknown; that he paid a heavy price for it, on the other hand, is crystal clear.

The story of Fassmann's sojourn in Berlin is the only part of his life that is relatively well known.[49] King Frederick William of Prussia agreed with much of Fassmann's negative evaluation of contemporary Baroque courts. He hated their theatricality, ostentatious display of power and riches, wastefulness, luxury, and flattery. Unlike some of his more flamboyant peers, Frederick William dressed in the blue uniform of an ordinary officer and surrounded himself with a small group of advisors in a so-called *Tabakskollegium*—a combination of advisory board and never-ending drinking and smoking party, where hierarchy was frowned upon and brutal honesty appreciated. In some respects, the Kollegium was an attempt to achieve in real life what for Fassmann only the dead could ever hope to accomplish: a completely honest conversation between a prince and his advisors. The parallels between the true and the fictional did not stop there. It was customary in the Kollegium for members to discuss current events in a way not dissimilar to the third part of a typical Fassmann *Conversation*. As an atlas lay open on one of the side tables as reference, the king and his advisors had the most interesting news of the day read to them by Fassmann or another member of the court. Then, "having been informed about the recent past, they discussed the present and tried to draw conclusions about the future."[50]

What was imitated in this situation, and who was the imitator? A commonsensical understanding of history today is that it follows life by reflecting or representing it in writing. The ancient Greeks called this function of writing *mimesis*, which roughly translates as "imitation." According to this approach, first comes a real event or situation (for example, Oppenheimer's activities in

Stuttgart), then its textual representation (Jäger's *species facti*). Viewed in this way, the first and most important question one can ask about a historical text is whether or not it tells the truth— whether or not it represents reality faithfully. Fassmann's *Conversations* certainly have this mimetic element to them. The fictional form of the dialogues of the dead notwithstanding, the *Conversations* recount real-life stories, or at least claim to do so.

At the same time, Fassmann's sojourn in Berlin shows that the *Conversations* created something in the world rather than merely representing it retrospectively. Just like Bernard's disputation with Oppenheimer, Fassmann's *Conversations* served simultaneously as a depiction and a script, a mold into which he poured what had already been and a device with which he shaped what was yet to come. After all, the scenes of a secretary reading newspaper articles to a powerful prince began appearing in the Leipzig *Conversations* before Fassmann performed exactly the same job at Frederick William's court. There is even reason to believe that the king invited Fassmann to Berlin precisely because of what Fassmann describes in his *Conversations*, including the brutal honesty and wild humor. By becoming a member of Frederick William's court, Fassmann and the king reversed what we often tend to view as the natural order of things. They imitated literature in life rather than the other way around.

Whatever else one might say about it, it is clear that Fassmann's experience in Berlin brought out the worst in him. While at the Prussian court, Fassmann drank profusely, smoked incessantly, got into fistfights, and composed vulgar verses. He employed his wit not for the education of the public but for the entertainment of the monarch and the humiliation of fellow courtiers. The same competition, distrust, and lying he so deftly describes in his earlier *Conversations* now became part of his own and very real daily life.

The situation reached its nadir in early April 1731, when another courtier, Jacob Paul von Gundling, died at Fredrick William's court. Gundling was a former history professor who over years of heavy drinking had turned into Frederick William's court fool. After Gundling's death, the king ordered that he be buried in a wine barrel—a vulgar allusion to Gundling's alcoholism—and that Fassmann deliver a mocking eulogy in the dead man's "honor." Fassmann performed his job well, but almost immediately thereafter began to fear that he would take Gundling's place and become the "Bouffon de la Cour," as he put it.[51] The thought of this ultimate degradation made Fassmann turn violent.[52] When a local court Jew by the name of Marcus crossed him around this time, Fassmann threw him on the ground, stepped on him, and grabbed the poor man's throat with such violence that "the Jew would have expired if other people had not intervened."[53] After this incident, Fassmann fled Berlin and eventually returned to Leipzig. Having first described court society in writing and then become one of its members, Fassmann now extricated himself from it and returned to his former life as a writer.

Four years after he left Berlin, Fassmann broke one of his rules and once again paid a price. In what seems to have been an ill-considered attempt to mollify his former Prussian employer, in 1735 Fassmann published a lengthy biography of King Frederick William. This was a clear breach of Fassmann's own maxim to only write biographies of dead people. Frederick William's reaction shows that Fassmann's original intuition was right. The book's portrayal of the king was flattering enough, but when Frederick William heard of its publication, he sent a note to all booksellers in his realm, forbidding them from selling the book and announcing that a failure to deliver any unsold copies would be punishable by a large fine and, where appropriate, a corporal punishment as well.[54] When these measures proved insufficient, the king sent agents to Deer's store in Leipzig with the intention of kidnapping Fassmann and bringing him back to Berlin. Fassmann made a narrow escape, fleeing to safety amid unknown relatives in southern Germany.[55] Though he would eventually return to Leipzig, he would never attempt to write a biography of a living prince again.

All of this is interesting in and of itself, but it is also quite significant for any interpretation of Fassmann's views of Oppenheimer's case. For one thing, Fassmann's stay in Berlin contains the only recorded incident in his life that shows him engaging in person with a court Jew. This exception proves a rule: Before Oppenheimer's trial, Fassmann never dedicated a *Conversation* to a Jew, nor did he ever show a sustained interest in the Jews as a people. Even his physical attack on Marcus was not unusual; Fassmann is known to have physically attacked other people as well, including Gundling—he was a wild spirit. Fassmann's later decision to describe Oppenheimer's fall from favor should be viewed in this light. For all we know, Fassmann's interest in the case of Jew Süss was motivated originally less by Oppenheimer's religion or ethnicity than by its being a good example of what court society does to its members, regardless of religious or confessional affiliation, as well as by its general sensationalist flavor.

Fassmann's decision to go to Berlin in 1726 and his five-year stay at the Prussian court are also of note because they highlight the tangled lines between fiction and reality in his own life story. Fassmann wrote fictional conversations about true-life stories. He began as an author of imaginary dialogues about court society, then crossed over to become a real-life courtier, and finally turned back into an observer. Representation, imitation, and reality were closely wound around each other in his life and work. This was true in the 1720s and 1730s, and it became evident again upon Fassmann's death in 1744.

Twenty-seven years after he moved to Leipzig and six years after he composed Oppenheimer's remarkable posthumous confession, Fassmann died while traveling in Saxony, not an hour away from his birthplace in Oberwiesenthal. Contemporary observers found it not a little amusing that Fassmann, the author of the famous *Conversations in the Realm of the Dead*, was now dead himself. The first news item published about Fassmann's death announces that "David Fassmann, who for so long stood in close correspondence with the Realm of the Dead . . . finally decided to visit that realm in person."[56] Then, in reference both to the long literary tradition to which Fassmann's *Conversations* belonged and to the Leipzig writer's controversial personality, the unnamed journalist quotes Virgil's famous lines from Book VI of the *Aeneid*: "The gates of hell are open night and day / Smooth the descent, and easy is the way // But to return, and view the cheerful skies / In this the task and mighty labor lies." This literary playfulness did not stop there. A few years after his death, the dead Fassmann appeared in a *Conversation of the Dead* published for the Leipzig fair by one of his many imitators. The Oberwiesenthal native might have appreciated the gesture. He became a character in a fictional world he staked his career on depicting.[57]

The story of Joseph Oppenheimer represents a similar kind of movement from the fictional to the historical and back. As the inventories of Oppenheimer's confiscated libraries in Stuttgart and Frankfurt make clear, the famous court Jew had been an avid consumer of popular literature long before he became its object. Oppenheimer owned tomes about ancient history and modern events, legal history, genealogy, exemplary historical speeches, travel literature, political newspapers and journals, and other similar pieces. Among the many items Oppenheimer possessed was also a copy of one of Fassmann's *Conversations in the Realm of the Dead* (which one we do not know).[58] The great French philosopher Jean-Jacques Rousseau once wrote how as a young man he read so many books that at one point, "I became the character whose life I read."[59] Oppenheimer's life story was a variation on the same theme. At first, he was the reader of a particular book, but then he found himself mentioned in two similar accounts, and finally even as a protagonist of a similar volume.

The Three Early Dialogues

Even before Oppenheimer himself passed on to the realm of the dead, Fassmann published three different *Conversations* that bore more or less directly on his case. These *Conversations* are of course fictitious, and because Fassmann lived many hundreds of miles away from Württemberg, he had no firsthand knowledge of any of the stories he let his interlocutors recount from beyond the grave. But despite their fantastical nature and their many other limitations as historical sources, Fassmann's three *Conversations* are also quite revealing. They shed light on the kind of literature Oppenheimer himself had been in the habit of reading; they inform us about the extent and high quality of information about Württemberg politics available outside of the duchy; and they help us follow the transformation in attitude toward Oppenheimer by one of Germany's most popular contemporary writers. This last point is worth emphasizing. It is not enough to say, as the previous chapters in this book have done, that Oppenheimer's case was depicted differently by different people. In Fassmann's case, a single person expressed several different views about the story of Jew Süss.

The first *Conversation* Fassmann devoted to the situation in Württemberg appeared in two parts in 1734 and 1735.[60] Its main protagonists are Eberhard Ludwig (Carl Alexander's predecessor) and the Duke of Berwyck, an English nobleman who died in battle while serving in the army of Louis XV of France. The dialogue between the two is of interest for two main reasons. First, it shows that Fassmann already had encyclopedic knowledge about Württemberg several years before Oppenheimer's trial. In over a hundred densely packed pages, Fassmann lets the dead Eberhard Ludwig cover many topics in great detail, including the complex genealogy of the House of Württemberg, Eberhard Ludwig's many military exploits, and the duke's amorous involvement with Christina Wilhelmina von Grävenitz, which had "caused so much gossip and scandal in the world."[61] Fassmann had clearly done his research. He demonstrates easy familiarity with the political and religious landscapes in Württemberg; he quotes verbatim from official Württemberg documents; and he knows the details of the Grävenitz case, down to the specifics of the financial deal that led to her release from prison. No less interesting is what is not present in Fassmann's rendering of Eberhard Ludwig's story. Nowhere in the *Conversation* does the dead Württemberg duke make any mention of Jews, either positively or negatively. An uninformed reader of this particular *Conversation* might conclude from it that the duchy had never hosted any Jews at all.

Two years after publishing Eberhard Ludwig's dialogue with the Duke of Berwyck, Fassmann picked up the topic of Württemberg's politics once again. The occasion was Carl Alexander's death, which, according to Fassmann, took the duke completely by surprise. "Where am I? Has someone cast a spell? One moment I was still in my palace in Ludwigsburg and the next I am here, in this strange place!"[62] Looking around at his new abode, Carl Alexander next identifies the figure of Eberhard Ludwig standing nearby, and the latter, recognizing Carl Alexander, rushes toward him, eager to receive news from home. "My beloved duke must remember well how things stood along the Rhine frontier upon your passing," Carl Alexander tells his predecessor, "as well as how, because of your amorous affair with the Countess von Grävenitz, her friends felt they could do whatever they pleased at court. . . . The Württembergers suffered greatly from both things, so I had plenty to do when I ascended to the throne."[63]

Of the two challenges Carl Alexander faced during the initial phase of his reign, he now feels that the Grävenitz-Würben affair was initially working in his favor. He reminisces how, upon entering Stuttgart in December 1733, the Württembergers were still celebrating the death of the hated Eberhard Ludwig and were therefore quite jubilant to see him. "Their hearts rejoiced," Carl Alexander reports to the annoyed ghost of Eberhard Ludwig. "Even children who could hardly speak cheered as I drove into the city."[64] But if the local population was expecting some peace and quiet after the previous duke's scandalous reign, it was in for a serious disappointment. The reason, Carl Alexander explains to his dead interlocutor, was Württemberg's strategic predicament.

For a very long time, the border between France and its neighbors in southwestern Germany had been in a state of turmoil. The powerful French army kept crossing the river and laying waste to its right bank, sometimes advancing as far as Württemberg itself. "Even as your body was carried to its grave, the French took over the fortress of Kehl and began to lay siege to Philippsburg."[65] Because these two Rhine fortresses were crucial to any defense of southwestern Germany against France, "it was crucial to construct as quickly as possible a series of fortresses for the defense of the country";[66] not doing so would have led to an immediate French invasion of neighboring territories in the Holy Roman Empire and eventually of Württemberg, too, and thus to "a disgrace upon my head, as its ruler." But where would the funds for such an expensive undertaking come from? Carl Alexander thought about raising taxes, but the Württemberg estates would have had none of it. What else could he do?

It was then, the ghost of Carl Alexander explains to Eberhard Ludwig, that a thought crossed his mind. What if the money for Württemberg's defense did not come from the estates but from elsewhere? What if it came from a Jew? The context of these statements makes it clear that by attributing them to Carl Alexander, Fassmann is not attempting to criticize the dead duke. On the contrary, throughout the *Conversation*, Fassmann portrays Carl Alexander as a ruler sensitive enough to his subjects' concerns to devise creative ways to defend the duchy without raising taxes. This is why the first mention of Oppenheimer in Fassmann's mythical realm of the dead is overwhelmingly positive. The court Jew solves problems rather than creating them. "I wish everyone would do what I had done in this respect," Carl Alexander meditates; "I went well beyond my means and duty in the defense of the land." Oppenheimer was crucial to that project. He was "loyal," "smart," "intelligent," "efficient," and "always at hand." "He might be a Jew, but he acted toward me in the most loyal way . . . he risked his entire fortune on my behalf."[67]

Unfortunately for Carl Alexander and his Jewish advisor, not all the duke's subjects were as devoted as Oppenheimer. Many in the population openly opposed their ruler's projects, and others, while pretending to be obedient subjects, in fact kept putting stumbling blocks in his path. "What could they possibly have been trying to achieve?" asks the exasperated Carl Alexander.

Only with "my good and loyal advisor, Süss," did things go well.[68] How tragic, then, that the Secretarius has just arrived in the realm of the dead with the news of Oppenheimer's arrest. "Oh, my good financial advisor, could it really be that this is the reward for all your faithful services to me?"[69]

About three months after the publication of Carl Alexander's dialogue with Eberhard Ludwig, Fassmann tackled the topic yet again. In a *Conversation* he composed toward the end of the summer of 1737, he reports that after Carl Alexander's first dialogue in the realm of the dead, the Württemberg duke retired to a remote corner in the netherworld in order to do some serious thinking. Upon his return, he revises his story, which he now shares with Ferdinand, the newly deceased ruler of Courland, a small duchy on the Baltic Sea, in modern-day Latvia. The two dead dukes share three main things in common: both had been soldiers long before they became rulers, both had not expected to succeed to the thrones of their respective duchies, and both had been born Lutheran but eventually converted to Catholicism. These basic similarities form the main axes of the ensuing dialogue between the two and consequently reveal what Fassmann set out to explore in writing it.

Carl Alexander is the first to recount his life story. He begins by recalling the time and manner of his own passing. "How strange death is! Sometimes it knocks on one's door when one is still very young and expects to live for many years. At other times, one awaits its arrival at any moment only to be visited by it years later, completely unprepared." Before becoming duke of Württemberg, Carl Alexander had been a famous soldier and spent much of his life in military campaigns, accompanied everywhere by the imminent threat of death. After he ascended to the throne, however, things had changed. "This, too, is extremely annoying about death," Carl Alexander explains to Duke Ferdinand, "that in battle, siege, and so many other dangerous occasions, one could escape death's claws with marks on one's back and chest, on all sides of the body, the right and the left, barely alive, but alive nonetheless. And then, years later, one finds oneself in one's palace, finally enjoying some peace and quiet amidst the world's many tribulations. And right there and then, just at that moment of peace, to be snatched away so cruelly from life as if by a tiger, pinned to the ground, suffocating, helpless."[70]

Fassmann puts these words in Carl Alexander's mouth for a reason. The constant threat of death before the move to Stuttgart and the radical change from the soldier's tent to the prince's palace help him explain Carl Alexander's particular temperament. During his conversation with Duke Ferdinand, Carl Alexander admits that his fiery temper provides one crucial explanation for the political tensions in Stuttgart after 1733. These were not related only to the issue of the land's defenses or to a duchy's benevolent yet misunderstood ruler, as in Carl Alexander's previous *Conversation* with Eberhard Ludwig. Rather, they were the result of the Württembergers' almost allergic reaction to a ruler who treated them more like soldiers than honorable subjects. "I admit it," Carl Alexander tells Duke Ferdinand, "my mood was often too heated, I commanded my men with all too much passion. When things did not go as I wished I was often beside myself with rage."[71] His courage was unmistakable, "but it was mixed with uncontrolled emotions. I had a certain impatience about me in all things. . . . I simply could not stand that someone objected to any decision I made. I wanted everyone to treat my will as the supreme and sole law of the land."[72]

With Carl Alexander's basic character flaw explained and one central moral of his biography clearly articulated, Fassmann then lets the deceased duke retell his whole life story from the beginning, including many aspects of his upbringing and military career, his decision to convert to Catholicism in 1712 ("I believed that one could reach heaven through the Catholic religion just as well as through the Lutheran one"[73]), and the tension this state of affairs caused once he ascended to the throne. In all these respects, Fassmann continues to show a deep familiarity with Württemberg's recent political history: he provides extensive quotations from contemporary sources and mentions all the main political players by name.

Toward the end of Carl Alexander's account, the dead duke finally reaches the topic of Jew Süss. "Oppenheimer served me well," Carl Alexander emphasizes in this *Conversation* just as he had done in his dialogue with Eberhard Ludwig: "I appreciated his services" and "he had my full and complete confidence."[74] But there was also something duplicitous about this supposedly loyal servant, a certain disconnect between his outer appearance and his inner self. Carl Alexander now reports that Oppenheimer "shaved his beard, behaved as if he was a Christian courtier, drank wine, and in general did all those things that are prohibited to Jews, except for eating pork."[75] What's more, Oppenheimer constantly mistreated other people, especially other courtiers. "Anyone who wanted to accomplish anything at all in Württemberg, be it political or even religious, had to go through Oppenheimer personally. . . . He was willing to help, but only after receiving bribes."[76]

The substantially more negative portrayal of Oppenheimer in this second *Conversation* involving Carl Alexander is only one aspect of a larger modification in the way Fassmann now tells the duke's story. Oppenheimer can be portrayed as possessing a strong but also duplicitous personality only if Carl Alexander has a weaker, more gullible character than previously assumed.[77] There is a certain psychological economics to their relationship. The evaluation of the Württembergers that Fassmann expresses via Carl Alexander, on the other hand, remains consistent. Carl Alexander views them as disobedient, hypocritical subjects who call their ruler's advisor "His Excellency" to his face, but an "arch-thief and traitor behind his back."[78] Duplicity is consequently not the court Jew's invention; it is endemic to the political culture in the duchy more generally.

In a crucial passage in his dialogue with Carl Alexander, Duke Ferdinand highlights the importance of the courtly setting to Oppenheimer's case:

> It is so, brave duke! Every time we are taken by surprise by the transformation that takes place at a court when one prince dies and another takes his place. Everything and everyone undergoes a remarkable transformation. A man who is addressed one day as His Excellency is a nobody the following day. One moment one has a special apartment in the princely palace and the next one he is left with nothing but a ramshackle abode in town. One week you thank your many secretaries, officers, cooks, pages, lackeys, and stable boys, and—lo and behold!—a short time later you are expelled from your land or incarcerated in a prison fortress.[79]

The moral from Fassmann's third Württemberg *Conversation* seems consequently quite clear. One could say many negative things about Oppenheimer's personality and his actions, and most of them would probably be true. But at the end of the day, Oppenheimer was not only, or even primarily, a problem. He was above all a symptom.

The Evil Jew

Half a year later, Fassmann was working on one of his run-of-the-mill *Conversations* when the news of Oppenheimer's execution reached him in Leipzig. He reports that the timing couldn't have been more propitious. When he received the dramatic news from Stuttgart, he was literally holding a quill in hand, writing a dialogue that was meant to highlight "the capriciousness of luck as well as its malice or even better put: heaven's favor and God's just judgment."[80] The original interlocutors were Johan Willem de Ripperda, a Dutch adventurer and diplomat who died under mysterious circumstances in Morocco in 1737, and Karl Heinrich Hoym, a Saxon diplomat (and possibly an acquaintance of Fassmann's)[81] who, after being accused of treason, committed suicide in a Dresden prison in 1736. The two men have been talking for a while when Fassmann suddenly introduces Oppenheimer. From that point on, the dead court Jew takes center stage and the original interlocutors only pose questions.

Fassmann introduces Oppenheimer to his *Conversation* by way of a detailed description of Oppenheimer's journey to the realm of the dead. After Oppenheimer's death, his spirit leaves the gibbet near Stuttgart and soars upward, toward a black spirit awaiting it in the sky. The two spirits then fly away from the execution site, over the Black Forest, across the Rhine, over the church steeples of the city of Strasbourg, and all the way to Burgundy, to the chateau of the disgraced French censor Germain Louis Chauvelin. "Your actions were worse than anything I had ever done myself,"[82] Oppenheimer's spirit tells the alarmed Chauvelin in what is perhaps Fassmann's attempt at settling scores with censors in general. Facing Oppenheimer's macabre apparition, Chauvelin remains speechless.

After encountering Chauvelin, the two spirits continue on their journey. They fly south from Burgundy, down to the Mediterranean coast, then eastward, past Sardinia and Corsica, toward Greece. After all, it was the ancient poets of this land who, in the Western tradition, first discovered the entrance to the realm of the dead. At long last, Oppenheimer and his companion reach the river Acheron and board Charon's ferry. Oppenheimer first claims a front seat on the boat, but when the black spirit tells the ferryman who its companion is, Charon goes to the dead court Jew, hits him on the head with a heavy oar, and tells him to seat himself at the back. This Lucianesque scene quickly morphs into one resembling an episode out of Dante's *Divine Comedy*. Cerberus, sitting at the entrance to the netherworld, growls disapprovingly at the approaching Oppenheimer, and throngs of creatures harass and ridicule the dead Jew as he passes through the gates of the netherworld.[83]

It is at this point that Hoym and Ripperda notice Oppenheimer in their vicinity, prostrate on the ground. Ripperda recognizes him by the rope still hanging around his neck, approaches him, and asks Oppenheimer to recount his life story while "keeping in mind that here, in this realm, there is no point in hiding anything. Also know that in my own life I was almost as bad as you were and that this man here, Hoym, is your equal in evil deeds if not even worse than you."[84] This last statement is not meant to trivialize Oppenheimer's soon-to-be-confessed "enormous crimes"; it is only intended to magnify Hoym's past actions, of which Ripperda was informed earlier in the *Conversation*.

The first part of the story Oppenheimer recounts to Hoym and Ripperda in the next thirty pages is a much more elaborate retelling of what Fassmann had laid out in his previous three *Conversations* about the situation in Württemberg. It begins with new information about Oppenheimer's family, the rumors about the exact identity of his father, and his youth, and continues with a detailed description of Oppenheimer's meeting with Carl Alexander, the events surrounding Eberhard Ludwig's death, and Oppenheimer's move to Württemberg. Oppenheimer also recalls the details of his activities in Stuttgart, Carl Alexander's death, his own arrest (complete with the mistress in the bedchamber and the household arrestees), and his incarceration.

Similar in many ways to Fassmann's earlier descriptions of Oppenheimer's case, Oppenheimer's *Conversation* with Hoym and Ripperda also differs from them in at least three important ways. First, Fassmann now highlights the Jewish aspect of Oppenheimer's story and does so in a very negative way. Oppenheimer's story is no longer just another instance of a courtly rise-and-fall drama, but a tale with very few contemporary parallels.[85] Oppenheimer possesses inherent and unshakable Jewish traits. He has a particularly "Jewish physiognomy"; like all Jews, he was taught from early childhood "to lie, cheat, and steal"; and "a Jew, even if he is ennobled, remains always and everywhere a Jew." Gone are adjectives such as "faithful," "loyal," or "good," common especially in Carl Alexander's dialogue with Eberhard Ludwig. Oppenheimer is now simply "the Jew," and Carl Alexander's decision to employ him is "neither just nor good," because Jews in general, and German and Polish Jews in particular, are "rogues, villains, and scoundrels."[86]

The second main difference between Fassmann's earlier dialogues and Oppenheimer's *Conversation* with Hoym and Ripperda has to do with Fassmann's use of the first person in telling the court Jew's story. This literary device allows him to achieve what at first glance seems an entirely paradoxical effect. On the one hand, the confessional tone of Oppenheimer's account allows

Fassmann to impart a unique sense of truthfulness to the court Jew's story. None of the other authors we examined in this book could achieve this, either because Oppenheimer refused to confess anything to them (for example, to Jäger or Bernard) or because they preferred not to say too much about it for their own reasons (as with Schloss and Seligmann). Fassmann's fictional account circumvents these obstacles. His Oppenheimer confesses in the afterlife to almost all the charges he denied while still alive: misuse and abuse of power, treason, theft, counterfeiting of coins, manipulation of state monopolies, and womanizing (though no rapes). His past life, Oppenheimer's spirit acknowledges, was led "without a single thought devoted to God or one's own conscience."[87] The only reason he could live with himself was that "according to the principles of the Jewish religion, it is no sin for a Jew to lie, cheat, take an unfair advantage of, or steal from a gentile."[88]

At the very same time that it allows Fassmann to tell Oppenheimer's story as a supposedly full and honest confession, the use of the first person singular also enables Fassmann to imagine the world through Oppenheimer's eyes. The resulting effect, at least from the perspective of a modern reader, is highly paradoxical: in none of his other *Conversations* about Württemberg does Fassmann depict Oppenheimer in a more negative light, but in none of the other dialogues does he seem as sympathetic to Oppenheimer as in this one. Thus, during his description of Oppenheimer's transfer from Stuttgart to Hohen Neuffen, Fassmann has Oppenheimer recount how, while the little convoy departed the city, "I had to listen to the most obscene language directed at me by both the young and the old. At one point, several men approached my carriage and hit me on the face with a swine's tail. I thought they would snatch me off the carriage and tear me to pieces." A little while later, "as we drove past the gallows, several young men yelled at me: His Excellency! You should rest here a while and take a good look at your surroundings. You shall come back to this place soon enough." "My heart bled as I experienced all of this," Oppenheimer's spirit recalls the scene; "it is a miracle I didn't shed blood instead of tears in that place."[89]

The seeming contradiction between vilification on the one hand and first-person narration on the other hand is evident even more strongly in the *Conversation*'s second part. At the very end of Oppenheimer's *Conversation* with Hoym and Ripperda, the secretary arrives from the world of the living, carrying with him news from various European courts. Taking his usual place among the spirits of the dead, he tells the three dead interlocutors about the firing of a general in the Prussian court and a few stories about political intrigues concerning the redrawing of boundaries between several European states. After that, Fassmann has his three dead interlocutors depart toward their final and eternal destination in the netherworld. Oppenheimer has the worst of the lot. He ends up locked up forever in the lowest and darkest part of hell, the bleak and terrifying Tartarus. According to Fassmann, it is the only fitting reward for Oppenheimer's enormous crimes.[90]

And yet just before this final scene, Fassmann does something very different. His previous *Conversation* about Württemberg had been written in the late summer of 1737 and consequently ended without a description of the last scene in Oppenheimer's life. Now that Oppenheimer was dead, Fassmann could finally bring his story to a close, complete with the humiliating transfer from Hohen Asperg to Stuttgart, the stay at the Herrenhaus, the reading of the verdict by the criminal court (of which Jäger, we remember, was a member), and the encounter with several visitors, including "a certain David Bernard" (*sic*) and two local Jews, with whom Oppenheimer asked to discuss matters of faith. So far in this book, we have been observing people observing Oppen-

heimer. Having studied Jäger's, Bernard's, Schloss's and Seligmann's accounts, we can now go even further and explore Fassmann observing *them*.

The Execution

This is how Oppenheimer, in Fassmann's *Conversation*, tells the
story of his own execution (figure 11):[91]

> On January 30 of this year [1738], I was transported from
> the prison fortress of Hohen Asperg to Stuttgart. The fol-
> lowing day, several members of the inquisition committee
> came to see me. It was a Friday and they told me that I
> should make preparations for my death between then and
> February 4. Should I finally come to my senses and decide
> to convert to the Christian religion, they would be happy to
> make the necessary arrangements and send for a pastor. But
> I should not conclude from this that a conversion would in
> any way change my death sentence. There was no mercy in
> the world, other than God's, which could free me from this
> just punishment.
>
> Despite my refusal to convert, the inquisition committee
> sent a pastor to see me. When I saw him, I stuck my head in
> my garment and refused to hear his discourse. Instead, I de-
> manded to see two Jews, which the committee in fact al-
> lowed, but only if the Tübingen lecturer and former rabbi,
> David Bernard, would be present in the room as well. They
> all arrived and Bernard tried to persuade me to convert, but
> I resisted all his attempts to discuss matters of faith. In the
> end, he just tried to prepare me to my death according to the
> principles of the Jewish religion. But I turned away, walked
> around the room, and asked repeatedly "What? I? A man of
> such riches, of so much intelligence and honor, should I die

FIGURE 11. J. G. Thelott and C. Pfandzelt. The hanging of Jud Süss, 1738.
Source: WLB, Grafische Sammlung.

such a shameful death? I? Who was surrounded my entire life with princes, counts, and other nobles, I, innocent and famous even many hundreds of miles from here, should my end be that shameful?" Needless to say, none of my vitupera- tions made any difference.

The execution day had finally arrived. Apart from the six hundred regular troops stationed in the Stuttgart barracks, six hundred militiamen marched to the city from the Würt- temberg countryside, assembling around the Herrenhaus and in the marketplace. At eight o'clock in the morning, the bell on top of the Herrenhaus began to toll and I was served two rolls of white bread for breakfast. Then they escorted me out of my cell and into the main hall of the Herrenhaus. There was a table in that hall, covered in red cloth, around which all my judges sat. Hardly was I in the room when I fell on my knees, then stood up, all the while asking and crying for mercy. I was ordered to stand still and listen to the verdict. The judges began reading it to me.

As soon as I heard that I was to be executed on the iron gallows because of my crimes, I began to cry and shout even more loudly than before. I got so excited that the hangman, who stood beside me, had to cover my mouth with his hand. I recoiled and told him to let me be, I shall fight for my life, all the while listening to the judges reading my ver- dict. As soon as the verdict had been read, one of the judges broke the staff and threw its pieces at my feet.* Then they

---

* This is done according the criminal custom in Germany. Compare *Peinliche Hals- gerichtsordnung Kaiser Karls V. (Constitutio Criminalis Carolina)*, §95. A connection to the broken lance of medieval statues of synagoga is indirect. *Handwörterbuch zur deutschen Rechtsgeschichte*, s.v. "Stab"; Nina Rowe, *The Jew, the Cathedral, and the Medieval City: Synagoga and Ecclesia in the Thirteenth Century* (New York: Cambridge University Press, 2011), esp. 40–78.

gave me over to the bailiff's men. The executioner bound me again—I had managed to take my shackles off during the exchange with the hangman—then led me back to my cell, where my last meal was prepared for me. But I refused to eat or drink.

Then I was escorted outside to the street. The executioner's carriage, drawn by a single horse, was waiting for me there. I wore a coat, undergarments, and pants—all bright red—and also a vest, white socks, a wig, and a hat. The executioner's assistants had to violently hoist me up, dressed in this manner, onto their carriage, because I would not climb on it voluntarily. My seat consisted of a cushion covered with plain-woven fabric and filled with straw, and my hands and one of my feet were tied to the carriage. Two of the executioner's men walked along the carriage on either side, the one carrying a jug, the other a wine cup. The executioner's other assistants followed us from behind. All around me were foot soldiers: a hundred marching in front of the carriage, a hundred at the back, and a hundred on each side, all with their bayonets drawn. A further hundred cavalry were already waiting at the execution site, arranged in a circle around the gallows. Several times along the way, the executioner stopped the procession, turned to me, and asked if I would like to have some of the wine. I replied: "You only want to mock me."

When we reached the execution site, I looked around in alarm. I saw the iron gallows on which I would be strangled. It was forty-eight feet high and stood on a platform eight feet wide and four feet tall. All the way up, at the top of the gallows, was a long iron handle in the shape of a weathercock or a flag. The gallows themselves were painted red, with touches of gold, and just as I caught sight of all their details, I noticed that attached to the weathercock was a strange-looking birdhouse or cage. It was six feet high and weighed no less than 300 pounds. Just like the rest of the gallows, it was painted red. I could easily guess the purpose of this cage. My heart became even heavier than before.

I could not but be amazed at the large crowd that assembled to witness my execution. I estimate its number at between fifteen and sixteen thousand souls. Surely, all these people could not have come from Stuttgart alone? Many must have traveled from the rest of Württemberg and perhaps also from other neighboring lands. All these people, just for my sake!

I was ordered to climb down from the carriage and was then forced to enter the area around the gallows. Someone took away my shoes. Two clergymen bothered me here with their religious discourse. I say "bothered" because at the time I felt that they were only trying to increase my anxiety, though now that I'm dead I regret not having listened to their admonitions. Earlier in the day, following the public reading of my verdict and my transport back to my room in the Herrenhaus, I had walked back and forth in my cell, confused and overwhelmed by anxiety. It was then that a pastor came to see me. He talked with me about God's grace and about man's refuge in the passion of Jesus Christ. But the only thing I was willing to hear was news about the revocation of my verdict. This was not meant to be. And so I cried in Hebrew at him "Adonai Elohim," etc., which in the German tongue means "My God! My God and Lord! Bestow your mercy upon me, I am so weak!" And because I wanted to get rid of the priest I told him that I would give him 2,000 gulden for his efforts on my behalf, as long as he gave some of it also to the poor. I thanked him for everything he had done for me, but wanted to be left alone. I was resolved to die as a martyr for my faith.

Now, standing close to the gallows, I saw that cleric again. He spoke to me once more about grace through the Lord Jesus Christ, also declared publicly that he had spared no effort in trying to save my soul. But I screamed back at him in Hebrew "Adonai Elohim," etc., and "Shema Israel"—"The Lord is our God," and "Hear Israel, the Lord is our God, the Lord is one." I started crying these words even beforehand. Indeed, they came out of my mouth throughout the journey from the Herrenhaus.

The executioner's assistants then held me and started dragging and pushing me up the ladder. As I was drawn up, I had a brief minute in which to say a few final words. I wanted to denounce Hallwachs, Bühler, and that Jew from Mannheim because of the false testimonies they had given against me. But the military drummers began to roll their instruments and my cries were drowned in the din. As I traveled up the ladder, a sudden gust of wind blew my hat and wig off my head. In the meantime, we reached the top of the gallows. They placed me next to the cage and tied a noose around my neck. Suddenly, the immense crowd grew quiet. Then I was hanged and two pastors led the crowd in reciting the Lord's Prayer, as the Christians are prone to do. As soon as I died, the executioners' assistant put my body in the gibbet, still dressed in my former clothes only without the shoes, the hat, and the wig. They bolted and locked my body inside. It was then that a black spirit came to me, took my spirit with it, and accompanied me to this place.

Epilogue

Only by reading a long excerpt from one of Fassmann's *Conversations of the Dead* can one fully appreciate the captivating force of his storytelling technique. To be sure, the basic facts of Oppenheimer's trial and execution were sensational in and of themselves. This is why thousands of people attended the public hanging outside Stuttgart and why so many people wrote about the court Jew in the months and years following his violent death. But by describing familiar events through the perspective of the executed himself, Fassmann manages to grab the reader's attention with a special force. For a few minutes, it is not altogether clear who is the captive here: the reader, who is entranced by Fassmann's incredible story, or the prisoner-protagonist, Oppenheimer himself.

A curious aspect of Fassmann's *Conversation* is that, not unlike Shakespeare's depiction of Shylock in *The Merchant of Venice*, it both helps us identify with Oppenheimer and vilifies him. At the same time that we are encouraged to view the world through Oppenheimer's eyes, Fassmann's series of *Conversations* also increasingly plunges into ever lower forms of Judeophobic language, turning the once true and loyal court Jew of the early *Conversations* into a thievish traitor condemned to the depths of Tartarus for all eternity. How can one explain this paradoxical coexistence of identification and vilification?

A widespread modern belief holds that adopting another person's perspective can bring about empathy, sympathy, and eventually perhaps even justice and social harmony. What turns human beings into moral creatures, we are often told, is their ability to imagine the world while walking in someone else's shoes. When they succeed in doing so, they open the door for reconciliation and mutual understanding; when they fail in this endeavor, they risk committing immoral actions. The eighteenth-century Scottish philosopher Adam Smith is perhaps the most famous person to have expressed this idea in theoretical terms, but many other thinkers, public figures, and even ordinary people before and after Smith have also subscribed to a version of it.[92] Indeed, Philipp Friedrich Jäger, Oppenheimer's own inquisitor, seems to have thought along very similar lines when he suggested to Oppenheimer that the latter's immoral actions were related to a failure to view the world through other people's eyes. After confronting Oppenheimer with the fact that the court Jew had introduced many foreigners to Carl Alexander's state administration, Jäger purportedly asked his prisoner, "What would he [Süss] feel if all these things were done to him?"[93]

The power of this moral theory notwithstanding, there are certain incidents in Oppenheimer's trial that raise doubts about the force with which it is sometimes asserted. According to Bernard's account, the Tübingen lecturer tried "to convince [Oppenheimer] by using the principles of his own religion [in order to] entangle him in his own web, as it were."[94] Here, Bernard uses his knowledge of his opponent's worldview for selfish polemical purposes, not for the sake of empathy. The same is probably also true in Fassmann's *Conversation* between Oppenheimer, Hoym, and Ripperda, which was written less in order to advance morality through empathy than to entertain by causing emotional excitement through a particular type of voyeurism. Thus, the most devastating depiction of Oppenheimer Fassmann ever wrote was also the one in which he demonstrated in full his uncanny ability to describe situations through his protagonist's eyes. The contradiction doesn't lie with Fassmann, but with us: perspective and empathy might be related, but they are not one and the same thing.

An equally important reason to reflect with care on Fassmann's description of Oppenheimer's story has to do with its similarities to works by modern historians. Fassmann placed Eberhard Ludwig, Carl Alexander, and eventually also Oppenheimer front and center in his *Conversations* about Württemberg. He consequently depicted these three figures in detail. Less interesting for the Leipzig writer were almost all the other characters involved in Oppenheimer's trial. The exact identity of the inquisition committee members is something Fassmann never discusses; he calls Schloss and Seligmann simply "the two Jews" in his account; and even Bernard, whom Fassmann does mention by name, does not emerge from the *Conversation* as a three-dimensional figure.

Modern historians, though they of course differ from Fassmann in many respects, are similar to him in this regard. Before the present book, no historian has ever shown sustained interest in Oppenheimer's judges as individuals, let alone in Schloss and Seligmann or any of the other members of the Jewish community in Stuttgart. This is true to some extent even of Bernard, who, although he is mentioned by Fassmann and by some modern historians, has hitherto never been treated as a flesh-and-blood figure. Both Fassmann and modern historians have tended to treat the actors in Oppenheimer's case less as human beings than as representatives of larger social entities ("judges," "Jews," "converts"). The personal stories of such actors and the particular relationships they forged among themselves have never received the kind of attention they deserve.

The parallels between Fassmann and modern historians go even deeper. Although Fassmann depicts Oppenheimer in three very different ways in his *Conversations*, in each case he attempts to capture the court Jew's figure once and for all. He shows no doubts, no hesitation; he is ever the omniscient narrator. The rhetorical device of a confessional speech from beyond the grave is crucial here, because in each case it imparts a sense of finality and definitive truthfulness to Fassmann's (changing) story. In their own separate ways, the other protagonists in the present book also engaged in similar practices. Schloss and Seligmann ordered their coreligionists not to reflect on Oppenheimer's guilt until the arrival of the Messiah; Bernard tried to ensnare the prisoner in a scholastic dispute from which Oppenheimer wouldn't be able to escape; and Jäger not only incarcerated Oppenheimer physically, in jail, but also refused to let him voice his own side of the story and indeed in his *species facti* showed not a shred of doubt about the extent of Oppenheimer's "treacherous machinations."

Modern historians write in a genre that is seemingly very different from those of the legalistic Relation, the printed scholarly disputation, the Yiddish pamphlet, or the imaginary dialogue of the dead. Their attempts to reconstruct Oppenheimer's saga have for the most part been genuine and based on the available documentation. This very book would not have been possible without them. And yet they, too, have often pretended to have captured Oppenheimer once and for all, to have kept him under lock and key. It is in this light that we need to assess recent statements by otherwise wonderful historians about Oppenheimer's case, such as the claim that Oppenheimer's trial was ultimately about cameralism (eighteenth-century political economy)[95] or the especially striking assertion that "by now, the case of Jew Süss should be considered thoroughly and definitively researched."[96] If this book has shown anything at all, it is the opposite: Oppenheimer's trial was about more than one thing, and our knowledge of it is very partial. How can a trial be considered thoroughly researched when the most basic facts about the judges, about Oppenheimer's coreligionists in Stuttgart, and about practically all key eyewitnesses (including Bernard) have never been seriously explored? What is it in the way we presently write history that makes even the best of us write about the past like this?

Repeated efforts to lay Oppenheimer's story to rest once and for all are not only misleading. They are also likely to fail today just as they did in Fassmann's time. Shortly after the Leipzig writer left Oppenheimer locked up in Tartarus apparently forever, the court Jew's elusive figure appeared elsewhere. Soon the ghost of the court Jew participated in several imitations of Fassmann's *Conversations*, including in a truly remarkable dialogue between Oppenheimer and the famous Jewish false messiah Shabbetai Zevi. (According to the *Conversation*'s author, Oppenheimer matched Zevi in his notoriety, falsehood, and treacherousness.[97]) In the following years and decades, these ghostly apparitions would never stop. Even today, almost three centuries after Oppenheimer's execution, the court Jew, transformed and metamorphosed in a thousand ways, keeps making his appearances among us: in cinema, the theater, and the opera; in novels, short stories, and poems; and in historical accounts, including the book you are now holding in your hands. No, Oppenheimer's case was not "all about" one thing and one thing only; and no, we cannot and should not say that the story of Oppenheimer's trial has already been told, thoroughly and definitively, once and for all.

Afterword

Composing this polyphonic history hasn't been easy, and this concluding section is no exception. The reason is not hard to grasp. The book contains four quite different stories, and these, while they all circle the same theme, also follow their own individual trajectories. Can the historian resist their separate pulls? Can he hold the cords to the work's different parts just tight enough so that they don't fly in all directions but also don't become hopelessly tangled and plummet to the ground? The trick is to strike the right balance, and pulling it off is not a simple task.

The book began by observing that Oppenheimer's case poses three main challenges for historians: (1) the elusiveness of many factual aspects of Oppenheimer's life; (2) the many different contemporary interpretations of what his story amounted to; and (3) the difficulty in coming up with a plausible description of Oppenheimer's own view of his rise and fall. By looking at the trial from four distinct perspectives and by digging up a great deal of archival material, we set out to shed new light on these three important issues. We first followed Jäger's career and examined his actions during Oppenheimer's trial. Doing so made us see for the first time the connections between von Grävenitz's and Oppenheimer's trials and identify the cultural code that guided the work of the inquisition committees in both cases. In an important sense, Oppenheimer's trial had begun already several years before his arrest; it was part of a longer campaign against corruption, led by a small group of state officials that Oppenheimer first opposed as Grävenitz's aid before he himself became its main target. Reading the documents Jäger and his associates created during Oppenheimer's trial made it furthermore clear that the court Jew's inquisition committee lacked incriminating evidence against him. This is why it worked so hard, interviewed so many witnesses, and bent accepted legal procedures in pursuit of its preconceived verdict. The inquisition committee, and Jäger in particular, had an open, personal account to settle with Oppenheimer. In the end, this account was settled in the cruelest way possible.

The polyphonic methodology we explored in the pages of this book proved valuable also in Bernard's, Schloss's, and Seligmann's cases. The stories of these men throw into sharp relief the nexus of relationships and prejudices that gave Oppenheimer's case its recognizable shape. There is no doubt that many Württembergers harbored strong anti-Jewish sentiments. This is why some of Bernard's contemporaries did not accept his conversion to Christianity as genuine, and this is also why Schloss and Seligmann feared for their lives in the wake of Oppenheimer's arrest. But anti-Semitism was not the unifying driving force behind Oppenheimer's trial, nor were all Württemberg Jews on good terms with Oppenheimer when he fell from power. The political fault lines that ran through early eighteenth-century Württemberg were more complex than that. Turning our gaze away from Oppenheimer toward figures like Bernard, Schloss, and Seligmann proved invaluable in seeing all of this. In order to assess the relationship between anti-Semitism and Oppenheimer's case, one cannot just rely on an examination of Oppenheimer's own story.

We need other test cases; Bernard, Schloss, and Seligmann provide us with three extremely revealing ones.

The book concluded with Fassmann's case, which further supported many of the same conclusions. The Leipzig litterateur and fabulist had more than one opinion about who Oppenheimer "really was"; his anti-Jewish sentiments, though in evidence, were ultimately secondary to his main motivation in publishing pieces about Oppenheimer's case; and his successive portrayals of Oppenheimer demonstrate both overconfidence about who the fallen court Jew really was and a great uncertainty about the same topic. Last but not least, examining Fassmann's successive reconstructions of Oppenheimer's story helped us appreciate the tangled relationship between history and fiction in Oppenheimer's (and Fassmann's own) case. Fiction is not only an echo that reverberates after the "real" event already happened. Sometimes, fiction precedes history by serving as its script.

These quick highlights from the book's four main parts bring us finally to the crucial question of Oppenheimer's own perspective on his life, trial, and execution. On the face of it, the book has avoided this issue almost completely. More than half of its pages are devoted to the life stories of people other than Oppenheimer, and heavy clouds of suspicion hang over the rest of the pages, which do deal with Oppenheimer more directly. We are left with a blank or negative space at the very center of the book: with a kind of Godot-like Oppenheimer who never shows up. Or does he?

The fact of the matter is that we don't need to observe Oppenheimer directly in order to understand something about his perspective. Consider this: we spent a great deal of time with Jäger and his associates; we met with Bernard, Seligmann, and Schloss in the Herrenhaus; we even read together long passages from

Fassmann's *Conversations in the Realm of the Dead*. We share these exact activities with Oppenheimer; he did all of them too. Thus, without our realizing it, the book's four chapters have led us to adopt something of Oppenheimer's perspective; they have invited us to see and read what he himself saw and read. This is a delicate but important point I urge the reader to spend some time pondering. The book has revealed many important facts about Oppenheimer's case and it has discussed several ways in which contemporaries made sense of it. But it has also viewed and imagined the world partly through Oppenheimer's eyes. That the court Jew hasn't appeared more often in our field of vision is no coincidence. In an important sense, we have stood in Oppenheimer's shoes all along.

* * *

My original intention in writing this book was to shed new light on the factual, interpretative, and psychological dimensions of Oppenheimer's notorious trial and execution. In the course of the writing, though, it became clear to me that I was also trying to develop a general methodology to help us deal with common historical dilemmas in which the contradictions in the sources seem frustratingly irreconcilable. My polyphonic methodology, such as it is, was composed of building blocks fellow historians would readily recognize—reading sources closely and against the grain, employing so-called speech act theory and second-order observation, and much more. Fellow historians would also admit, I believe, that though my building blocks are familiar, only very rarely in the field of historical scholarship do they appear as they do in this unusually structured book. It is both fitting and necessary that I say at this point a few words about this aspect of the book. My story will not be complete otherwise.

Historians disagree about almost everything. They have competing personal preferences and motivations in exploring the past, and they use a remarkably diverse toolbox in analyzing their findings. Some historians choose to explain past events and processes through the prism of diplomacy and high politics, while others believe in the primacy of the economy, culture, or abstract ideas. But while competing works of history are often strikingly different in terms of their ideology and content, the basic literary (narratological) structure they follow is almost always the same. The basic blueprint for such structures includes a beginning, a middle, and an end, in that order; it contains a single plotline that traces a process of change; and it involves a narrator—the historian him- or herself—who hardly ever admits that he or she does not know all the relevant facts about the matter at hand. Linearity, unity, and omniscience are almost universal characteristics of contemporary historical writing.

That even in the early twenty-first century historians keep writing books as if they were nineteenth-century European novelists should give us pause. Why is it that while we disagree about almost everything else, we mimic one another in our narrative structures? Viewed in this light, the problem with contemporary historical writing is not, as is commonly believed, its postmodern inclinations. Rather, it is that historical writing hasn't ever entered the phase of literary *modernity* as such. In the early twenty-first century, we still write like Hugo and Austen, narratologically speaking. Woolf, Faulkner, Joyce, and Beckett, who have influenced every other mode of artistic production over the past hundred years, have left hardly any mark on us at all. Note that I do not claim that historians do not embrace modernist and postmodernist modes of argumentation—of course they do. Rather, I argue that they don't use modernist narratological structures, or do so only very rarely indeed.

I now raise my eyes from the computer screen and look at the book-laden shelves in my library. What an incredible diversity! What a monument to human ingenuity, industry, and thought! What a shame, then, that so few among the authors of all these wonderful books of history could ever admit in writing that they do not know or understand something; what a pity that, though in their teaching they must have always looked at topics from different angles, repeated their story more than once in order to make sense of it, and on occasion changed their minds—what a pity, I say, that though they did all these things in the classroom, historians have so seldom reproduced the same polyphony in their written work. Between the Scylla of false omniscience and the Charybdis of "post-truth" relativism lies a whole world of possibilities. We historians inhabit it in our daily work but explore it all too rarely in our published essays and books. As I write the last sentences in this book, I wish to recall for a final time one such world of polyvocal contradictions and possibilities, the world my book has so persistently sought to conjure. This world contains Stuttgart, Tübingen, Schorndorf, and Frankfurt's Judengasse; it stretches all the way to the black pit of Tartarus from King Saul's ancient Hebrew land. Giving it life and meaning are our four storytellers and countless others, a gallows' shadow, and you and me and a large—stupefyingly large—horrendous end.

Princeton, New Jersey, January 2016

Illustrations

1. Central Europe in the early eighteenth century xii

2. Württemberg and its environs, ca. 1730 xii

3. Bruno Rehab, poster for the first screening of the film *Jud Süss,* 1940 xiv

4. J. A. Fridrich, d. J., portrait of Philipp Friedrich Jäger, 1745 24

5. Unknown artist, three scenes from Oppenheimer's trial, 1738 54

6. Elias Beck, Oppenheimer in the Herrenhaus and the reading of his verdict, 1738 102

7. Mordechai Schloss and Callman Seligmann, *The Story of the Passing of Joseph Süss, May the Memory of the Righteous Be a Blessing,* 1738 176

8. Unknown artist, *Portrait of the Württemberg Court Jew Elias Hayyum,* ca. 1735 199

9. Unknown artist, frontispiece to volume 16 of David Fassman, *Gespräche in dem Reiche derer Todten,* 1737 230

10. Unknown artist, "The Court Fool" (caricature of David Fassmann), ca. 1736 235

11. J. G. Thelott and C. Pfandzelt, the hanging of Jud Süss, 1738 270

Abbreviations

I. PRINTED SOURCES

ET: Shlomo Ettlinger, *Ele Toldot*, 32 volumes (Leo Baeck Institute, http://digital
.cjh.org:80/R/-?func=dnom-jump-full&object_id=258967&amp
;silo_library=GEN01).

GRdT: David Fassmann, *Gespräche in dem Reiche derer Todten* (Wolfgang Deer:
Leipzig, 1718–1740). Quoted are always the respective Conversation and
page numbers (for example, GRdT 15:12).

II. ARCHIVAL AND LIBRARY COLLECTIONS

AFSt/H: Archiv der Franckeschen Stiftungen zu Halle

BSB München: Bayerische Staatsbibliothek, München

CAJP: Central Archives of the Jewish People

EvStA Tübingen: Archiv des Evangelischen Stifts, Tübingen

GLA Karlsruhe: Generallandesarchiv, Karlsruhe

GStA PK: Geheimes Staatsarchiv Preußischer Kulturbesitz

HStA Stuttgart: Hauptstaatsarchiv, Stuttgart

IStG Frankfurt am Main: Institut für Stadtgeschichte, Frankfurt am Main

JMNY: Jewish Museum, New York

LKA Stuttgart: Landeskirchliches Archiv, Stuttgart

NLI: National Library of Israel

SächsHStA Dresden: Sächsisches Hauptstaatsarchiv, Dresden

StdA Heidelberg: Stadtarchiv, Heidelberg

StdA Kirchheim unter Teck: Stadtarchiv, Kirchheim unter Teck

StdA Leipzig: Stadtarchiv, Leipzig

StdA Nürnberg: Stadtarchiv, Nürnberg

StdA Schorndorf: Stadtarchiv, Schorndorf
StdA Tübingen: Stadtarchiv, Tübingen
UAJ: Universitätsarchiv, Jena
UA Tübingen: Universitätsarchiv, Tübingen
UB Halle: Universitätsbibliothek, Halle
UB Tübingen: Universitätsbibliothek, Tübingen
WLB: Württembergische Landesbibliothek, Stuttgart

Notes

INTRODUCTION

1. HStA Stuttgart A48/14 Bü 12, Nr. 10.
2. A good general introduction to the early modern history of Jews in the Holy Roman Empire, including court Jews, is Mordechai Breuer, "The Early Modern Period," in *German-Jewish History in Modern Times*, ed. Michael A. Meyer, 4 vols. (New York: Columbia University Press, 1996), 1: 79–260.
3. HStA Stuttgart A48/14 Bü 12, Nr. 10.
4. For example, Daniel Jütte, *Das Zeitalter des Geheimnisses: Juden, Christen und die Ökonomie des Geheimen (1400–1800)* (Göttingen: Vandenhoek & Ruprecht, 2011), 158–163.
5. HStA Stuttgart A48/14 Bü 12, Nr. 10.
6. For a short overview of the archival material in the Stuttgart archives, see Robert Kretzschmar, "Tradition und Überrest: Die Überlieferung zum Kriminalprozess gegen Joseph Süß Oppenheimer," in *Die Quellen sprechen lassen: Der kriminalprozess gegen Joseph Süss Oppenheimer 1737/38*, ed. Gudrun Emberger and Robert Kretzschmar (Stuttgart: Kohlhammer, 2009), 6–26.
7. An excellent example for the reconstruction of Oppenheimer's activities prior to his arrival in Württemberg is Jürgen Rainer Wolf, "Joseph Süß Oppenheimer ('Jud Süß') und die Darmstädter Goldmünze, ein Beitrag zur hessen-darmstädtischen Finanzpolitik unter Landgraf Ernst Ludwig," in *Neunhundert Jahre Geschichte der Juden in Hessen* (Wiesbaden: Kommission für die Geschichte der Juden in Hessen, 1983), 215–262.
8. Johann Heinrich Zedler, *Grosses vollständiges Universal-Lexicon aller Wissenschaften und Künste*, s.v. "Süß Oppenheimer, Joseph," www.zedler-lexikon.de, accessed January 9, 2015.
9. Zedler, *Universal-Lexicon*, ibid.
10. Zedler, *Universal-Lexicon*, ibid.

11. This and many other examples are covered in Barbara Gerber's remarkably detailed study *Jud Süß: Aufstieg und Fall im frühen 18. Jahrhundert: Ein Beitrag zur historischen Antisemitismus- und Rezeptionsforschung* (Hamburg: H. Christians, 1990), esp. 151–249.

12. Manfred Zimmermann, *Josef Süß Oppenheimer, ein Finanzmann des 18. Jahrhunderts: Ein Stück Absolutismus- und Jesuitengeschichte* (Stuttgart: Rieger, 1874); Curt Elwenspoek, *Jud Süß Oppenheimer, der große Finanzier und galante Abenteurer des 18. Jahrhunderts* (Stuttgart: Süddeutsches Verlagshaus, 1926); Selma Stern, *Jud Süss: Ein Beitrag zur deutschen und zur jüdischen Geschichte* (Berlin: Akademie-Verlag, 1929); Heinrich Schnee, "Der Geheime Finanzienrat Joseph Süß Oppenheimer als Württembergischer Hoffaktor," in *Die Hoffinanz und der Moderne Staat: Geschichte und System der Hoffaktoren an deutschen Fürstenhöfen im Zeitalter des Absolutismus* (Berlin: Duncker & Humblot, 1963), 4: 109–148.

13. Gerber, *Jud Süß*; Hellmut G. Haasis, *Joseph Süss Oppenheimer, genannt Jud Süss: Finanzier, Freidenker, Justizopfer* (Reinbek: Rowohlt, 1998); Alexandra Przyrembel and Jörg Schönert, eds., *"Jud Süss": Hofjude, literarische Figur, antisemitisches Zerrbild* (Frankfurt am Main and New York: Campus, 2006); Emberger and Kretzschmar, eds., *Die Quellen sprechen lassen*.

14. Wilhelm Hauff, "Jud Süß," in *Sämtliche Werke*, ed. Sybille von Steinsdorff (Munich: Winkler, 1970), 2: 476–538; Lion Feuchtwanger, *Jud Süss* (Munich: Drei Masken Verlag, 1925); *Jew Süss*, directed by Lothar Mendes (1934; Chicago: International Historic Films, 2004), VHS; *Jud Süss*, directed by Veit Harlan (1940; Chicago: International Historic Films, 2008), DVD; Detlev Glanert, *Joseph Süß* (1999); Yehoshua Sobol, *Jud Süß: Der Kaufmann aus Stuttgart*, directed by Dieter Wedel (Worms Festspiele, 2013).

15. Apart from the coedited volume with Robert Kretzschmar, Emberger added short but very valuable contributions to the literature about Oppenheimer. See, for instance, Gudrun Emberger, "Verdruß, Sorg und Widerwärtigkeiten. Die Inventur und Verwaltung des Jud Süßchen Vermögens 1737–1772," *Festschrift für Hansmartin Decker-Hauff zum 65. Geburtstag* (Stuttgart: Kohlhammer, 1982), 369–375; and Gudrun Emberger and Rotraud Ries, "Der Fall Joseph Süß Oppenheimer: Zum historischen Kern und den Wurzeln seiner Medialisierung," in Przyrembel and Schönert, eds., *"Jud Süß,"* 29–55.

16. For example, Stern, *Jud Süss*, IX; Haasis, *Joseph Süss Oppenheimer*, 7; Emberger and Ries, "Der Fall Joseph Süß Oppenheimer."

17. Wolfgang Iser in Germany and Stanley Fish in the United States are two of the leading theoreticians behind this approach to the study of literary texts.

Wolfgang Iser, *Der Akt des Lesens. Theorie ästhetischer Wirkung* (Munich: Fink, 1976); Stanley Fish, *Is There a Text in This Class?* (Cambridge, MA: Harvard University Press, 1980).

18. Susan Tegel, *Jew Süss: Life, Legend, Fiction, Film* (London and New York: Continuum, 2011).

19. Richard Price, *Alabi's World* (Baltimore, MD: Johns Hopkins University Press, 1990); Laura Otis, *Müller's Lab* (Oxford and New York: Oxford University Press, 2007); James Goodman, *Stories of Scottsboro* (New York: Pantheon Books, 1994). Two recent examples for this approach, the latter developed (independently) along very similar lines to what I do in the pages of this book, are Karl Jacoby, *Shadows at Dawn: A Borderlands Massacre and the Violence of History* (New York: Penguin Press, 2008); and Joshua Piker, *The Four Deaths of Acorn Whistler: Telling Stories in Colonial America* (Cambridge, MA: Harvard University Press, 2013). Readers fluent in German may also find two older multiperspectival examples to be of interest: Dieter Kühn, *N.* (Frankfurt am Main: Suhrkamp, 1970); and Hans Magnus Enzensberger, *Der kurze Sommer der Anarchie. Buenaventura Durrutis Leben und Tod* (Frankfurt am Main: Suhrkamp, 1972).

CHAPTER 1

1. Wilhelm Jeremias Jacob Cleß, *Wie es eine Seele mit Jesu meinen müsse, die ein Schäflein in dieses guten Hirtens sein wolle: wurde bey ansehnlicher Leich-Begräbniss des Philipp Friedrich Jägers vorgestellt* (Stuttgart: Gedrückt in der Stollischen Buchdruckerey, 1745), 30.

2. Basic details about the funeral are taken from Cleß, *Wie es eine Seele*. About typhus (also known as "jail fever") in early modern prisons, see, for instance, Mary J. Dobson, *Contours of Death and Disease in Early Modern England* (Cambridge: Cambridge University Press, 1997), 248–250.

3. Wilhelm Jeremias Jacob Cleß was Jäger's wife's cousin. Eberhard Emil von Georgii-Georgenau, *Biographisch-Genealogische Blätter aus und über Schwaben* (Stuttgart: Verlag Emil Müller, 1879), 118–120, 410.

4. A short introduction to Leichenreden with a list of relevant literature is *Theologische Realenzyklopädie*, s.v. "Leichenpredigt." A specific discussion of the Leichenpredigt in Württemberg is Horst Schmidt-Grave, *Leichenreden und Leichenpredigten Tübinger Professoren 1550–1750* (Tübingen: J.C.B. Mohr, 1970).

5. Cleß, *Wie es eine Seele*, 4–5.

6. Cleß, *Wie es eine Seele*, 3, 30. (The references are to Psalm 77 and Job 1.)

7. Cleß, *Wie es eine Seele*, 27–28.

8. Cleß, *Wie es eine Seele*, 50.

9. Why such positions tended to run in families will be discussed later in this chapter.

10. The genealogical information about Philipp Friedrich Jäger's family is taken primarily from Georgii-Georgenau, *Biographisch-Genealogische Blätter*, esp. 407–416. Very helpful also is Hans Helmut Jaeger, *Familienchronik Jaeger*, 6 vols. (Erlangen: Selbstverlag, 1979–2008). About district ducal commissioners in Württemberg, see James Allen Vann, *The Making of a State: Württemberg 1593–1793* (Ithaca, NY: Cornell University Press, 1984), 39–40.

11. About the Ehrbarkeit, see Gabriele Haug-Moritz, *Die württembergische Ehrbarkeit: Annäherungen an eine bürgerliche Machtelite der Frühen Neuzeit* (Tübingen: Jan Thorbecke Verlag, 2009). An older and often still very valuable account is Peter H. Wilson, *War, State, and Society in Württemberg, 1677–1793* (New York: Cambridge University Press, 1995). My discussion of the political institutions in Württemberg is also deeply indebted to Vann, *The Making of a State*, esp. 58–88.

12. The original estimate is in Vann, *The Making of a State*, 299. The latest and much more detailed analysis is Sabine Holtz, *Bildung und Herrschaft: zur Verwissenschaftlichung politischer Führungsschichten im 17. Jahrhundert* (Leinfelden-Echterdingen: DRW-Verlag, 2002), 67–80.

13. The best account of early modern Schorndorf is Uwe Schmidt, *Geschichte der Stadt Schorndorf* (Stuttgart: Theiss, 2002), 31–72. The view of the town is from 1686. It is reproduced in Schmidt, plate 4. I take the notion of German hometowns from Mack Walker's classic, *German Home Towns: Community, State, and General Estate, 1648–1871* (Ithaca, NY: Cornell University Press, 1971).

14. Noted in Hans Helmut Jaeger, *Familienchronik Jaeger*, 1.3: 240.

15. Johann Georg Rösch, *Schorndorf und seine Umgebung nebst einer statistischen Übersicht des Königreichs Württemberg* (Stuttgart: Metzler, 1815), 75.

16. Kirchenregisteramt Schorndorf, *Tauf- Ehe- und Totenbuch 1683–1752* (entry for October 14, 1707); Cleß, *Wie es eine Seele*, 23.

17. Cleß, *Wie es eine Seele*, 24, 86.

18. Today, Kirchplatz 1. I am deeply grateful to Uwe Jens Wandel for clarifying for me many issues about Schorndorf's history and architecture.

19. All quotes are taken from Sigmund Wisshack, "Vorrede," in *Zwei Christliche Gespräche oder Schul-Dialogi, Darinnen abgehandelt wird, wie die Unterweisung der Töchtern besser einzurichten seye?* (Stuttgart: Christoph Erhard,

1742). For background, see Adolf Palm, "Das alte Unrecht an den Frauen: Der Schorndofer Prezäptor Sigmund Wisshack (1679–1751) zwischen Pietismus und Aufklärung," *Heimatblätter. Jahrbuch für Schorndorf und Umgebung* 2 (1984): 46–98.

20. Cleß, *Wie es eine Seele*, 23.

21. Cleß, *Wie es eine Seele*, 52.

22. Cleß, *Wie es eine Seele*, 52.

23. Sigmund Wisshack, "Historische kurze Beschreibung des Ewangelischen Jubelfests allhier Schorndorf Anno 1717." StdA Schorndorf, RB 55.

24. All quotes are taken from Wisshack, "Historische kurze Beschreibung," fols. 19–21.

25. The brothers' names were Carl Friedrich Jäger, deacon in Bad Canstatt; Georg Friedrich Jäger, physician in Nürtingen; and Johann Friedrich Jäger, councilor and ducal commissioner in Göppingen. Cleß, *Wie es eine Seele*, 79, 86.

26. The two were Johann Wendel Bardili and Matthäus Konrad Hochstetter. Information taken from Cleß, *Wie es eine Seele*, 24; and Walter Pfeilsticker, *Neues Württembergisches Dienerbuch* (Stuttgart: Cotta, 1963), 2: 2363, 2131.

27. The best account of Grävenitz-Würben's case is Sybille Oßwald-Bargende, *Die Mätresse, der Fürst und die Macht: Christina Wilhelmina von Grävenitz und die höfische Gesellschaft* (Frankfurt am Main: Campus Verlag, 2000).

28. Philipp Friedrich Jäger, *Als an des Durchlauchtigsten Fürsten und Herren . . . Eberhard Ludwig, Hertzogen zu Würtemberg und Töck, Grafen zu Mömpelgardt . . . In einer Oratione Valedictoria zugleich öffentlich gratulirte, Wollte in nachgesetzter Cantata seine . . . Pflicht ferner abstatten* (Stuttgart: Rößlin, 1723), n.p.

29. For the history of hometowns like Schorndorf, see Walker, *German Home Towns*.

30. Jürgen Sydow, *Geschichte der Stadt Tübingen* (Tübingen: Laupp, 1974), II: 19.

31. Cleß, *Wie es eine Seele*, 25; Heinrich Hermelink, ed., *Die Matrikeln der Universität Tübingen*, vol. 3, *1710–1817* (Tübingen: Universitätsbibliothek, 1953), 53 (Nr. 32192).

32. Cleß, *Wie es eine Seele*, 25.

33. A general introduction to the education of jurists in German-speaking Europe is Gerhard Köbler, "Zur Geschichte der juristischen Ausbildung in Deutschland," *JuristenZeitung* 26, no. 23/24 (1971): 768–773. About *collegia privata* in early eighteenth-century Tübingen, see Gabriele Nieder, *Ferdinand*

Christoph Harpprecht (1650–1714) (Tübingen: Mohr Siebeck, 2011), 29–30.

34. Cleß mentions some of the professors in *Wie es eine Seele*, 25. Further information is to be found in Ernst Conrad, "Die Lehrstühle der Universität Tübingen und ihre Inhaber (1477–1927)" (PhD Dissertation: Tübingen, 1960). On the constitution and different roles of the law faculty in Tübingen, see Hans-Wolf Thümmel, *Die Tübinger Universitätsverfassung im Zeitalter des Absolutismus* (Tübingen: J.C.B. Mohr, 1975), esp. 185–212.

35. Conrad, "Die Lehrstühle der Universität Tübingen," 158. The materials about Scheffer's trial are in HStA Stuttgart A48/13.

36. General information about the court is taken from Ferdinand Graner, "Zur Geschichte des Hofgerichts in Tübingen," *Württemberigische Vierteljahrshefte für Landesgeschichte, Neue Folge* 32 (1925/1926): 36–89; the court's location is specified in Theodor Knapp, "Das württembergische Hofgericht zu Tübingen 1514–1805," *Tübinger Blättern* XVIII (1925–1926): 60–62.

37. Cleß, *Wie es eine Seele*, 25; Michaele Grassus, *Decanus et collegium facultatis iuridicae in alma eberhardina hacce l.s.* (Tübingen: Sigmund, 1730).

38. Nieder, *Ferdinand Christoph Harpprecht*, 29–30.

39. Short and very informative discussions of the Relation are Heinrich Gehrke, "Die Rechtsprechungs- und Konsilienliteratur Deutschlands bis sum Ende des Alten Reichs" (PhD Dissertation: Berlin, 1972), esp. 48–49, 78–79; and Erich Döhring, *Geschichte der deutschen Rechtspflege seit 1500* (Berlin: Duncker & Humboldt, 1953), 255–277.

40. Cleß, *Wie es eine Seele*, 25.

41. UA Tübingen 13/17, fol. 5 (Zulassungsprüfung für die Lizentiaten- oder Doktorpromotionexam); and Heinrich Hermelink, ed., *Die Matrikeln der Universität Tübingen*, vol. 3, *1710–1817*, 53 (Nr. 32192).

42. Eberhard Friedrich Moser, *Real-Index und Auszug der Herzoglich-Württembergischen Hofgerichts-Ordnung . . .* (Tübingen: Jacob Friedrich Heerbrandt, 1784), 351.

43. A copy of the dissertation was published as Philipp Friedrich Jäger, *Dissertatio juridica inauguralis de arbitriis familiae erciscundae, . . . d. [ ] maii anno 1728 . . .* (Tübingen: H. Franck, 1728).

44. StdA Kirchheim unter Teck, Kirchliche Familienkartei Blatt 2371, and Taufregister der Evangelischen Kirche Kirchheim unter Teck, entry for May 23, 1709. The couple married in Kirchheim unter Teck on August 15, 1730. I am grateful to Renate Schattel of the Stadtarchiv und Museum Kirchheim unter Teck for this information.

45. Graner, "Zur Geschichte," 51–52; Knapp, "Das württembergische Hofgericht," 53–58; Wolfgang Adam Schöpff, *Tractatus theoretico-practicus de processu summi appellationum tribunalis, ducatus Würtembergici, quod Tübingæ est* (Stuttgart: Johann Benedikt Metzler, 1720).
46. Knapp, "Das württembergische Hofgericht," esp. 98–100; Graner, "Zur Geschichte," 87.
47. Moser, *Real-Index*, 336, 344.
48. Graner, "Zur Geschichte," 59; Moser, *Real-Index*, 305 n. (l).
49. I am grateful to Andrea Heck of the HStA Stuttgart for clarifying the history of the Hofgericht's archive in the twentieth century.
50. HStA Stuttgart A398 L Bü 31.
51. Wisshack, "Historische kurze Beschreibung," fol. 21.
52. In her fascinating biography of von Grävenitz-Würben, Sybille Oßwald-Bargende does not consider Oppenheimer's story at all, and Helmut Haasis touches on von Grävenitz-Würben's case only in passing. Peter Wilson mentions similarities without recognizing the clear continuities between the cases. Oßwald-Bargende, *Die Mätresse*; Haasis, *Joseph Süss Oppenheimer*; Wilson, *War, State and Society*, esp. 126.
53. On the criminal justice system in eighteenth-century Württemberg, see Helga Schnabel-Schüle, *Überwachen und Strafen im Territorialstaat: Bedingungen und Auswirkungen des Systems strafrechtlicher Sanktionen im frühneuzeitlichen Württemberg* (Köln: Böhlau, 1997).
54. HStA Stuttgart A48/05 Bü 56, Nr. 15.
55. HStA Stuttgart A48/05 Bü 56, Nr. 21.
56. *Summarische Peinliche Anklage des . . . Fiskals Moritz David Harpprechts contra Christina Wilhelmine, verwittibte Gräfin von Würben . . .* , WLB, cod. hist., 2° 739, IV, 3a.
57. WLB cod. hist. 2°, 275, fol. 75. The entire catalogue follows, fols. 75–103.
58. For a full discussion of this topic, see chapter 3 of this book.
59. All quotations in the previous paragraphs are taken from WLB cod. hist. 2°, 275, fols. 75–103.
60. Oßwald-Bargende, *Die Mätresse, der Fürst und die Macht*, 17.
61. HStA Stuttgart A48/05 Bü 38, Nr. 71 (Letter from January 29, 1734); HStA Stuttgart A48/14 Bü 81, Nr. 3.
62. HStA Stuttgart A48/14 Bü 6, fols. 37–38.
63. HStA Stuttgart A48/05 Bü 57, Nr. 54.
64. HStA Stuttgart A48/05 Bü 57, Nr. 65, Bl. 2.

65. HStA Stuttgart A48/05 Bü 57, n.n., "Schreiben aus Schorndorf, 12 August 1736."

66. Jaeger, *Familienchronik Jaeger*, 1.7: 170.

67. HStA Stuttgart A48/14 Bü 15, fols. 831ff.

68. HStA Stuttgart A48/14 Bü 2, Nr. 79.

69. HStA Stuttgart A48/14 Bü 14, fol. 1.

70. The order to transfer the three prisoners to Hohen Neuffen was not given in writing or did not survive. Nevertheless, a complaint letter by Bühler's wife regarding the events of the "previous day" pinpoints the date. The letter is dated March 21. HStA Stuttgart A48/01 Bü 19, Nr. 1.

71. Von Pflug's official appointment to the inquisition committee is not documented. On March 23, however, he is already mentioned as a member. HStA Stuttgart A48/14 Bü 10, fol. 1.

72. HStA Stuttgart A14/14 Bü 14, fols. 1–6. The said library was in all likelihood the one belonging to the administrative council.

73. HStA Stuttgart A14/14 Bü 14, fols. 308, 6, 19, and 267, respectively. The issue of Oppenheimer's domestic servants will be discussed in full in chapter 3 of this book.

74. The arrival is documented in HStA Stuttgart A48/14 Bü 14, fol. 1. On April 7, Jäger still interrogated Bühler in Hohen Neuffen, but by April 8, he was back in Stuttgart. Compare HStA Stuttgart A48/14 Bü 14, fol. 250.

75. HStA Stuttgart A48/14 Bü 2, fol. 1.

76. HStA Stuttgart A48/14 Bü 2, fol. 1.

77. For a general discussion of the role of "voice" in historical research, see Alessandro Portelli, "The Peculiarities of Oral History," *History Workshop Journal* 12, no. 1 (1981): 98. Two important discussions on the role of the scribe, both dealing with Württemberg, are Sabine Kienitz, *Sexualität, Macht und Moral. Prostitution und Geschlechterbeziehungen Anfang des 19. Jahrhunderts in Württemberg* (Akademie Verlag: Berlin, 1995), 59ff; and David Sabean, "Soziale Distanzierung. Ritualisierte Gestik in deutscher bürokratischer Prosa der Frühen Neuzeit," *Historische Anthropologie* 4 (1996): 216–233.

78. Haasis, *Joseph Süss Oppenheimer*, 324. Compare Kretzschmar, "Tradition und Überrest," 18, where the author claims that the protocols allow us to witness directly the captive Oppenheimer.

79. Most importantly, *Kurze doch gesetzmäßige Abhandlung von denen Würtembergischen Statt- Amt- und Gerichtsschreibereyen*. WLB, cod. iur. 4° 218 a.

80. HStA Stuttgart A48/14 Bü 2, fols. 2–3.

81. On this and other issues relating to the "invention" of the modern crimi-

nal, see Richard Wetzell, *Inventing the Criminal: A History of German Criminology, 1880–1980* (Chapel Hill: University of North Carolina Press, 2000).

82. HStA Stuttgart A48/14 Bü 2, fols. 3–4.

83. HStA Stuttgart A48/14 Bü 2, fol. 5.

84. About this episode, see Haasis, *Joseph Süss Oppenheimer*, 215–216.

85. HStA Stuttgart A48/14 Bü 2, fols. 5–6.

86. HStA Stuttgart A48/14 Bü 2, fols. 10–18.

87. HStA Stuttgart A48/14 Bü 2, fols. 10–18.

88. HStA Stuttgart A48/14 Bü 2, fol. 18.

89. HStA Stuttgart A48/14 Bü 2, n.n.

90. HStA Stuttgart A48/14 Bü 14, fols. 81–90 (Hallwachs); A48/01 Bü 1, fol. 90 (Bühler); HStA Stuttgart A48/14 Bü 2, fol. 53 (Oppenheimer).

91. The protocols of Hallwachs's preliminary interrogation can be found in HStA Stuttgart A48/14 Bü 14, fols. 97ff. Bühler's first questioning is documented in HStA Stuttgart A48/01 Bü 1.

92. HStA Stuttgart A48/14 Bü 14, fol. 96; A48/14 Bü 2, Nr. 58.

93. HStA Stuttgart A48/14 Bü 14, fol. 117.

94. According to one account sent by Oppenheimer's warden to the inquisition committee in September 1738, Oppenheimer asked explicitly for "paper, ink, and feathers" in order to write down his story, but his request was denied. UB Tübingen, Handschriftenabteilung, Mh 468, Wolfgang Conrad Glaser to the inquisition committee, September 28, 1737.

95. HStA Stuttgart A48/01 Bü 1, fols. 57–60; HStA Stuttgart A48/14 Bü 11 (11/4, *species facti*), fols. 15–16.

96. HStA Stuttgart A48/01 Bü 1, fols. 62, 65.

97. HStA Stuttgart A48/01 and HStA Stuttgart A48/06.

98. HStA Stuttgart A48/01 Bü 19, Nr. 1; Bü 13, Nrs. 6a, b; HStA Stuttgart A48/01 Bü 2, Nr. 6.

99. HStA Stuttgart A48/01 Bü 2, Nrs. 15, 21.

100. So, for instance, the selling of Oppenheimer's wine in mid-April and his horses later that month. HStA Stuttgart A48/14 Bü 2, Nrs. 89, 95, 116.

101. Tuesday, April 9—the day after Jäger's return from Hohen Neuffen—was a typical day in this phase of the trial. Von Pflug was still in Hohen Neuffen, dealing with some unspecified business; the committee charged with taking an inventory of Oppenheimer's property was confronting complicated legal issues; and the ducal commissioner in Stuttgart was hard at work interrogating some of Oppenheimer's domestic servants who were still being kept under guard in Oppenheimer's home in the city. Jäger, too, was busy. That

day, he composed a report about the interrogations of Hallwachs and Bühler (having already completed one on Oppenheimer on March 31), and he read and responded to yet another written complaint from Bühler's wife. In the afternoon, Jäger joined Faber, Dann, and Gabler at Forstner's house to discuss plans to release some of Oppenheimer's domestic servants and move the others to a different location. This reconstruction is based on HStA Stuttgart A48/14 Bü 2, Nr. 85; Bü 14, fols. 147, 250, 279; and HStA Stuttgart A48/01 Bü 13, Nrs. 6a, b.

102. HStA Stuttgart A48/14 Bü 2, Nrs. 92, 107, 110.

103. HStA Stuttgart A48/14 Bü 14, fol. 308.

104. HStA Stuttgart A48/14 Bü 3, Nr. 185a, fol. 1.

105. These and other interrogations are documented in HStA Stuttgart A48/14 Bü 10, fols. 200ff.

106. All quotes are taken from HStA Stuttgart A48/14 Bü 3, Nr. 185a, fols. 2–4.

107. HStA Stuttgart A48/14 Bü 3, Nr. 185a, fol. 4.

108. All quotes are from HStA Stuttgart A48/14 Bü 3, Nr. 185a, fol. 5.

109. HStA Stuttgart A48/14 Bü 3, Nr. 185a, fols. 4–9.

110. HStA Stuttgart A48/14 Bü 3, Nr. 185a, fol. 8.

111. HStA Stuttgart A48/14 Bü 3, Nr. 185a, fol. 8.

112. HStA Stuttgart A48/14 Bü 3, Nr. 185a, fol. 3 (rescript), and Nr. 214, fol. 1.

113. HStA Stuttgart A48/14 Bü 3, Nr. 185a, fol. 3 (rescript).

114. HStA Stuttgart A48/14 Bü 14, fol. 306; Bü 15, fol. 321.

115. In November 1737, the inquisition committee refers directly to the editing of the documents. HStA Stuttgart A48/14 Bü 8, letter of November 6, 1737, n.p.

116. All quotes from HStA Stuttgart A48/14 Bü 4, fols. 11ff.

117. HStA Stuttgart A48/14 Bü 4, fol. 116.

118. HStA Stuttgart A48/14 Bü 4, fol. 138.

119. HStA Stuttgart A48/14 Bü 3, Nr. 222.

120. HStA Stuttgart A48/14 Bü 4, fols. 147–161.

121. HStA Stuttgart A48/14 Bü 11 (11/4 *species facti*), fol. 8.

122. HStA Stuttgart A48/14 Bü 15, fol. 681.

123. Wisshack, "Historische kurze Beschreibung," fol. 20.

124. About the countess of Sponek, see Haasis, *Joseph Süss Oppenheimer*, 217.

125. HStA Stuttgart A48/14 Bü 75, Ehefrau Faber, fol. 1.

126. All quotes from HStA Stuttgart A48/14 Bü 75, Ehefrau Faber, fol. 2.

127. Most dramatically in "Fund bestätigt Justizmord am Juden Oppenheimer," *Die Welt*, June 7, 2011. See also Haasis, *Joseph Süss Oppenheimer*, 371.

128. HStA Stuttgart A48/14 Bü 17, fol. 1593.

129. HStA Stuttgart A48/14 Bü 48, Nr. 178; Bü 50, Nr. 229; Bü 59, Nr. 519; Bü 62, Nr. 570.

130. HStA Stuttgart A48/14 Bü 15, fols. 691–692.

131. HStA Stuttgart A48/14 Bü 11 (11/4, *species facti*), fol. 17.

132. HStA Stuttgart A48/14 Bü 8, Nr. 358a.

133. HStA Stuttgart A48/14 Bü 8, Nr. 358b.

134. HStA Stuttgart A48/14 Bü 8, Nr. 358a (rescript).

135. All quotes are from HStA Stuttgart A48/14 Bü 8, Nr. 373.

136. HStA Stuttgart A48/14 Bü 8, Nr. 373.

137. *Das jetzt lebende Württemberg unter der glorwürdigsten Administrations-Regierung des Durchlauchtigsten Herrn Herzogs Karl Friedrichs* . . . (Esslingen: Gedruckt bei Gottfried Mäntelrn, 1739), 3.

138. HStA Stuttgart A48/14 Bü 8, Nr. 373 (rescript).

139. On Harpprecht: HStA Stuttgart A48/14 Bü 8, Nrs. 384 and 389, as well as the unnumbered letter in this file, dated Tübingen, November 3, 1737.

140. HStA Stuttgart A48/14 Bü 11 (11/1), esp. fols. 1–2.

141. HStA Stuttgart A48/14 Bü 11 (11/1), fols. 1–2.

142. HStA Stuttgart A48/14 Bü 8, n.p., "Schreiben an den Herzog, 6/8.11.1737." Mögling's complete document is at HStA Stuttgart, A48/14 Bü 122.

143. Haasis, *Joseph Süss Oppenheimer*, 389.

144. HStA Stuttgart A48/14 Bü 11 (11/3 Nr. 6), fol. 2.

145. It can be found in HStA Stuttgart A48/14 Bü 11 (11/4 *species facti*).

146. The original protocol is in HStA Stuttgart A 14/48 Bü 112. Schöpff's hesitation is documented on fol. 50: "Es frage sich ob eine Todesstraffe statthabe."

147. HStA Stuttgart A48/14 Bü 11 (11/4, *species facti*), fol. 3. Cf. Wolf, "Joseph Süß Oppenheimer"; Haasis, *Joseph Süss Oppenheimer*, 74–90.

148. HStA Stuttgart A48/14 Bü 11 (11/4, *species facti*), fol. 3.

149. See earlier, introduction.

150. Georg Konrad Rieger, *Gute Arbeit gibt herrlichen Lohn: in einer Predigt über das Evangelium am Sonntage Septuagesimae,* . . . *mit einer eingeflossenen Anweisung, wie die vorseyende Execution des verurtheilten Juden Joseph Süss Oppenheimers, christlich anzusehen und zu gebrauchen seye. Samt einer Nachricht von dessen* . . . *schmählichen Ende* (Frankfurt am Main: Wolfgang Christoph Multzen, 1738), 13.

151. HStA Stuttgart A48/14 Bü 11 (11/4, *species facti*), fol. 3.

152. HStA Stuttgart A48/14 Bü 11 (11/4, *species facti*), fol. 4.

153. HStA Stuttgart A48/14 Bü 11 (11/4, *species facti*), fol. 8.

154. HStA Stuttgart A48/14 Bü 11 (11/4, *species facti*), fol. 8.

155. HStA Stuttgart A48/14 Bü 11 (11/4, *species facti*), fol. 24.

156. HStA Stuttgart A48/14 Bü 11 (11/4, *species facti*), fol. 12.

157. HStA Stuttgart A48/14 Bü 11 (11/4, *species facti*), fol. 12.

158. HStA Stuttgart A48/14 Bü 11 (11/4, *species facti*), fol. 17.

159. HStA Stuttgart A48/14 Bü 11 (11/4, *species facti*), fol. 73.

160. HStA Stuttgart A48/14 Bü 11 (11/4, *species facti*), fol. 79.

161. HStA Stuttgart A48/14 Bü 11 (11/3 Nr. 6), fol. 2.

162. HStA Stuttgart A48/14 Bü 100, fol. 82 (Nr. 206).

163. HStA Stuttgart A48/14 Bü 11 (11/4, *species facti*), fol. 12.

CHAPTER 2

1. Christoph David Bernard, *Ausführlicher Discurs mit einem seiner guten Freunde, von allem, was ihme in den drey letzten Tagen des unglücklichen Jud Süß Oppenheimers, vornemlich von seiner Beicht, Glaubens-Bekanntniß, und Ablaß, auch zukünftigen Sünden und andern merckwürdigen Vorfallenheiten bekannt worden . . .* (Tübingen: Sigmund, 1738), 11.

2. Bernard, *Ausführlicher Discurs*, 10.

3. Bernard, *Ausführlicher Discurs*, 11–12.

4. Bernard, *Ausführlicher Discurs*, 22.

5. Three examples: Stern, *Jud Süss*, 173; Haasis, *Joseph Süss Oppenheimer*, 422–426; Emberger and Kretzschmar, eds., *Die Quellen sprechen lassen*, 84–86.

6. Emberger and Kretzschmar, eds., *Die Quellen sprechen lassen*.

7. A crucial starting point for the following research into Bernard's life is Martin H. Jung, *Die Württembergische Kirche und die Juden zur Zeit des Pietismus (1675–1780)* (Berlin: Institut Kirche und Judentum, 1992), 253–258. Later, I give the references only to the primary sources, which I have always consulted in person, but my debt to Jung is considerable throughout.

8. Christoph David Bernard, *Hütte Davids / Welche in sich hält alle Grammaticalische Reguln der Hebräischen Sprache . . .* (Tübingen: Sigmund, 1722), "Vorrede" (n.p.). Storr's biography is largely unexplored, although he was the author of a massive handbook about converting Jews. Johann Philipp Storr, *De veritate religionis christianae oder evangelische Glaubenskraft* (Tübingen: n.p., 1703).

9. Bernard, *Ausführlicher Discurs*, 39.

10. Schnee, "Der Geheime Finanzienrat," 112–113; Stern, *Jud Süss*, 8–9, Haasis, *Joseph Süss Oppenheimer*, 19.

11. About Bernard's parents: LKA Stuttgart KB 111 (10.9.1713). All other infor-

mation is summarized by August Friedrich Bök, *Geschichte der herzoglich Würtenbergischen Eberhard Carls Universität zu Tübingen im Grundrisse* (Tübingen: Cotta, 1774), 181.

12. LKA Stuttgart A 3/17, fol. 988 (11.7.1713).

13. HStA Stuttgart A 282 Bd. 1449, 193v, where it also says that Bernard enjoyed exactly 152 meals between July 8 and September 22, 1713. On the location of the Geistliche Herberge: Karl Pfaff, *Geschichte der Stadt Stuttgart* (Stuttgart: Sonnewald, 1846), 2: 136.

14. LKA Stuttgart A 3/17, fol. 1034 (25.8.1713).

15. LKA Stuttgart KB 111 (10.9.1713). No sources were left about the actual ceremony. A detailed example of a contemporary ceremony is Jakob Biber, *Die ohnumgänglich nothwendige Verbindung der Tauffe zu einem heiligen Leben* . . . (Ludwigsburg: Eberhard Friderich Dieterich, 1732), 19–20. Chaijm David was assisted in his conversion by Bernard himself. It is also clear that at least at first, Bernard spent time with other converts. HStA Stuttgart A 21 Bü 697, Nr. 4, document from May 25, 1717.

16. Searches in the collections of the Center for the Study of the History of the Jews at the Central Archives of Historical Records in Warsaw; various Polish state archives (for example in Rzeszów, Piotrkow, and the Vinnytsia Oblast); and the Ukrainian state archives in Lviv and Kiev yielded the same disappointing result. I am grateful to Iwa Nawrocki for her assistance in exploring these archives.

17. Elisheva Carlebach, *Divided Souls: Converts from Judaism in Germany, 1500–1750* (New Haven, CT: Yale University Press, 2001), for example, 42–45. One such person, a Joseph Levi from Wildau, was exposed in Tübingen half a century before Bernard's conversion. Another convert, Christian Philipp by name, was also a suspect in this regard in 1710. HStA Stuttgart, A209 Bü 1922; UA Tübingen, 84, Juristische Fakultät, Consiliensammlung, Bd. 17, 381ff. Further examples in HStA Stuttgart C3 2306 (I/J 1711), for example, the story of Gottfried Hermann/Levi Polach.

18. LKA Stuttgart A3/17, fol. 1172 (19.12.1713).

19. Fundamental to an understanding of the complex position of Jewish converts in eighteenth-century Lutheranism is Martin Jung, "Judentum und Christentum im Pietismus des 17. und 18. Jahrhunderts," in *Kirche und Synagoge: Handbuch zur Geschichte von Christen und Juden, Darstellung mit Quellen*, ed. Karl Heinrich Rengstorf and Siegfried von Kortzfleisch (Stuttgart: Ernst Klett Verlag, 1970), II: 87–128.

20. Biber, *Die ohnumgänglich nothwendige Verbindung der Tauffe zu einem heiligen Leben* . . . , 19.

21. Christoph David Bernard, *Davids Stab oder gründliche Unterweisung worin-nen man denen Unglaubigen, insonderheit aber denen Juden, zeigen kann . . .* (Tübingen: Flick, 1730), 76.

22. Totenregister Tübingen 3.5.1751 (LKA Stuttgart KB 1643).

23. Bernard, *Hütte Davids*, title page. Other occurrences throughout the archival material cited in this essay.

24. Bernhard's official request to Regent Carl Rudolf to do something about this situation was granted (tellingly!) a day after Oppenheimer's execution. UA Tübingen 29/1, 2–43, Nr. 4.

25. Cited in M. Duncker, "Aus Visitationsakten: Die anatolische Schule in Tübingen in den Jahren 1670–1748," *Tübinger Blätter* X, no. 1/2 (1907): 6; HStA Stuttgart A 281 Bü 1279 (1743).

26. LKA Stuttgart A 3/17, fol. 1039 (5.9.1713).

27. Bernard, *Ausführlicher Discurs*, 14–15.

28. The following description of the seminary is based on a detailed account from the 1740s. Andreas Christoph Zeller, *Ausführliche Merckwürdigkeiten der Hochfürstl. Würtembergischen Universitaet und Stadt Tübingen . . .* (Tübingen: David Bauhof, 1743), 203–210.

29. EvStA Tübingen, E1 9/1 (Testimonia Alumnorum Ducalis Stipendy Theologi), Sebastiani 1714.

30. About daily life in the seminary, including the meals, see Martin Leube, *Geschichte des Tübinger Stifts* (Stuttgart: Steinkopf, 1954), II: 186–198. A typical weekly menu is reproduced in Joachim Hahn and Hans Mayer, *Das Evangelische Stift in Tübingen: Geschichte und Gegenwart* (Stuttgart: Konard Theiss, 1985), 267 and Abb. 198/199.

31. Johann Adam Gottfried, *Wahrhafter Bericht von M. Johann Adam Gottfrieds sonderbaren Bekehrung vom Judenthum zum Christenthum . . .* (n.p.: n.p., 1776), 3.

32. For a floor plan of the seminary in the eighteenth century, including the *Convertitenstube*, see F. Fritz and A. Schneiderhan, *Baugeschichte des Tübinger Stifts* (Stuttgart: Verlag für Volkskunst und Volksbildung, 1919), 91.

33. These and other incidents are cited in Hahn and Mayer, *Das Evangelische Stift*, 170–171. The prohibition on cohabitation of converts is from 1704: Carl Hirzel, ed., *Sammlung der württembergischen Schul-Gesetze, Teil 2, . . . für die Mittel- und Fachschulen bis zum Jahr 1846* (Tübingen: Fues, 1846), 191.

34. Fritz and Schneiderhan, *Baugeschichte*, 35 n. 69. More generally about the typical daily schedule of the students, see Hirzel, ed., *Sammlung*, 186–191.

35. LKA Stuttgart A26/456 1, Nr. 11 and A3/17, fol. 1172 (19.12.1713).

36. LKA Stuttgart A3/17, fol. 1172 (19.12.1713).

37. EvStA Tübingen E1 9/1 Georgii and EvStA E1 151/Bernard.

38. Stephan Schultz, *Leitungen des Höchsten nach seinem Rath auf den Reisen durch Europa, Asia und Africa . . . Aus eigener Erfahrung beschrieben . . .* (Halle: Hemmerde, 1771–1775), 1: 137; UA Tübingen 44/118, 2, 51, Nr. 3. About Stephan Schultz more generally, see Johann F. A. de Le Roi, *Stephan Schultz: Ein Beitrag zum Verständniss der Juden und ihrer Bedeutung für das Leben der Völker* (Gota: F. A. Perthes, 1871).

39. On the importance of disputations for all seminary students, see Leube, *Geschichte*, II: 90; Hahn and Mayer, *Das Evangelische Stift*, 131–132. The fundamental study about disputations in early modern German universities is still Ewald Horn, *Die Disputationen und Promotionen an den deutschen Universitäten, vornehmlich seit dem 16. Jahrhundert* (Leipzig: O. Harrassowitz, 1893). More recent literature is covered in Martin Gierl, *Pietismus und Aufklärung: Theologische Polemik und die Kommunikationsreform der Wissenschaft am Ende des 17. Jahrhunderts* (Göttingen: Vandenhoek & Ruprecht, 1997), 125–45.

40. On this aspect of the early modern disputation, see Ignacio Angelelli, "The Techniques of Disputation in the History of Logic," *Journal of Philosophy* 67 (October 22, 1970): 806–807.

41. Indeed, even among Jewish medieval scholars, the *pilpul* was sometimes criticized as an intellectual trap or a sign of arrogance. Talya Fishman, *Becoming the People of the Talmud: Oral Torah as Written Tradition in Medieval Jewish Cultures* (Philadelphia: University of Pennsylvania Press, 2011), 162. On the history of the *pilpul* more generally, see for instance H. Dimitrovsky, "Al derekh ha-pipul," in *Salo Wittmayer Baron Jubilee Volume on the Occasion of His Eightieth Birthday*, ed. Saul Lieberman and Arthur Hyman (Jerusalem: American Academy of Jewish Research, 1975), III: 111–181.

42. *Wöchentliche Gelehrte Neuigkeiten* (Tübingen: Cotta, 1738), 645.

43. Christoph David Bernard, *Der in der Lüfften schwebende neue Jüdische Heilige Joseph Süß Oppenheimer, oder: Das von der Würtembergischen Judenschafft herausgegebene merckwürdige Canonisations-Manifest . . .* (Tübingen: Johann Georg Cotta, 1738), 6; see also 79.

44. *Ordo Studiorum in Universitate Anno MDCCXXIV* (Tübingen: Schramm, 1734), n.p. On the importance of disputations in private *collegia,* see Horn, *Die Disputationen,* 38–46.

45. According to Andreas Christoph Zeller, the historian of the University of Tübingen and a contemporary of Bernard's, the latter even prepared a whole publication refuting Albo's arguments. Its title was *Emunat David/Davids*

Glaub ("David's faith"), but it was never published. Zeller, *Ausführliche Merckwürdigkeiten*, 514–515.

46. WLB, cod. or. 40° 26, fol. 174. Another book copied by Bernard was the eleventh-century *Chovot ha-Levavot* by Bahya ibn Paquda. WLB cod. or. 40° 27.

47. Bernard, *Ausführlicher Discurs*, 15.

48. Bernard, *Ausführlicher Discurs*, 11–12.

49. EvStA Tübingen 151/Bernhard (4.5.1714).

50. Hillel Levine, "Gentry, Jews, and Serfs: The Rise of Polish Vodka," *Review* 4, no. 2 (1980): 223–250; Magdalena Opalski, *The Jewish Tavern-Keeper and His Tavern in Nineteenth Century Polish Literature* (Jerusalem: Zalman Shazar Center for the Furtherance of the Study of Jewish History, 1986); Glenn Dynner, *Yankel's Tavern: Jews, Liquor, and Life in the Kingdom of Poland* (New York: Oxford University Press, 2014).

51. This reconstruction is based on UA Tübingen 15/13 (Matricula, 1625–1748); HStA Stuttgart A21 Bü 697, Nr. 4; UAJ M48–51; J.F.A. De Le Roi, *Die evangelische Christenheit und die Juden in der Zeit der Herrschaft christlicher Lebensanschauungen unter den Völkern* (Leipzig: Zentralantiquariat der DDR, 1974), I: 388; Bök, *Geschichte*, 181; and LKA Stuttgart A3/19, fol. 179 (29.3.1718).

52. Christoph David Bernard, *Hütte Davids*; Bernard, *Die erstere Worte Davids welche in sich halten die Menschenwerdung Christi . . .* (Tübingen: Pflick, 1724); Bernard, *Unpartayische Beurtheilung des Eyd-Schwurs Eines Juden gegen einem Christen . . .* (Tübingen: Cotta, 1728); Bernard, *Davids Stab*.

53. The reconstruction of this part of Bernard's life is based on UA Tübingen, Acta Senatus XLVI 1720–1725, 4/7, fol. 161; LKA Stuttgart 3/23 fol. 1247 (8.10.1726); and *Catalogus Lectionum publicarum, et privatarum, quas in universitate tubingensi, omnium ordinum preofessores, qui praesentes sunt, per semestre hoc hybernum habent, habebuntque. Anno MDCCXXXVII* (Tübingen: Schramm, 1737), n.p.

54. Augustine, *Expositions of the Psalms, 51–72*, ed. John E. Rotelle, trans. Maria Boulding (New York: New City Press, 2001), 13.

55. Edward A. Gosselin, *The King's Progress to Jerusalem: Some Interpretations of David during the Reformation Period and Their Patristic and Medieval Background* (Malibu, CA: Undena Publications, 1976), esp. 67–89.

56. Bernard, *Die erstere Worte Davids*, "Vorrede" (n.p.).

57. LKA Stuttgart A 3/19, fol. 179.

58. StdA Tübingen A20/S216 (Gerichtsprotokoll 1724–30), fols. 381b, 386 (4/11.12.1726).

59. StdA Tübingen, E 202 (Tübinger Häuserbuch von Reinhold Rau), fasc. 1015.

60. University records show that when the town tried to put up soldiers in Bernard's house in late 1736, he had enough cash to buy them out. UA Tübingen, Acta Senatus XLVIII, 1736–1740, 4/11, fl. 17–18 (20.12.1736). In two letters written by Bernard shortly before Oppenheimer's trial, he complains about his meager salary: UA Tübingen 29/1, 2–43, Nrs. 1 and 2.

61. StdA Tübingen, E101/131. More about Bernard's inventories later.

62. One reichsthaler was worth two gulden in Württemberg that year. *Die Archivpflege in den Kreisen und Gemeinden: Lehrgangsbericht und Hilfsbuch für Arbeiter in Württemberg und in Hohenzollern* (Stuttgart: W. Kohlhammer Verlag, 1952), 90. For the sum of 3,000 reichsthaler, see Bernard, *Ausführlicher Discurs*, 40–41, and later, chapter 3.

63. LKA Stuttgart A 3/20, fol. 758 (7.5.1720); Biber, *Die ohnumgänglich nothwendige Verbindung der Tauffe zu einem heiligen Leben . . .* , 19–20.

64. "Gesuch des Lektors Christoph David Bernard in Tübingen um Abhaltung eines Religionsgesprächs mit einigen jüdischen Notabeln in der Karlsruher Synagoge, 1730." GLA Karlsruhe 206 Nr. 2198.

65. GLA Karlsruhe 206 Nr. 2198.

66. Georg Konrad Rieger, *Gute Arbeit gibt herrlichen Lohn*, 6.

67. About Pfaff, see Wolf-Friedrich Schäufele, "Christoph Matthäus Pfaff (1686–1760) als Tübinger Universitätskanzler und Professor," in *Die Universität Tübingen zwischen Orthodoxie, Pietismus und Afuklärung*, ed. Ulrich Köpf (Tübingen: Jan Rhotbecke Verlag, 2004), 123–156.

68. Christoph Matthäus Pfaff, introduction to Bernard, *Hütte Davids*, n.p.

69. De Le Roi, *Die evangelische Christenheit*, I: 396–397; Karl Christian Eberhard Ehmann, *Friedrich Christoph Oetinger, Leben und Briefe: Als urkundlicher Commentar zu dessen Schriften* (Stuttgart: J. F. Steinkopf, 1859), 51, 429.

70. Bök, *Geschichte*, 181.

71. The information is based on the preamble to the couple's inventory upon Maria Margaretha's death. StdA Tübingen, E101/131.

72. StdA Tübingen, E 202, fasc. 1015 (Tübinger Häuserbuch von Reinhold Rau).

73. StdA Tübingen A20/S217 (Gerichtsprotokoll 1727–1730), fols. 102b, 117, 118b, 135 (January–May 1728).

74. The information is based on the second inventory of Bernard's property (at his death) and his and his second wife's joint last will and testament of 1743. StdA Tübingen, E101/133, 5.2.1743; 14.4.1752.

75. StdA Tübingen, E101/133, 5.2.1743.

76. Bernard, *Ausführlicher Discurs*, 21–23.

77. Among his books, we find both in 1728 and at his death in 1751 the Geneva

Bible and Johannes Buxendorf's *Biblia Hebraica* (4 vols., 1618–1619); Isaac Abrabanel's exegesis on the Pentateuch and the Former Prophets; and Thomas à Kempis's *Imitatio Christi* and Johann Arendt's *True Christianity*. StdA Tübingen, E101/131 6.2.1728, 14.4.1752.

78. Zeller, *Ausführliche Merckwürdigkeiten*, 514–515; StdA Tübingen, E101/133 (14.4.1752).

79. Johann Albrecht Bengel, *Welt-Alter darin die Schriftmässige Zeiten-Linie bewiesen und die Siebenzig Wochen samt andern wichtigen Texten und heilsamen Lehren erörtert werden . . .* (Esslingen: Schall, 1746), 260–261. Bernard's response to this criticism has survived in a very submissive letter to Bengel. WLB Stuttgart, cod. hist. 4° 689, I: 19–21.

80. Bernard, *Ausführlicher Discurs*, 5–6.

81. HStA Stuttgart A48/14 Bü 2, Nr. 150, fol. 1.

82. HStA Stuttgart A48/14 Bü 2, Nr. 150, fol. 1 (rescript).

83. Bernard, *Ausführlicher Discurs*, 6–7.

84. It can be found in HStA Stuttgart A48/14 Bü 118/1.

85. HStA Stuttgart A48/14 Bü 44, Fasz. XVI holds almost exclusively letters addressed to Oppenheimer. The other three fascicles of the same Signatur (XVII, XVIII, XIX) contain letters to and by treasurer Levi.

86. These were published in Haasis, *Joseph Süss Oppenheimers Rache*, 121–124.

87. HStA Stuttgart A48/14 Bü 44, Fasz. XVI, Nrs. 28, 30.

88. Respective examples from HStA Stuttgart A48/14 Bü 44, Fasz. XVI: Nrs. 41; 20, 62, 73, 81, 110; 63; 76, 102.

89. For example, HStA Stuttgart A48/14 Bü 44, Fasz. XVI, Nrs. 53–59.

90. For example, HStA Stuttgart A48/14 Bü 44, Fasz. XVI, Nr. 4; Fasz. XVII, Nr. 68; Fasz. XIX, Nr. 7.

91. HStA Stuttgart A48/14 Bü 44, Fasz. XVI, Nr. 1; Fasz. XVI, Nr. 101; Fasz. XIX, Nr. 76.

92. Christoph Matthäus Pfaff, introduction to Bernard, *Hütte Davids*, n.p.

93. The relevant documents are all in HStA Stuttgart A48/14 Bü 7, Nr. 324. They are not numbered.

94. All quotes are from HStA Stuttgart A48/14 Bü 7, Nr. 324, n.p.

95. HStA Stuttgart A48/14 Bü 7, Nr. 324, n.p.

96. "So bitte ich, daß ihr sollt mir den befallen zu erweisen, und zu Hajum zu gehen, und ihme zu sagen alles was ich euch schreibe, da mit einerley Rede möchte geführt werden." HStA Stuttgart A48/14 Bü 7, Nr. 324, n.p.

97. All quotes are from HStA Stuttgart A48/14 Bü 7, Nr. 324, n.p.

98. HStA Stuttgart A48/14 Bü 8. Letter by von Gaisberg, Faber, and Jäger to Carl Rudolf, November 8, 1737.

99. HStA Stuttgart A48/14 Bü 11, Nr. 4, fol. 12.

100. HStA Stuttgart, A48/14 Bü 98, 1, Oktober 1737. It was from this apartment, in the so-called Posthaus in the Friedbergergasse, that some of Oppenheimer's correspondence survived in its original form, reaching the state archives in Stuttgart only in 1928. Reproduced in Stern, *Jud Süss*, 299, 302.

101. Indeed, in Bernard, *Der in der Lüfften schwebende Jüdische Heilige*, 4, the reference is direct.

102. This was a common understanding of Saul's story as understood by early modern theologians, including in several books found in Bernard's house upon his death. These include, among others, Johannes Arndt's influential *Vom wahrem Christenthumb* (Magdeburg, 1610), 1: 110, and Heinrich Müller's *Der Himmlische Liebeskuss* (Hof: Johann Christoph Leidenfrost, 1737), 147. Compare the list of books in Bernard's library at StdA Tübingen, E101/133, 14.4.1752.

103. Augustine, *The City of God against the Pagans*, ed. and trans. R. W. Dyson (Cambridge: Cambridge University Press, 1998), 785–790. On the reception of St. Augustine's work in the early modern period, see especially Heiko A. Oberman, "'Tuus sum, salvum me fac': Augustinréveil zwischen Renaissance und Reformation," in *Scientia Augustiniana*, ed. Cornelius Petrus Mauer and Willigis Eckermann (Würzburg: Augustiner-Verlag, 1975), 349–394.

104. Luther emphasized Matthew 21:43 in his interpretation of Jona, one of the minor prophets. It is perhaps no coincidence that the latter was the topic of Bernard's lectures in the semester immediately before Oppenheimer's execution. Martin Luther, *Die Auslegungen derer grossen und kleinen Propheten* (Halle: Johann Justinus Gebauer, 1741), 2689.

105. Augustine, *The City of God*, 788.

106. Bernard tells this story in *Der in der Lüfften schwebende Jüdische Heilige*, 4, 51–52, 58. The original pamphlet has surfaced very recently after almost three centuries in which it has been presumed to be lost. Its reproduction and German translation can be found in Hellmut G. Haasis, ed., *Totengedenkbuch für Joseph Süss Oppenheimer* (Worms: Worms-Verlag, 2012), 10–20. For full evaluation, see chapter 3 of this book.

107. Bernard, *Der in der Lüfften scwebende Jüdische Heilige*, 58–59, 64.

108. Bernard, *Der in der Lüfften scwebende Jüdische Heilige*, 58.

109. Bernard, *Der in der Lüfften scwebende Jüdische Heilige*, 5.

110. Christoph Matthäus Pfaff, *Einleitung in die dogmatische Theologie oder die Grund-Wahrheiten der Christlichen Religion* (Tübingen: Cotta, 1747), for example, 45, 98, 415–422. That Pfaff also taught Augustine to his students

is evident from dissertations written under his supervision—for example, Heinrich Lisching, Johann Dannenberger, and Christoph Kausler, *Diss. theol. de ecclesia sanguinem non sitiente* . . . (Tubinga: Pflicke atque Bauhof, 1740), 2–3, 16–17.

CHAPTER 3

1. General information about the Judengasse is from Isidor Kracauer, *Geschichte der Juden in Frankfurt am Main (1150–1814)*, 2 vols. (Frankfurt am Main: in Komission bei Kaufmann, 1925–1927); Fritz Backhaus, ed., *Die Frankfurter Judengasse: Jüdisches Leben in der Frühen Neuzeit* (Frankfurt am Main: Societätsverlag, 2006); Cilli Kasper-Holtkotte, *Die Jüdische Gemeinde von Frankfurt/Main in der Frühen Neuzeit* (Berlin: De Gruyter, 2010); and Gerald Soliday, *A Community in Conflict: Frankfurt Society in the Seventeenth and Eighteenth Centuries* (Hanover, NH: University Press of New England, 1974). Unless indicated otherwise, genealogical information about Mordechai Schloss's family is taken from Alexander Dietz, *Stammbuch der Frankfurter Juden* (Frankfurt am Main: J. St. Goar, 1907), 261–264, and especially Shlomo Ettlinger's remarkable *ET* (see list of abbreviations).
2. According to the protocols of the inquisition committee, Schloss was 63 years old in 1737. HStA Stuttgart, A 48/14 Bü 66, fol. 51.
3. "Hier kann auf 24 Fragen, der Jud kein Wort mehr sagen," Karten und Grafik Sammlung, WLB Stuttgart.
4. WLB cod. hist. fol. 1022, IV: Versteigerung des Süß'sche Besitzes, 1737, for example, Nr. 20. Compare also figures 5 and 8 in this book.
5. "Visitation der Judengasse, Ao. 1694, 1703, 1709," IStG Frankfurt am Main, Juden Akten, 17; IStG Frankfurt am Main, Rechneiamt: Bücher, 700, fols. 28, 64, 99, 136; *The Frankfurt Memorbuch*, Jerusalem, NLI, ms. Heb. 1092, fols. 114, 310. Also very helpful in reconstructing these details is the database of Jewish gravestones in Germany: http://steinheim-institut.de/cgi-bin/epidat, accessed January 23, 2015.
6. See also Soliday, *A Community in Conflict,* 175–197.
7. *The Frankfurt Memorbuch*, fol. 114.
8. Three examples are documents from March 25, 1721; March 9, 1722; and April 9, 1732; HStA Stuttgart A 6 Bü 168. About Schloss's death and his wife's return to Frankfurt, see IStG Frankfurt am Main, Juden wider Fremde, 910.
9. *The Frankfurt Memorbuch*, fol. 310.
10. Houses 170 and 181 (Wilder Mann), "Visitation der Judengasse, Ao. 1694, 1703, 1709," IStG Frankfurt am Main, Juden Akten, 17.

11. "Visitation der Judengasse, Ao. 1694, 1703, 1709," IStG Frankfurt am Main, Juden Akten, 17.

12. For an introduction, see Chava Turniansky, "Ha-limud ba-cheder ba-et ha-chadasha ha-mukdemet," in *ha-Cheder: mehkarim, te'udot, pirke sifrut ve-zikhronot*, ed. Immanuel Etkes and David Assaf (Tel-Aviv: Bet Shalom Alekhem, 2010).

13. On this topic, see H. C. Zafren, "Hebrew Printing by and for Frankfurter Jews—to 1800," in *Jüdische Kultur in Frankfurt am Main von den Anfängen bis zur Gegenwart*, ed. Karl. E. Grözinger (Wiesbaden: Harrassowitz, 1997), 231–271.

14. For example, Chava Turniansky, "Yiddish 'Historical' Songs as Sources for the History of the Jews in Pre-partition Poland," *Polin, A Journal of Polish-Jewish Studies* 4 (1989): 42–52.

15. For many examples, see Cilli Kasper-Holtkotte, *Die jüdische Gemeinde von Frankfurt/Main in der Frühen Neuzeit: Familien, Netzwerke und Konflikte eines jüdischen Zentrums* (Berlin and New York: De Gruyter, 2010), 59ff.

16. HStA Stuttgart A 48/05 Bü 18, Num. XX, response to question 11; IStG Frankfurt am Main, Juden wider Fremde, 910.

17. About von Grävenitz's story, see Oßwald-Bargende, *Die Mätresse, der Fürst und die Macht*.

18. For an overview, see Schnee, *Die Hoffinanz und der moderne Staat*, 4: 87–109. About the history of Jews in Stuttgart, see Paul Sauer, *Geschichte der Stadt Stuttgart. Bd. III: Vom Beginn des 18. Jahrhunderts bis zum Abschluß des Verfassungsvertrags für das Königreich Württemberg 1819* (Stuttgart: Kohlhammer, 1995), 171–194. Later, I go against some aspects of Sauer's description of the communal life of Württemberg's court Jews. The crucial archival collections about the topic are HStA Stuttgart, A 6 Bü 168, and HStA Stuttgart A 211 Bü 410, Bü 411, and Bü 412.

19. As Löw explains in HStA Stuttgart A 5 Bü 151, document from November 4, 1720, p. 1.

20. About the involvement of Jews in the construction of the Ludwigsburg palace, see Walter Baumgärtner, *Die Erbauung des Ludwigsburger Schlosses: Ein Beispiel staatlicher Bauwirtschaft im 18. Jahrhundert* (Würzburg-Aumühle: Konrad Triltsch, 1938), 47–49.

21. HStA Stuttgart A 6 Bü 168; HStA Stuttgart A 211 Bü 410.

22. Attested by his wife after her return to Frankfurt in 1744. IStG Frankfurt am Main, Juden wider Fremde, 910, document from December 22, 1744.

23. About the commercial connection between Schloss and Seligmann, see, for instance, HStA Stuttgart A 6 Bü 173, passport issued July 17, 1732.

24. HStA Stuttgart A 48/05 Bü 38, Nr. 7.
25. Some examples are HStA Stuttgart A 256 Bd. 202, Nr. 641; HStA Stuttgart A 256 Bd. 211, Nr. 647; HStA Stuttgart A 256 Bd. 216, Nrs. 851 and 871.
26. HStA Stuttgart A 21 Bü 701, Nr. 5, document from April 13, 1723.
27. HStA Stuttgart A 21 Bü 701, Nr. 5, document from April 13, 1723.
28. HStA Stuttgart A 21 Bü 701, Nr. 5; HStA Stuttgart A 6 Bü 168, documents from January 12, 1722; March 9, 1722; February 27, 1728; and February 13, 1730.
29. Britta Wassmuth, *Im Spannungsfeld zwischen Hof, Stadt und Judengemeinde: Soziale Beziehungen und Mentalitätswandel der Hofjuden in der kurpfälzischen Residenzstadt Mannheim am Ausgang des Ancien Régime* (Ludwigshafen am Rhein: Pro Message, 2005), 126.
30. HStA Stuttgart A 21 Bü 701, Nr. 5, letter of April 13, 1723, fol. 4.
31. The crucial documents about the syndicate are collected in HStA Stuttgart A 21 Bü 701, Nr. 4.
32. Roland Fischer (archivist of pre-1848 documents, IStG Frankfurt am Main) in discussion with the author, July 2014.
33. Ludwig, who converted to Lutheranism in 1699, shared a similar life story to Christoph David Bernard's. In a letter he composed in 1712, Ludwig complains about his Christian neighbors, who constantly call him a "baptized Jew," although he had converted a long time ago. "Es seye ein Schandname, mit dem ich mich nimmer lassen wolle." HStA Stuttgart A 210 II Bü 238.
34. HStA Stuttgart A 21 Bü 697, Nr. 4, document from May 25, 1717.
35. HStA Stuttgart, C 3 Bü 2307 (I/J 1716), Jahre 1723/1724.
36. HStA Stuttgart A 6 Bü 168, document from January 12, 1722; *The Frankfurt Memorbuch*, fol. 310; Leopold Löwenstein, *Beiträge zur Geschichte der Juden in Deutschland* (Kauffmann: Frankfurt am Main, 1895) I: 218–219.
37. HStA Stuttgart A 21 Bü 701, Nr. 5, document from December 5, 1718.
38. HStA Stuttgart A 21 Bü 701, Nr. 5, document from June 23, 1723.
39. HStA Stuttgart A 21 Bü 701, Nr. 5, document from March 8, 1724.
40. HStA Stuttgart A 21 Bü 701, Nr. 5, document from April 13, 1724.
41. HStA Stuttgart A 5 Bü 151, document from November 4, 1720.
42. HStA Stuttgart C 3 Bü 2306 (I/J 1711), Jahre 1723–1726.
43. HStA Stuttgart C 3 Bü 2306 (I/J 1711), Jahre 1723–1726.
44. HStA Stuttgart A 21 Bü 701, Nr. 4, document from June 24, 1727.
45. HStA Stuttgart A6 Bü 168, document from April 12, 1729; HStA Stuttgart A48/05 Bü 18, Nr. XX, response to question 1.
46. Heinrich Völker, "Joseph Süss Oppenheimer und seine Beziehungen zu Frankfurt am Main," *Alt-Frankfurt. Geschichtliche Zeitschrift für Frankfurt*

und seine Umgebung, 2 (1929): 51–54, 83–85; Haasis, *Joseph Süss Oppenheimer*, 91–104.

47. Haasis, *Joseph Süss Oppenheimer*, 95.
48. Haasis, *Joseph Süss Oppenheimer*, 98.
49. HStA Stuttgart A 48/05 Bü 18, Nr. XX. act. d. 19. Febr. 1734.
50. HStA Stuttgart A 48/05 Bü 18, Nr. XX. act. d. 19. Febr. 1734.
51. HStA Stuttgart A 48/05 Bü 18, Nr. XX. act. d. 19. Febr. 1734.
52. HStA Stuttgart A 48/05 Bü 18, Nr. XX. act. d. 19. Febr. 1734.
53. HStA Stuttgart A48/14 Bü 75, Staat und Ordnung für Süss. Stuttgart, den 18. März 1734.
54. IStG Frankfurt am Main, Juden wider Fremde, 910.
55. See the interrogation of Elias Hayum in HStA Stuttgart A48/14 Bü 75.
56. Löwenstein, *Beiträge zur Geschichte der Juden in Deutschland*, I: 218, n. 1.
57. HStA Stuttgart A 6 Bü 168, document from December 11, 1725, mentions Hayum as Schloss's soon-to-be son-in-law.
58. HStA Stuttgart A 21 Bü 907.
59. Especially HStA Stuttgart A 210 III Bü 136, Nr. 6.
60. Compare with figure 5.
61. Seligmann received the status of a protected Jew (Schutzjude) only once Schloss was dead. HStA A404 Bü 26, document from June 16, 1744.
62. HStA Stuttgart A 211 Bü 412, n.p. (extractus dassigen Stadtvotamts, 29. Aprilis 1747).
63. HStA Stuttgart A 21 Bü 700 and Bü 701 (for example, Nr. 1). Compare the very different description in Sauer, *Geschichte der Stadt Stuttgart*, III: 174–176.
64. *The Frankfurt Memorbuch*, fol. 409.
65. HStA A404 Bü 26 (document of 1747) and HStA Stuttgart A 211 Bü 412, n.p. (extractus, 29. Aprilis 1747).
66. HStA Stuttgart A 6 Bü 173 (passport for Callman Seligmann).
67. Bernard, *Ausführlicher Discurs*, 41.
68. *The Frankfurt Memorbuch*, fol. 409; ET, 14.VI.1683; 27.I.1737; 28.VIII. 1764.
69. This was the house "Strauss." The building was subdivided in 1608 into three smaller houses: restlicher Straus, Krachbein, and Reifenberg. Kasper-Holtkotte, *Die jüdische Gemeinde von Frankfurt/Main*, 553.
70. About Michal (or Michele) Oppenheimer, see Haasis, *Joseph Süss Oppenheimer*, 131–138; about Daniel Oppenheimer, see Haasis, *Joseph Süss Oppenheimer*, 315–318.
71. IStG Frankfurt am Main, Criminalia: Akten, 4.740.

72. Their names and the details of their depositions are documented in HStA Stuttgart, A48/14 Bü 10.

73. HStA Stuttgart, A 48/14 Bü 10, fol.18.

74. HStA Stuttgart A 48/14 Bü 2, Nr. 90.

75. HStA Stuttgart A 48/14 Bü 10, fols. 330–350. About Oppenheimer's recorded response to these allegations, see HStA Stuttgart A 48/14 Bü 6, fol. 90 (question 338).

76. HStA Stuttgart A 48/14 Bü 10, fols. 337–338.

77. Bernard, *Ausführlicher Discurs*, 36.

78. HStA Stuttgart Bü 66, Articuli defensionales, fol. 22.

79. HStA Stuttgart A 48/14 Bü 75. The letter by his wife is attested (but not quoted) in HStA Stuttgart, A 48/14, Bü 85, Akten den Elias Hayum betr., Nr. 6.

80. See earlier, chapter 2.

81. HStA Stuttgart, A 210 III Bü 134: "Belästigung eines Juden (Marx Nathan)."

82. HStA Stuttgart A 48/14 Bü 2, Nrs. 89, 95, 116; and especially WLB cod. hist. fol. 1022, IV: Versteigerung des Süß'sche Besitzes, 1737. The records indicate that among local Jews, Nathan Maram invested the most in buying Oppenheimer's property.

83. HStA Stuttgart A48/14 Bü 66, fol. 14.

84. HStA Stuttgart A 48/14 Bü 66, fol. 15.

85. HStA Stuttgart A 48/14 Bü 66, fols. 15–16.

86. HStA Stuttgart A 48/14 Bü 66, fol. 14.

87. HStA Stuttgart A 48/14 Bü 66, fol. 13.

88. A copy of *The Story of the Passing of Joseph Süss*, including a transcription in Hebrew letters and a German translation by the author, can be found in Haasis, ed., *Totengedenkbuch*, 10–20. All further references to *The Story of the Passing of Joseph Süss* are based on this reproduction.

89. Hebrew and Yiddish do not normally distinguish between Catholic priests and Lutheran pastors. I retained the ambiguity in the translation.

90. HStA Stuttgart A48/14 Bü 12, Nr. 33; HStA Stuttgart A48/14 Bü 71, fols. 516–519.

91. Callman Seligmann, Isaac Seligmann his brother, and Gideon Seligmann.

92. Bernard, *Ausführlicher Discurs*, for example, 23; Bernard, *Der in der Lüfften schwebende Jüdische Heilige*, esp. 65; HStA Stuttgart A48/14 Bü 100, Nr. 216; UA Tübingen 38/10, 1–Nr. 7.2.

93. Chava Turniansky, "The Events in Frankfurt am Main (1612–1616) in *Megillas Vints* and in an Unknown Yiddish 'Historical' Song," in *Schöpferische*

Momente des europäischen Judentums in der frühen Neuzeit, ed. Michael Graetz (Heidelberg: C. Winter, 2000), 122; Elisheva Carlebach, *The Death of Simon Abeles: Jewish-Christian Tension in Seventeenth-Century Prague* (New York: Center for Jewish Studies, Queens College, 2001), 35, n. 92.

94. Elisheva Carlebach, *The Death of Simon Abeles*, 35–38.

95. Bernard, *Der in der Lüfften schwebende Jüdische Heilige*, 4.

96. *The Story of the Passing of Joseph Süss.*

97. Bernard, *Der in der Lüfften schwebende Jüdische Heilige*, 4–5.

98. Bernard, *Der in der Lüfften schwebende Jüdische Heilige*, 63.

99. *The Story of the Passing of Joseph Süss.* The receipt for Seligmann's (also known as Salomon Schächter's) trouble is in HStA Stuttgart A 48/14 Bü 100, Nr. 216.

100. *The Story of the Passing of Joseph Süss.*

101. Several contemporary poems, all identified by Barbara Gerber, make this comparison. "Ein Joseph war vorlängst Ägypten wohlbekannt / Ein Joseph kam zu uns ins Württembergerland"; "Das schöne Württemberg war fast Ägypten"; Oppenheimer sei "ein wahrhafter Joseph unserer Zeiten / Jenem Joseph in Ägypten so gleich wie ein Tag dem anderen," and so on. WLB cod. hist. fol. 348. Nrs. 15, 16, 27, and 82; Gerber, *Jud Süß*, 443, n. 156.

102. Haasis, *Joseph Süss Oppenheimer*, 448.

103. *Der Jüdische Schelmische Heilige und Schand Märterer Joseph Süss, oder: Abdruck und Übersetzung Eines unter denen Juden herumgehenden öffentlichen Hebräischen Ausschreibens* (Frankfurt and Leipzig, 1738), 9.

104. Chava Turniansky summarizes some of this literature in Glikl of Hammeln, *Glikl: Zikhronot, 1691–1719*, trans. and ed. Chava Turniansky (Jerusalem: Merkaz Zalman Shazar, 2006), 250, n. 17.

105. "Mekhirot Yossef (1707?)," in *Mahazot mikra'iyim be-Yiddish, 1697–1750*, ed. Chone Shmeruk (Jerusalem: Israeli Academy of Sciences, 1979), 533–621.

106. Selma Stern, *The Court Jew: A Contribution to the History of the Period of Absolutism in Central Europe*, trans. Ralph Weiman (Philadelphia: Jewish Publication Society of America, 1950), 73.

107. For an English version, see Yaakov ben Yitzchak Ashkenazi, *Tz'enah ur'enah: The Classic Anthology of Torah Lore and Midrashic comment [Tse'enah u-re'enah]*, ed. Meir Holder, trans. Miriam Stark Zakon (Brooklyn, NY: Mesorah Publications, 1983), 356–357.

108. HStA Stuttgart A 48/14 Bü 1, Nr. 92.

109. Many relevant examples can be found in the entries dedicated to Joseph's story in the *Jewish Encyclopedia* (1904) and *Encyclopedia Judaica* (2007).

110. And compare Bernard, who has this to say about Oppenheimer: "He told me, I shall forgive my fellow human beings and my coreligionists who gave a false testimony against me." See earlier, chapter 2.

CHAPTER 4

1. Existing literature on David Fassmann's life is uneven and based almost solely on Fassmann's own (often very spurious) claims. Of the older literature about Fassmann mentioned in the excellent entry of the *Allgemeine Deutsche Biographie*, the dissertation by Kaschmieder is still valuable and the one by Damberg extremely useful. More recent works include the third chapter in Routledge's volume and the equally valuable discussion of some primary sources in Agatha Kobuch's book. Eckhardt's and Matthes's dissertations tackle specific topics within Fassmann's large corpus and as such are often helpful. Several brief discussions in Arndt's recent book are useful as well, though the author's focus is very far from being Fassmann himself. The most recent discussion of Fassmann's work is the dissertation by Stephanie Dreyfürst. Excellent as a literary scholar, Dreyfürst takes at face value Fassmann's description of his own life story. For reasons that will become clear in the rest of this chapter, this is misguided and in fact constitutes a misreading of Fassmann's own views on such self-descriptions. Wilmont Haacke, "Fassmann, David," in *Neue Deutsche Biographie* 5 (1961): 28; Käthe Kaschmieder, "David Fassmanns 'Gespräche im reiche der Toten' (1718–1740): Ein Beitrag zur deutschen Geistes- und Kulturgeschichte des 18. Jahrhunderts" (PhD Dissertation, Breslau, 1934); Wilhelm Damberg, "Die politische Aussage in den Totengesprächen David Fassmanns: Ein Beitrag zur Frühgeschichte der politischen Zeitschrift" (PhD Dissertation, Münster, 1952); John Rutledge, *The Dialogue of the Dead in Eighteenth-Century Germany* (Frankfurt am Main: Herbert Lang, 1974); Agatha Kobuch, *Zensur und Aufklärung in Kursachsen: Idealogische Strömungen und politische Meinungen zur Zeit der sächsisch-polnischen Union, 1697–1763* (Weimar: Hermann Böhlaus nachfolger, 1988); Nils Eckhardt, "Arzt, Medizin und Tod im Spiegel der von David Faßmann (1683–1744) in den Jahren 1718 bis 1739 herausgegebenen Zeitschrift 'Gespräche in dem Reiche derer Todten'" (PhD Dissertation, Düsseldorf, 1987); Eckhard Matthes, *Das veränderte Russland: Studien zum deutschen Russland-verständnis im 18. Jahrhundert zwischen 1725 und 1762* (Frankfurt am Main: Peter D. Lang, 1981); Johannes Arndt, *Herrschaftskontrolle durch Öffentlichkeit: Die publizistische Darstellung politischer Konflikte im Heiligen Römischen Reich, 1648–1750* (Göttingen: Vandenhoeck & Ru-

precht, 2013); Stephanie Dreyfürst, *Stimmen aus dem Jenseits: David Fassmanns historisch-politisches Journal "Gespräche in dem Reiche derer Todten" (1718–1740)* (Berlin: De Gruyter, 2014).

2. According to the records of Oberwiesenthal's Lutheran church, David Fassmann was baptized on September 20, 1685. He was the eldest son of Alexander Fassmann, a merchant, and Dorothea (née Rhyle), the local pastor's daughter. The parents had six other children and the grandfather died on March 1, 1699. Pfarramt Oberwiesenthal, *Tauf-, Trau- und Sterbebuch 1678–1737*, 30b, 36a, 44a, 50a, 60a, 71b, 385, 597, 634, 694.

3. Teaching at Altdorf at the time was the famous anti-Jewish Hebraist Johann Christoph Wagenseil. Whether Fassmann heard or read Wagenseil during his sojourn in Altdorf is unknown, but later in life, Fassmann did mention Wagenseil in his writings. For example, David Fassmann, *Des glorwürdigsten Fürsten und Herrn, Herrn Friedrich Augusti, des Großen, Königs in Pohlen und Churfürstens zu Sachsen . . . Leben und Helden-Thaten* (Leipzig: Wolfgang Deer, 1734), 194.

4. The two accounts of Fassmann's life, like all other eighteenth-century sources, seem to repeat are the first obituary of 1744 and Fassmann's autobiographical notes from 1737. *Neue Leipziger Zeitungen von Gelehrten Sachen* LXII (1744): 557–559; GRdT 225, "Vorrede."

5. GRdT 225, "Dedication," 7.

6. StdA Nürnberg B11 Nr. 125; SächsHStA Dresden, 10026 Geheimes Kabinett, Loc. 3116/3; AFSt/H, D 11b, 11c, 11e.

7. Friedrich August Hackmann, *Der, im Wein-Faß begrabene Paul Gundling, Geheimer Staats- Kriegs- und Domainen-Rath, raisonniret mit David Faßmann . . .* (Freybourg, 1736?), frontispiece.

8. The description of Leipzig is based on *Die vornehmsten europäischen Reisen* (Hamburg: Benjamin Schillers Wittwe, 1713), 33–34.

9. *Das jetzt lebende und jetzt florirende Leipzig: welches die Nahmen, Characteren, Chargen, Profeßionen und Wohnungen derer Personen . . . aufrichtig vorstellet* (Leipzig: Boetio, 1723), 61.

10. *Die vornehmsten europäischen Reisen*, 33.

11. About this expert report, see Jakub Goldberg, "Leipziger Theologen gegen die Ritualmorde. Das Gutachten vom Jahre 1714," *Herbergen der Christenheit. Jahrbuch für deutsche Kirchengeschichte* 23 (1999): 65–72.

12. On these and other aspects of the book trade in the first half of the eighteenth century, see Johann Goldfriedrich, *Geschichte des deutschen Buchhandels*, vol. 2, *Vom Westfälischen Frieden bis zum Beginn der klassischen Litteraturperiode, 1648–1740* (Leipzig: Börsenverein, 1908); and Reinhard Wittmann,

Geschichte des deutschen Buchhandels (Munich: Beck, 1991), 82–121. A good introduction in English to Germany's peculiar situation is Jeffrey Freedman, *Books without Borders in Enlightenment Europe* (Philadelphia: University of Pennsylvania Press, 2012), 16–42.

13. Heinrich Engelbert Schwarz, *Etwas Altes und Neues bestehende in kurtzer Vergleichung der . . . Zwo Städte Jericho und Leipzig . . .* (Leipzig: Christian Ehrenfried Förster, 1748), 37.

14. Quoted in Volker Rodekamp, *Leipzig Stadt der wa(h)ren Wunder* (Leipzig: Stadtgeschichtliches Museum Leipzig, 1997), 11.

15. Gotthold Ephraim Lessing, *Gesammelte Werke,* ed. Paul Rilla, vol. 9, *Briefe* (Berlin: Aufbau-Verlag, 1957), 10.

16. A distant second was Frankfurt am Main with 75 journals before 1750. See Joachim Kirchner, *Die Grundlagen des deutschen Zeitschriftenwesens,* 2. Teil, *Die Bibliographie der deutschen Zeitschriften bis zur Französischen Revolution. Statistische Ergebnisse* (Leipzig: Hiersemann, 1931), 323–330.

17. On censorship in Saxony during Fassmann's lifetime, see Kobuch, *Zensur und Aufklärung in Kursachsen.*

18. The head censor in Frankfurt, known as the *Buchkommissar,* reported to the archbishop of Mainz and through him to the highest legal echelons in the Holy Roman Empire. The kommissar had often an overtly Catholic, counter-Reformation agenda, which made the publication of non-Catholic materials in Frankfurt so difficult that many publishers resettled in Leipzig. Peter Weidhaas, *Zur Geschichte der Frankfurter Buchmesse* (Frankfurt am Main: Suhrkamp, 2003), 73–98.

19. Wittmann, *Geschichte des deutschen Buchhanderls,* 97.

20. "Fassmann an den König, dem 16. April 1731." Quoted in Friedrich Christoph Förster, *Friedrich Wilhelm des I. König von Preussen* (Potsdam: Ferdinand Riegel, 1834), I: 282.

21. The story of Fassmann's stay in Berlin as well as some documents about it were published by Friedrich Christoph Förster, the nineteenth-century biographer of the Prussian king Friedrich Wilhelm I. Förster, *Friedrich Wilhelm des I,* I: 272–286. Förster does not mention his sources, but they can be found in GStA PK, II. HA GD Abt. 4, Tit. 21, Nr. 24. Further documents about Fassmann's time in Berlin, not mentioned by Förster, are in the Archiv der Berlin-Brandenburgsichen Akademie der Wissenschaften, Signatur I-III-1a, Bl. 251, 256, 258–260, 267.

22. Fassmann does not mention the Lord Chancellor's relative by name, though he does mention that he died in Naples in 1715. Extensive research about the possible identity of this (supposed?) relative revealed no such individual.

Among the sources consulted were the index to "Overseas Births, Marriages, and Deaths, 1627–1960" at the British National Archives; the alumni registers for the universities of Oxford and Cambridge; Lord Chancellor Cowper's personal papers at the Hertfordshire local archives, relevant probate records, and other miscellaneous sources.

23. A full list of Fassmann's writings can be found in Haacke, "Fassmann, David," V: 26.

24. GRdT 225:20.

25. On the reception of Lucian's dialogues before and after Fassmann, see, most importantly, Hansjörg Schelle, "Totengespräch," *Reallexikon der deutschen Literaturgeschichte* (Berlin: Walter de Gruyter, 1984), IV: 475–513. More recent treatment of the subject is Dreyfürst, *Stimmen aus dem Jenseits*, chapter 3.

26. Lucian, "Dialogues of the Dead," in *Lucian in Eight Volumes*, ed. A. M. Harmon et al., vol. 7 (New York: Macmillan, 1967), 125, 157, and 175, respectively.

27. Lucian, "Dialogues," 55.

28. This was Fassmann's own argument. GRdT 33: "Vorrede."

29. Lucian, "Dialogues," 11.

30. Lucian, "Dialogues," 101–118.

31. Lucian, "Dialogues," 3.

32. Lucian, "Dialogues," 67.

33. Most clearly in GRdT 12:889, which Fassmann highlights by referring to it in the index of his *Conversations* under "politics": "Eure Frage aber zu beantworten, so wisest, dass die Politique eine Wissenschaft ist, sich klug und verschlagen zu stellen und aufzuführen. Simuliren und Dissimuliren sind sehr wesentliche Stücke der Politique, ohne welche sie nicht bestehen kann."

34. GRdT 1: Vorbericht.

35. *Neue Zeitung von Gelehrten Sachen*, Nr. LXXI, September 3, 1718, 568; "Libri historici philosophici et aliarum artium humanarum," *Catalogus universalis, sive designatio eorum librorum, qui hisce nundinis autumnabilus Francofurtensibus et Lipsiensibus anni MDCCXVIII . . . sunt prodituri* (Leipzig: Johann Großen seel. Erben, 1718), n.p.

36. GRdT 33: "Vorrede."

37. Four representative examples: *Freymüthige Nachrichten von neuen Büchern und andern zur Gelehrtheit gehörigen Sachen* 1 (1744), XXIV: 272; *Göttingische Zeitungen von Gelehrten Sachen*, Band 1742: 629–630 and Band 1744: 781–782; *Niedersächsische Nachrichten von Gelehrten neuen Sachen*, Band 1736: 119.

38. Five examples: GRdT 7, 19, 27, 43, 54.

39. Some examples are mentioned in Ulrich Schmidt, "Gespräche in dem Reiche derer Todten (1718–1740)," in *Deutsche Zeitschriften des 17. bis 20. Jahrhunderts*, ed. Heinz-Dietrich Fisher (Pullach bei München: Verlag Dokumentation, 1973), 54.

40. David Fassmann, *Die neu-entdeckten Elisäischen Felder und was sich in denselben sonderbares zugetragen* (Frankfurt and Leipzig, 1735), 7. Other comments on his imitators in GRdT 41: 686 and GRdT 225, "Dedication," 3.

41. David Fassmann, *Interviews in the Realms of Death: or, Dialogues of the Dead between Several Great Personages Deceas'd* (London: Printed by W. Hunter for J. Hooke, 1718), title page.

42. GRdT 225: "Vorrede," 7.

43. GRdT 97: 6; GRdT 145: 6.

44. David Fassmann, *Sechzehender Band zu denen Gesprächen in dem Reiche derer Todten, worinnen enthalten: I. Die Historie nach denen Monarchien, Reichen und Staaten . . . II. Die Summarien, oder ein kurtzer Inhalt aller 240 Entrevüen . . . III. Ein General-Register, über alle sechzehen Bände . . .* (Leipzig: Wolfgang Deer, 1740).

45. Fassmann tells his side of the story in GRdT 240: 1202. The description later is based on the documents in StdA Leipzig, Tit. XLVI (F) 174.

46. StdA Leipzig, Tit. XLVI (F) 174.

47. GRdT 7: 514.

48. GRdT 7: 517.

49. So, for instance, in Christopher Clark, *Iron Kingdom: The Rise and Downfall of Prussia, 1600–1947* (Cambridge, MA: Harvard University Press, 2006), 80. More detailed descriptions of Fassmann's time with Frederick William I are Martin Sabrow, *Herr und Hanswurst: Das tragische Shicksal des Hofgelehrten Jacob Paul von Gunling* (Stuttgart: Deutsche Verlags-Anstalt, 2001), 77–92; and Förster, *König Friedrich Wilhelm des I.*, I: 281–286.

50. David Fassmann, *Leben und Thaten des Allerdurchlauchtigsten und Großmächtigsten Königs von Preußen Friederici Wilhelmi* (Hamburg and Breslau, 1735), I: 960.

51. Richard Wolff, ed., *Vom Berliner Hofe zur Zeit Friedrich Wilhelms I.: Berichte des Braunschweiger Gesandten in Berlin, 1728–1733* (Berlin: Verlag des Vereins für die Geschichte Berlins, 1914), 241.

52. See especially the letter to the king from April 16, 1731, as quoted in Förster, *Friedrich Wilhelm des I.*, I: 281–282.

53. Wolff, *Vom Berliner Hofe*, 241–242.

54. GStA PK, I. HA Geheimer Rat, Rep. 9 Allgemeine Verwaltung F 2 a Fasz. 5, Nr. 43, fols. 1–2.

55. GStA PK I HA Rep. 49Q, Fasz. 5.
56. *Freye Urtheile und Nachrichten zum Aufnehmen der Wissenschaften und der Historie überhaupt*, LXI (1744), 489.
57. *Freundschafftliche Unterredung der Seelen David Faßmanns und Thomas Hobbes durch welche beyder Caracter moralisch zergliedert warden* (n.p., 1751).
58. Selma Stern reproduced the inventory in *Jud Süss*, 298–303.
59. Jean-Jacques Rousseau, *The Confessions*, trans. J. M. Cohen (Harmondsworth, UK: Penguin, 1953), 21.
60. GRdT 193; GRdT 194.
61. GRdt 193: 66.
62. David Fassmann, *Besondere Entrevue der Gespräche in dem Reich der Todten zwischen denen zwey letzt-verstorbenen regierenden Herzogen von Würtemberg, Herrn Eberhard Ludwig und Herrn Karl Alexander . . .* (Frankfurt and Leipzig: Wolfgang Deer?, 1737), 4.
63. Fassmann, *Besondere Entrevue*, 6.
64. Fassmann, *Besondere Entrevue*, 12.
65. Fassmann, *Besondere Entrevue*, 12.
66. Fassmann, *Besondere Entrevue*, 20.
67. Fassmann, *Besondere Entrevue*, 26, 32.
68. Fassmann, *Besondere Entrevue*, 36.
69. Fassmann, *Besondere Entrevue*, 45.
70. GRdT 225: 22–23.
71. GRdT 225: 24.
72. GRdT 225: 25. This explanation for Carl Alexander's problems in Stuttgart has been repeated recently in Joachim Brüder, *Herzog Karl Alexander von Württemberg und die Landschaft (1733 bis 1737): Katholische Konfession, Kaisertreue und Absolutismus* (Stuttgart: Kohlhammer, 2010).
73. GRdT 225: 42.
74. GRdT 225: 70b.
75. GRdT 225: 70c.
76. GRdT 225: 70d.
77. An insightful reformulation of the same claim can be found in Peter H. Wilson, "Der Favorit als Sündenbock. Joseph Süss Oppenheimer (1698–1738)," in *Der zweite Mann im Staat: Oberste Amtsträger und Favoriten im Umkreis der Reichsfürsten in der Frühen Neuzeit*, ed. Michael Kaiser and Andreas Pečar (Berlin: Duncker & Humboldt, 2003).
78. GRdT 225: 70e-d.
79. GRdT 226: 75–76.

80. David Fassmann, *Merkwürdige Staats Assembleé in dem Reiche derer Todten zwischen einem ganz besonderem Klee-Blatt; oder dreyen unartigen Staats-Ministern, nemlich dem Duc de Ripperda, den Grafen von Hoymb, und dem Juden Süss-Oppenheimer* . . . (Amsterdam: Hermann van der Hauer, 1738), "Vorbericht."

81. Thus, Hoym headed the Saxon delegation to Frankfurt in which Fassmann claimed he had taken part in 1711. SächsHStA Dresden, 10687 Geheimer Rat (Geheimes Archiv) Loc. 10687/3, Das Quartier Wesen zu Frankfurt am Mayn bey dem Kayserl. Wahl-Tage betr., Anno 1711, fol. 202.

82. Fassmann, *Merkwürdige Staats Assembleé*, 143.

83. Fassmann, *Merkwürdige Staats Assembleé*, 145–147.

84. Fassmann, *Merkwürdige Staats Assembleé*, 148–149.

85. Fassmann, *Merkwürdige Staats Assembleé*, "Vorbericht."

86. Fassmann, *Merkwürdige Staats Assembleé*, 151, 152, 156.

87. Fassmann, *Merkwürdige Staats Assembleé*, 168.

88. Fassmann, *Merkwürdige Staats Assembleé*, 182.

89. Fassmann, *Merkwürdige Staats Assembleé*, 172–173.

90. Fassmann, *Merkwürdige Staats Assembleé*, 192.

91. The following is a translation, with very minor editorial interventions, in Fassmann, *Merkwürdige Staats Assembleé*, 173–181. For a description of the usual stages of an execution in early modern Germany, see Evans, *Rituals of Retribution*, 65–108.

92. Adam Smith, *The Theory of Moral Sentiments*, ed. D. D. Raphael and A. L. Macfie (Indianapolis: Liberty Fund, 1976). Two important formulations of the same idea as it pertains to reading are Martha Nussbaum, *Poetic Justice: The Literary Imagination and Public Life* (Boston: Beacon Press, 1995); and Lynn A. Hunt, *Inventing Human Rights: A History* (New York: Norton, 2007). Compare also President Barack Obama's remarkable eulogy for Clementa Pinckney, www.whitehouse.gov/the-press-office/2015/06/26/remarks-president-eulogy-honorable-reverend-clementa-pinckney, accessed July 1, 2015.

93. HStA Stuttgart A48/14 Bü 15, fol. 681.

94. Bernard, *Ausführlicher Discurs*, 15.

95. Andre Wakefield, *The Disordered Police State: German Cameralism as Science and Practice* (Chicago: University of Chicago Press, 2009), 1–2, 143.

96. Jütte, *Das Zeitalter des Geheimnisses*, 161.

97. *Curieuse Nachrichten aus dem Reich der Beschnittenen, zwischen Sabathai Sevi* . . . *und dem fameusen württembergischen Avanturier, Jud Joseph Süß Oppenheimer* . . . (Gedruckt zu Cana in Galiläa, 1737).

Index

Aeneid, 240, 255

Agag, biblical figure, 151–53, 163, 165–66, 171

Albo, Joseph, 119, 122, 127, 305n45

Andler, Phillip Heinrich, 81–82, 96

Ansbach, 202, 232–33

anti-Semitism, 1, 16, 20, 77, 98–99, 178, 236, 275, 281

Aristotle, 16

Augsburg, 198

Augustine, 117, 124, 166–68, 171–73, 309n103

Austen, Jane, 284

Bach, Johann Sebastian, 234

Bad Canstatt, 33, 295n25

Baden, 126

Bardili, Eberhard Ludwig, 48, 52, 56, 67, 72–73, 87–88, 97

bar Kokhba, Simon, 9

Bavaria, 2

Beck, Elias, 102, 287

Beckett, Samuel, 284

Bengel, Johann Albrecht, 130

Berlin, 47, 134, 240, 251–54, 318n21

Bernard, Christoph David, 131–74, 193, 198, 204–5, 213–19, 227, 238, 267–69, 276–79, 281–82; baptism of, 112, 114; books by, 123–24, 126–27, 130; conver-
sion from Judaism, 104–11, 117; and conversions of other Jews, 126; disputational method of, 118–21, 252; first meeting with Joseph Süss Oppenheimer, 113, 144–55, 164; lecturer at Tübingen, 20, 103, 122–31; marriages of, 128–29; parents of, 107, 129; and Schloss, Mordechai, 184, 189, 200; and schnapps distilling, 125–26, 135; second meeting with Oppenheimer, 155–63; at theological seminary, 112, 115–17, 122

Bible, 162–63; canon of, 116, 130, 182, 211; exegesis of, 127, 165; references to, 9, 104, 123, 152, 194, 218–23, 226–27. *See also* David, biblical king; Exodus; Genesis; Joseph, biblical figure; Saul, biblical king

Bing, Callman. *See* Seligmann, Callman

Bingen-on-the-Rhine, 134, 201, 203

blood libel, 77, 236

Bök, August Friedrich, 127, 302n11

Braunschweig, 134

Bühler, Johann Christoph, 56–57, 64–67, 69–70, 76–77, 81, 94, 274

Calvin, John, 124

Calvinism, 4, 115, 148

Cambridge Yiddish Codex, 221

Canz, Isaac Abraham, 136, 138–40
Carl Alexander, duke of Württemberg, 66, 77, 89, 197–98, 206–7, 209, 233, 276; acquaintance with Oppenheimer, 4, 193; ascent to throne, 5, 47, 93, 131, 194; and Catholicism, 46; death of, 52, 55–56, 85, 257, 266; and Fassmann, David, 257–63, 277; and Grävenitz-Würben case, 48, 51–52, 94, 194; and Landau, Isaac Salomon, 204
Carl Eugen, duke of Württemberg, 89
Carl Rudolph, regent in Württemberg, 56, 136; and trial of Joseph Süss (Jew Süss) Oppenheimer, 68–69, 72, 75, 80–81, 83–84, 86–87, 89, 92, 132
Carolina. See Holy Roman Empire
Catherine I, empress of Russia, 250
Catholicism, 4–5, 46, 55, 92, 113–14, 148, 202, 260, 262, 318n18
Charon, 231, 240–42, 265
Chauvelin, Germain Louis, 264–65
Chazan, Selmele, 107, 161
The City of God, 168
Cleß, Wilhelm Jeremias Jacob, 25–28, 40, 42, 53, 293n3; eulogy for Philipp Friedrich Jäger, 31, 34, 36, 38, 99
Conversations in the Realm of the Dead, 231, 249–51, 279, 283; and death of David Fassmann, 255; and Oppenheimer, Joseph Süss, 256, 264–65, 267, 275, 277; reception of, 248; structure of, 246–47, 252. See also Fassmann, David
Courland, 260
court Jews, 1, 4–5, 8, 13, 221; and Fassmann, David, 253–54; in Holy Roman Empire, 4–5; in Württemberg, 50–51, 189–94, 197, 199, 201, 203–4, 224
Cracow (Krakow), 126

Daniel, Jakob, 126
Dann, Johann Jakob, 56–57, 67, 69, 72–74, 76, 78, 82–83, 131, 206; deliberations in Stuttgart, 86–88, 96–97
Darmstadt, 4, 60–61, 92, 192, 203
David, Benjamin, 134
David, biblical king, 9, 27, 124, 166–67
David, Chaijm (Haim), 126
Deer, Wolfgang, 230, 236, 238–39, 247, 250, 254
Die europäische Fama, 237
disputation, 39–41, 117–19; and Bernard, Christoph David, 116–21, 123, 149, 152, 165, 175; and Fassmann, David, 242; and Oppenheimer, 147, 152
Divine Comedy, 240, 265
Dresden, 232–33, 264
Duke of Berwyck, 257

Easter, 236, 238–39
Eberhard Ludwig, duke of Württemberg, 37, 50–51, 108, 183–86, 190, 257–62, 266, 277; affair with Christina Wilhelmina von Grävenitz, 37, 45–47, 65, 257; and court Jews, 50, 184–85; death of, 193, 257–58
Ehrbarkeit, 30, 36, 49, 92, 99, 294n11; and court of Württemberg, 45, 47; as pastors, 33; tensions with dukes, 31, 76
Emerson, Ralph Waldo, 172–73
Engerer, Johann Helwig, 168
England, 107–10, 233, 237, 239, 245
Epstein, Yehiel Michel ben Avraham Halevi, 212
Exodus, 211, 219, 221, 227

Faber, Johann Friedrich, 78
Faber, Wilhelm Eberhard, 57, 64, 72–74, 76, 78, 82–88, 96–97, 206; and Hofgericht, 56; in Stuttgart, 64, 67–69, 131
Faberin, Christina Dorothea, 78–79, 81, 100
Fassmann, David, 21, 230–57, 259–69,

275–79, 282–83; and Catherine I, 250; death of, 255; depiction of, 235, 287; early life, 232–34; and Leipzig, 21, 234–40, 279; and Lucian's dialogues with the dead, 240–46; and Fredrick William of Prussia, 250–54. See also *Conversations in the Realm of the Dead*

Faulkner, William, 284

Fénelon, François, 243, 245

Ferdinand, duke of Courland, 260

Fettmilch, Vincenz, 179

Feuchtwanger, Lion, 12, 16, 19

Fischerin, Luciana, 78, 154

Fontenelle, Bernard Le Bovier de, 243, 245

Forstner, Christoph Peter von, 57, 68–70, 299n101

France, 32–33, 233, 236–37, 245–46, 257–59

Francke, Hermann August, 233

Fränkel, Gabriel, 185

Fränkel, Levin, 189, 191, 194–95

Frankfurt am Main, 2, 40, 151, 236, 255, 285; and Chazan, Selmele, 107, 161; fairs of, 183, 238, 245; and Fassmann, David, 233; and Grävenitz-Würben, Christina Wilhelmina von, 47, 51, 183–84; *Judengasse* (ghetto or Jewish Lane) of, 177–78, 180, 182, 184, 192, 201; and Oppenheimer, Joseph Süss, 5, 7–8, 60–63, 125, 132, 134, 164, 192–94, 197; and Schloss, Mordechai, 177–80, 183–87, 206; and Seligmann, Callman, 200–201, 203, 221

Frederick William, king of Prussia, 251–53

Friedrich Carl, duke of Württemberg, 185

Fürth, 168, 202, 216

Gabler, Christoph Ludwig, 55–57, 67, 69, 73, 76, 87–91; and Carl Rudolph, 75;

and Grävenitz-Würben case, 51–52, 88; and *Hofgericht*, 44, 48

Gaisberg, Ernst Conrad von, 72, 75, 87–88, 96, 141–42; and Grävenitz-Würben case, 48, 52; and *Hofgericht*, 44, 48, 52; and interrogation of Joseph Süss Oppenheimer, 73, 76, 80

Genesis, 223–24, 226–27

Genesis Rabbah, 222

Georgii, Friedrich Heinrich, 72, 83

Gilgamesh, epic of, 240

Glikl of Hammeln, 186

Goebbels, Joseph, 16

Goebel, Anna Catharina, 128

Goebel, Margaretha Agnesa, 128

Grävenitz, Christina Wilhelmina von, 94, 194–95, 281; affair with Eberhard Ludwig, 37, 45–46, 183–84, 257–58; incarceration of, 46–47; trial of, 47–53, 56, 62, 65, 67, 70, 77, 82, 88, 94, 98, 198, 207, 280

Grävenitz, Friedrich Wilhelm von, 194–95

Grimmaische Lane (Leipzig), 236, 238

Gundling, Jacob Paul von, 235, 253–54

Hackmann, Friedrich August, 235

Halle, 134, 233, 235

Hallwachs, Jacob Friedrich, 56–57, 64–66, 69–70, 76–77, 94, 274, 299n101

Hammel, Hertz, 185, 189

Harlan, Veit, 11–12, 16, 19

Harpprecht, Georg Friedrich, Sr., 28, 44, 48, 71, 86–87, 89–90, 96, 141; and interrogation of Joseph Süss Oppenheimer, 73–76; and Jäger, Philipp Friedrich, 40–42

Harpprecht, Moritz David, 48–49

Hauff, Wilhelm, 12, 16, 19

Hayum, Elias, 138–40, 185–86, 198–99, 204–5, 222, 287

Hechinger, Abraham, 185

Heidelberg, 8, 92, 133, 151, 155; and Oppenheimer, Joseph Süss, 1, 4, 58, 60, 63, 170, 231; university of, 42
Heidenheim, 63
Heitersdorf, General von, 92
Herodotus, 1, 19
Hesse-Darmstadt, 4, 192
Hochstetter, Johann Heinrich, Sr., 58–59, 63, 66
Hohen Asperg, 72–74, 76–77, 136, 141, 203, 205–6, 209–10, 225, 268–69; and Bühler, Johann Christoph, 66, 77; and Grävenitz-Würben, 46
Hohen Neuffen, 56–57, 64, 66, 68, 70, 73, 267, 298n70; and Grävenitz-Würben, 46
Holy Roman Empire, 2–3, 148, 211, 237, 245–46, 259, 318n18; and Imperial knights, 30; Jews of, 4, 8; legal system of, 40–41, 47, 66, 72, 75, 87, 151, 202
Hoym, Karl Heinrich, 264–66, 268, 276
Hugo, Victor, 284

Imperial free cities. See Frankfurt am Main; Nuremberg
inquisitorial system (of Holy Roman Empire), 3, 58
Isaac, Simon, 93
Israelites, 152, 166, 172, 212, 219–20, 222–23
Italy, 233–34

Jacob, biblical patriarch, 194, 224, 226
Jäger, Anna Friderika, 55
Jäger, Anna Maria, 29, 32
Jäger, Charlotte Regina, 55
Jäger, Charlotte Regina (née Cleß), 26, 42
Jäger, David Friedrich, 37
Jäger, Georg Friedrich, 29, 34
Jäger, Maria Rosine, 55, 96
Jäger, Philipp Friedrich, 21, 55–59, 61, 63–70, 82–91, 100–101, 107, 131, 173,

221, 267–69, 276, 278, 280–82; death and funeral of, 25–28, 34, 40, 95–96, 99; early life, 29–33, 35–36; education, 36–42; family of, 55; and Grävenitz-Würben case, 45–53, 56, 62, 94, 194; and Hofgericht, 43–45; at Hohen Asperg, 72–82; and Oppenheimer verdict, 20, 29, 238; portrait of, 24, 287; and Rieger, Georg Konrad, 93, 114; and Schloss, Mordechai, 171, 198, 207; and species facti, 91–99, 218, 228, 252
Jena, 111, 123, 127, 189
Jew Süss (Nazi propaganda film), 11
Joseph, biblical figure, 194, 218–29
Joyce, James, 284
Judeophobia. See anti-Semitism

Kabbalah, 116
Kahn, Maram, 136, 138–40, 160, 189, 203–4, 222
Karlsruhe, 119, 126, 144, 192, 203
katabasis, 240
Kehl, 258
Kirchheim unter Teck, 42
Koblenz, 132
Krieger, Maria Margaretha (née Wagenknecht), 127–28

Landau, 93, 133
Landau, Isaac Salomon, 204, 222
Langenschwalbach, 106–8, 110
Lehmann, Berend, 221
Leichenrede, 26, 293n4
Leipzig, 232–34, 250, 264, 279, 282; and book trade, 238–39, 245; and Fassmann, David, 21, 232–34, 236–37, 239–40, 243, 246–47, 252–55; and Schloss, Mordechai, 187; and Wolfgang Deer (printing house), 236, 254
Lemberg. See Lviv (Ukraine)
Leopold I, Holy Roman emperor, 246
Leser, Isaac, 203

Lessing, Gotthold Ephraim, 237
Levi, Hirsch, 185
Levi, Isaac Samuel, 69, 131, 133–34, 136–
    37, 140, 202
Levin, Fränckel, 185, 187
London, 237
Louis XIV, king of France, 233, 236,
    245–46
Louis XV, king of France, 257
Löw, Model, 185, 190–91, 194, 196
Low Countries, 42
Lucian, 240–46, 265, 319n25
Ludwig, Christian, 188–89
Ludwig, Friedrich, 46
Ludwig, Johanna Elisabetha, 37, 46, 108
Ludwigsburg, 30, 72, 111, 136, 160, 188,
    203; ducal palace, 8, 37, 52, 185, 257,
    311n20; Jews in, 8, 111, 136, 185, 188,
    203
Luther, Martin, 3, 124, 168, 309n104
Lutheranism, 26, 35, 46, 113, 115, 117,
    232, 303n19; and Bernard, Christoph
    David, 106, 148, 312n33; and Catholi-
    cism, 4, 46, 202, 260, 262; and Rieger,
    Georg Konrad, 36; in Schorndorf, 33–
    34; and Storr, Johann Philip, 106; in
    Tübingen, 37
Lviv (Ukraine), 107, 109–10, 120

Ma'assebuch, 221
Mainz, 106, 184, 318n18
Mändel, Abraham Joseph, 185
Mann, Thomas, 229
Mannheim, 60, 63, 133, 136–37, 160, 187,
    203, 274
Maram, Nathan, 69, 314n82
Margalith Family (Margolis or Margaliot),
    134
Marx, Nathan (Nathan the Jew). See
    Schloss, Mordechai (Marx Nathan or
    Nathan the Jew)
Mayer, Salomon, 203

Mendes, Lothar, 12
Merchant of Venice, 2, 275
Mez, Johann Albrecht, 69
Mögling, Michael Andreas, 80–81, 84, 87
Mühringen, 126
Munich, 134

Nathan the Jew. See Schloss, Mordechai
    (Marx Nathan or Nathan the Jew)
Neckarsulm, 133
Nuremberg, 2, 168, 202, 232–33

Oberwiesenthal, 232–33, 255, 317n2
Odyssey, 240
Oetinger, Friedrich Christoph, 127
Oppenheimer, Daniel, 133, 202
Oppenheimer, Issachar Süsskind, 4, 107,
    110, 210
Oppenheimer, Joseph Süss (Jew Süss), 20–
    21, 57–61, 63–82, 84–85, 87–101, 130–
    31, 174, 189, 279; and Bernard, Chris-
    toph David, 103–7, 111–13, 116–18,
    120–25, 129, 131–71, 173, 184, 238; and
    Callman, Seligmann, 200–201; as court
    Jew, 4–5, 9, 65, 185; death sentence and
    execution, 5, 103, 118, 163, 186, 269–74;
    depictions of trial, 54, 102, 287; and
    Fassmann, David, 231–32, 239, 245,
    247–48, 251–74, 275, 277, 282–83; and
    von Grävenitz case, 46–47, 51; and
    Gütliches Verhör, 80, 82; and Hayum,
    Elias, 199, 205; in history, 1–2, 7–8, 10–
    19, 191, 278, 280; and Jäger, Philipp
    Friedrich, 29, 33, 35–41, 44–45, 50–53,
    55–56, 276, 281; Jewish responses to ar-
    rest of, 201–5; and Rieger, Georg Kon-
    rad, 114, 126; and Schloss, Mordechai,
    177–79, 192–94, 197–99, 206–8; and The
    Story of the Passing of Joseph Süss, ZT"L,
    208–14, 216–28; torture of, 90; and trial
    documents, 6–7; verdict in case, 29, 97;
    in Zedler's Universal-Lexicon, 7–8

Oppenheimer, Michal (Michele), 4, 107, 202, 313n70

Palatinate, 4
Papal Inquisition, 3
Paris, 237
Passover, 68, 181–82, 210, 218–19, 221
Paul, apostle, 9, 168
performativity, 170
Pfaff, Christoph Matthäus, 127, 135, 167, 172
Pfeil, Joachim Friedrich von, 194–96
Pfersee, 198
Pflug, Johann Christoph von, 48, 52, 63–66, 69, 72–74, 87–88, 96, 206; and death sentence in Oppenheimer trial, 91; on inquisition committee, 56–58, 61, 76, 131
Philippsburg, 258
Poland, 109, 122, 266, 303n16
polyphonic history, 19–22, 23, 232, 280–81, 283, 285
Prague, 8, 134, 216
Pregizer, Johann Philipp, 96, 100, 103, 104, 112, 144, 147–48, 155, 169; and Bühler, Johann Christoph, 67; and Jäger, Philipp Friedrich, 29, 53, 69, 206
Protestantism, 4, 236, 238
Protestant Reformation, 3, 35, 124
Prussia, 239–40, 250–54, 268
Purim, 182, 221

Rabbi Akiva, 154
Rashi (Rabbi Shlomo Yitzchaki), 226
Regensburg, 232
Relation (document), 65, 70, 74, 79–80, 82, 91, 97, 278; and Carl Rudolph, 83, 89, 92; definition of, 41
Renz, Günther Albrecht (Councilor), 28, 83, 87–88, 96
Rezeptionsgeschichte ("history of reception"), 17–19

Rieger, Georg Konrad, 36, 89, 93, 114, 126
Ripperda, Johan Willem de, 264–66, 268, 276
Rosh Hashana, 112–13, 149, 181, 210
Rothschild Family, 134
Rousseau, Jean-Jacques, 256
Russia, 233, 237, 250

Samuel, biblical prophet, 103, 152, 162–63, 166–67
Sattler, Christian Friedrich, 29, 43–44, 87, 96
Saul, biblical king, 152, 162–63, 165–68, 170–72, 285
Saxony, 2, 233–34, 236–38, 250, 255, 264, 318n17
Schächter, Salomon. See Seligmann, Callman
Schechter, Seligmann. See Seligmann, Callman
Scheffer, Johann Theodor, 39, 43–44
Schlachter, Seligmann. See Seligmann, Callman
Schloss, Leyb, 185–86
Schloss, Mordechai (Marx Nathan or Nathan the Jew), 21, 150, 155–56, 168–71, 176, 183–97, 216–25, 227–28, 238, 267, 269, 277–78, 281–82, 287; and Bernard, Christoph David, 143–44, 169–70; family and origins, 177–81, 204; and Frankfurt ghetto, 177–79, 201; and Grävenitz-Würben case, 82; and Jewish community in Stuttgart, 103; and meeting with Joseph Süss Oppenheimer, 212–14; at trial of Joseph Süss Oppenheimer, 205–8. See also The Story of the Passing of Joseph Süss, ZT"L
Schloss, Moshe (son of Mordechai Schloss), 185–86, 191
Schloss, Nateh (father of Mordechai Schloss), 180

Schloss, Nateh (son of Mordechai Schloss), 185

Schloss, Rachel (Rehle), 184–85, 198, 200

Schloss, Yudle (Yehudit), 185–86, 192, 198, 204–5

Schloss, Yule (Yoela), 185–86, 192, 199–200

Schnee, Heinrich, 12

Schöpff, Wolfgang Adam, 28, 40–44, 48, 52, 71–76, 87, 89–91, 96; and *Hofgericht*, 43–44; and interrogation of Joseph Süss Oppenheimer, 73–76; and Jäger, Philipp Friedrich, 40–44; and Oppenheimer verdict, 91–92

Schorndorf, 29, 31, 95, 285; and Burgschloss; 32, 35; and Jäger, Philipp Friedrich, 37–38, 42, 44, 46, 77, 81–82, 92, 99; and Jews, 36; Latin school of, 33–34, 96; town hall of, 34; and trial of Joseph Süss Oppenheimer, 81–82, 95

Schwabach, 168

Schwartz, Löw (Leyb), 184

second-order observation, 101, 283

Sefer ha-ʿIkkarim ("The Book of Principles"), 119, 121–22

Seligmann, Callman, 168–69, 176, 185, 287; and Bernard, Christoph David, 155, 200, 215–22; and Schloss, Mordechai, 200–201, 204–5, 224–28, 238, 267, 269, 277–78, 281–82; wife of (Yule), 186, 199–200

Smith, Adam, 276

Spain, 119, 245

Spanish Inquisition, 3, 94

species facti, 41; in Oppenheimer case, 55, 77, 91–95, 99–100, 218, 228, 252, 278

Stemann, Justus Valentin, 69

Stern, Selma, 12, 14–15, 17–19

Storr, Johann Philip, 106, 108, 302n8

The Story of the Passing of Joseph Süss, ZT"L (May the Memory of the Righteous Be a Blessing), 176–77, 208–25, 227–29,

287, 314n88. *See also* Schloss, Mordechai (Marx Nathan or Nathan the Jew)

Strassburger, Hayum, 185

Stuttgart, 5, 7–8, 23, 60, 71, 83, 90, 137, 197–200, 211, 231, 252, 255, 261, 264, 266–69, 271, 273, 277–78, 285; archives, 6, 15, 52; and Bernard, Christoph David, 108, 111–13, 125, 130–32, 135, 137, 142; Consistory in, 110, 122, 126; Herrenhaus of, 97, 106–7, 131, 140, 164, 169, 171, 208, 215, 223, 238, 268, 271, 282; and Hohen Asperg, 72, 76–77, 141, 225; and Hohen Neuffen, 56; and Jäger, Philipp Friedrich, 25, 29, 33, 36–38, 42–43, 55, 57, 67, 82, 89; Jews in, 21, 103; and Schloss, Mordechai, 180, 185, 193–94, 205, 208, 213; Spitalkirche, 26, 36, 40, 53, 87, 95–96, 99; town hall of, 86, 91

Switzerland, 198

Talmud, 117–18, 124, 143, 156, 159–60, 182

Thirty Years' War, 246

Torah, 181–82, 218–20, 222, 228

Tseno Ureno (Tsʾena u-Rʾena), 221

Tübingen, 24, 52, 71–72, 76, 128, 193, 269, 276, 285; as administrative center, 38; and Bernard, Christoph David, 105, 111–13, 117, 119, 122, 131, 133, 135–36, 140–41; Harpprecht, Georg Friedrich, Sr., 86; and *Hofgericht* of, 48, 56; and Jäger, Philipp Friedrich, 36–43; and Mögling, Michael Andreas, 80; and university of, 26, 36–42, 48, 96, 127; and Zeller, Christian, 108

Tübinger Vertrag, 30

Tympe, Johann Gottfried, 127

Ulmann, David, 185, 187

Ulmann, Jacob, 203, 222

Ulmann family, 134

University of Altdorf, 232, 317n3
University of Tübingen, 103, 127, 164, 172, 305n45
Urach, 29, 46

Versailles, 245–46
Vienna, 8, 134, 246

Wannweil, 128
Warsaw, 232, 303n16
Weinmann, Abel, 48, 52, 56–57, 67
Wetzlar, 202
Wilder Mann, 179–80, 183–84, 186
Wisshack, Sigmund, 33–35, 96
Woolf, Virginia, 284
World War II, 11
Worms, 181
von Würben, Christina Wilhelmina. See Grävenitz, Christina Wilhelmina von
Württemberg, 4, 13, 21, 25, 30, 55, 57, 70, 72, 75–77, 90, 95, 97, 271, 273, 287; anti-Jewish sentiment in, 281; and Bernard, Christoph David, 106–10, 112, 115, 126, 129, 137–38, 140, 148, 165, 167, 170; and Carl Alexander, 5, 46, 85, 93, 233, 258–61; and Carl Rudolph, 81; constitution of, 30; court Jews, 51, 185, 188–89, 191, 193, 199, 224; and Eberhard Ludwig, 183–85; and Fassmann, David, 21, 256–57, 262–63, 265–68, 277; *Hofgericht* of, 40, 42–44, 96; and Jäger, Philipp Friedrich, 20, 25, 29–30, 92, 99; Jewish settlement in, 76, 89, 91, 170; *Landtag* of, 30; mint of, 65; and Oppenheimer, Joseph Süss, 1–2, 13, 15, 47, 59–62, 66, 74, 85, 88, 125, 164, 206–7, 209, 218, 231; penal code of, 87; and Sattler, Christian Friedrich, 29; and Schloss, Mordechai, 180, 183–91, 194, 197–99; State Library of, 119; and *The Story of the Passing of Joseph Süss*, 218, 225

Yiddish, 181–83, 210, 212, 215–16, 220–21, 278, 314n89; and letters of Joseph Süss Oppenheimer, 131, 133, 136–37, 142, 168, 205
Yom Kippur (Day of Atonement), 113, 149

Zedler, Johann Heinrich, 7–8, 92
Zeller, Andreas Christoph, 130, 305n45
Zeller, Christian, 108, 114
Zevi, Shabbetai, 279